JN057193

The Tokara Islands

Culture, Society, Industry and Nature

Kagoshima University
International Center for Island Studies

The Tokara Islands

Culture, Society, Industry and Nature

Edited by

Yasushi OTSUKA, Ryuta TERADA and Satoru NISHIMURA

Takara-jima Island. Photo: Ryuta TERADA

Kagoshima University International Center for Island Studies

国立大学法人
鹿児島大学
KAGOSHIMA UNIVERSITY

Kagoshima University
International Center for Island Studies

© Kagoshima University International Center for Island Studies (KUICIS) 2020

First published: March 2020

Kagoshima University International Center for Island Studies
  1-21-24 Korimoto, Kagoshima City, 890-8580 Japan
  Phone +81 99 285 7394
  Fax   +81 99 285 6197

For bibliographic purposes this book should be cited as follows:
Yasushi OTSUKA, Ryuta TERADA and Satoru NISHIMURA (eds.) 2020. The Tokara Islands: Culture, Society, Industry and Nature. Hokuto Shobo Publishing, Tokyo. xii + 163 pages; 26.6 cm. Published on 10 March, 2020. Publisher: Hokuto Shobo Publishing.

ISBN 978-4-89290-054-9

Technical editing, graphic design and DTP: Ryuta TERADA

The Kagoshima University International Center for Island Studies (KUICIS) focuses on the studies on island-zones in Kagoshima, Oceania and its surroundings. An island-zone, consisting of an area that encompasses a group of islands, is a space where networks of people, things and information are formed and interaction among islands take place. An aggregation of island-zones comprises an island-sphere.

   The KUICIS aims to promote interdisciplinary studies on islands and islands zones in Oceania and its surroundings. The results of the studies are combined to promote comprehensive understanding of islands and islands zones and to further the welfare of people in Oceania and its surroundings. **KUICIS website.** http://cpi.kagoshima-u.ac.jp/index.html

Printed in Japan

Contents

Part I Culture and Society

Part II Industry

Part III Nature

Notes on Contributors

Editors

Yasushi OTSUKA is an associate professor in International Center for Island Studies, Kagoshima University. He specializes in medical zoology, and has conducted researches on blackfly and mosquito in Asia and Micronesia.

Ryuta TERADA is a professor at the United Graduate School of Agricultural Sciences, Kagoshima University. His scientific interests are in the biodiversity of marine plants including coastal ecosystems, and in the sustainable utilization of seaweed resources worldwide.

Satoru NISHIMURA is a professor of Economics at Kagoshima University. He has conducted research on land tenure systems in the Philippines since 1990. He has recently extended his areas of research to Fiji and Federal States of Micronesia.

Contributors

Shuji ANDO is a chief of Department of Virology-1, National Institute of Infectious Diseases. His interests include epidemiology and etiology of rickettsiosis and zoonoses.

Masako ANDOH is an associate professor in the Joint Faculty of Veterinary Medicine, Kagoshima University. Her interest is pathogenicity and epidemiology of zoonotic intracellular bacteria.

Hiromi FUJITA is a research fellow in the Medico-Field Study and Support Fukushima, a visiting professor in the University of Shizuoka, a hunter of ticks, mites, and acari-borne microorganisms in the field of medical acarology.

Mutsuyo GOKUDEN is a former Chief of Microorganism Section of the Kagoshima Prefectural Institute for Environmental Research and Public Health. Her current interest is in the fieldwork for acari-borne diseases.

Toshiro HONDA is a Chief of Microorganism Section of the Kagoshima Prefectural Institute for Environmental Research and Public Health. He specializes in diagnoses and epidemiology of infectious diseases included acari-borne disease in Kagoshima prefecture.

Teruki KADOSAKA is a former senior lecturer in Parasitology Division, Department of Infection and Immunity, Aichi Medical University School of Medicine. His interest is infection dynamics of *Orientia tsutsugamushi*, the etiological agent of scrub typhus.

Kenichi KANAI is a member of the Kagoshima Entomological Society. Focusing on insects in islands, they conduct distribution surveys.

Hiroki KAWABATA a chief of Department of Bacteriology-1 of the National Institute of Infectious Diseases. His primary research interest is the epidemiology of tick-borne infectious diseases.

Kei KAWAI is a professor at International Center for Island Studies, Kagoshima University. He specializes in marine biology and has conducted fieldwork in the islands of the Pacific and Kagoshima.

Motohiro KAWANISHI is an associate professor of the Faculty of Education, Kagoshima University. He specializes in vegetation science and has conducted researches on riparian vegetation in the Nansei islands and mainland of Japan.

Sueo KUWAHARA is a professor of Anthropology at Kagoshima University. He has conducted fieldwork in Malaysia over a number of years and more recently commenced research on the culture(s) of Japan's southwestern archipelago.

Masato MASUYA is a professor of Computing and Communications Center, Kagoshima University. His research interests include protein tertiary structure prediction and Information Communication

Technology utilization.

Taiji MORIYAMA is a member of the Kagoshima Entomological Society, and have been collecting and studying butterflies for many years. Recently, he has been surveying the distribution of butterflies on islands in Kagoshima Prefecture.

Hiroshi MORIWAKI is a professor emeritus of Kagoshima University. He specializes in physical geography, in particular geomorphologic development and Quaternary environmental history. Recently he has been interested in an integration of Quaternary environmental aspects in various regions.

Hiroyuki MOTOMURA is a professor of Ichthyology in the Kagoshima University Museum. He has worked on systematics and biogeography of marine and freshwater fishes in the Indo-Pacific region.

Hirohiko NAKAMURA is a professor of Physical Oceanography in the Faculty of Fisheries, Kagoshima University. His research interests are in the dynamics of oceanic motions with special emphasis on the Kuroshio and deep flows in the Okinawa Trough.

Yoshitaka NAKANISHI is a professor at the Faculty of Agriculture, Kagoshima University. He specializes in animal science and his research interests are animal behavior and management, conservation and utilization of native domestic animals, and active use of unused resources as feedstuff. He is also around as a president of Japan Goat Network.

Akio TACHIKUI is a former curator of the Kagoshima Prefectural Museum. He specializes in botany and has conducted researches on plant diversity and flora in the various islands and mainland of Kagoshima.

Ai TAKANO is an associate professor in the Joint Faculty of Veterinary Medicine, Yamaguchi University. She focuses on the biology and evolution of tick-borne pathogen in vector ticks.

Takayuki SHINZATO is an assistant Professor in the Research Center for Archaeology, Kagoshima University. He specializes in archaeology of pre-and proto-historic culture and society in the Ryukyu Islands.

Nobuhiro TAKADA is a former professor in Department of Pathological Sciences, Faculty of Medical Sciences, University of Fukui. His interest is the biology of medically important acari and the epidemiology of acari-borne infectious diseases.

Hiroto TAKAMIYA is a professor in International Center for Island Studies, Kagoshima University. He is specialized in prehistoric anthropology. He has been working on prehistory of the Central Ryukyus (Amami and Okinawa Archipelagos).

Jinshi TERADA is a former curator of the Kagoshima Prefectural Museum. He specializes in vegetation science and has conducted researches on various vegetation in the Nansei Islands and Kagoshima.

Takashi TORII is an associate professor of Faculty of Fisheries, Kagoshima University. He specializes in fisheries and economics, and has conducted fieldwork in the islands of Fiji and Kagoshima.

Seigo YAMAMOTO is a former head of Department of Microbiology of the Miyazaki Prefectural Institute for Public Health and Environment. His interests include infectious cycle of tick-borne infectious diseases.

Sota YAMAMOTO is an associate professor in International Center for Island Studies, Kagoshima University. He specializes in ethnobotany and tropical agriculture. His current interests include crop diversity, distribution, and dispersal routes in the Asia-Pacific region.

Yasuhiro YANO is an assistant professor in Department of Pathological Sciences, Faculty of Medical Sciences, University of Fukui. He is trying to determine the presence of various tick-borne pathogens in the tissues of ticks using electron microscopy.

Yoshiro WATANABE is a professor of the Faculty of Law, Economics and Humanities at Kagoshima University. He specializes in archaeology of ceramics in early modern Japan.

Preface

Kagoshima is an island prefecture with the second-highest number of islands in Japan—605, including 28 residential islands; these are primarily located in the sub-tropical zone. The distance between Kagoshima's north and south ends is approximately 600 kilometers.

The Kagoshima University International Center for Island Studies (KUICIS) published the books "*The Islands of Kagoshima, 2nd edition*" in 2015, "*The Amami Islands*" in 2016, and "*The Osumi Islands*" in 2017. The islands of Kagoshima were formed by the Koshiki Islands, Osumi Islands, Tokara Islands, and Amami Islands. The Project Planning Committee at KUICIS plans to publish the Islands book in English in Kagoshima to generate global awareness about these remarkable islands. In the book's fourth edition, we will introduce the Tokara Islands.

Because the Tokara Islands are located north of the Nansei Islands and stretch southwest from Kagoshima to Taiwan, they were governed by only one local government headquartered in Toshima Village. Toshima Village extends about 160 km from north to south and consists of seven populated and five uninhabited islands. About 700 people inhabit Nakano-shima, Kuchino-shima, Taira-jima, Suwanose-jima, Akuseki-jima, Kodakara-jima, and Takara-jima islands. People have inhabited these islands since the Jyomon period and created their own unique culture. These islands comprise smaller volcanic and uplifted islands, creating quite an unusual scenery. The islands are home to diverse flora and fauna, such as lily (*Lilium nobilissimum* [Makino]) and the Tokara horse. This shows that the Tokara Islands have a rich diversity from the natural, cultural, economic, and social points of view.

To conclude, we would like to thank the Project Planning Committee members, Kagoshima University, the Kagoshima local government, public office on each island, and local islanders for their support. We hope this book will help readers know the islands of Kagoshima better.

KAWAI Kei

Director
International Center for Island Studies
Kagoshima University

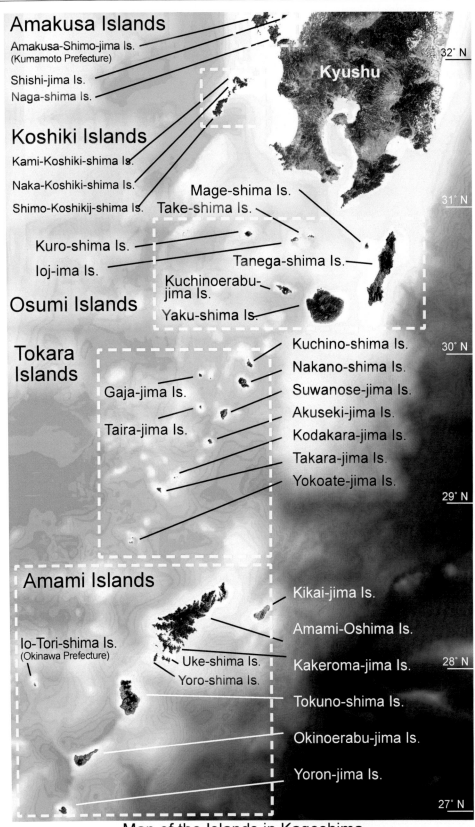

Amakusa Islands

Amakusa-Shimo-jima Is.
(Kumamoto Prefecture)

Shishi-jima Is.

Naga-shima Is.

Koshiki Islands

Kami-Koshiki-shima Is.

Naka-Koshiki-shima Is.

Shimo-Koshikij-shima Is.

Kuro-shima Is.

Ioj-ima Is.

Osumi Islands

Mage-shima Is.

Take-shima Is.

Tanega-shima Is.

Kuchinoerabu-jima Is.

Yaku-shima Is.

Tokara Islands

Gaja-jima Is.

Taira-jima Is.

Kuchino-shima Is.

Nakano-shima Is.

Suwanose-jima Is.

Akuseki-jima Is.

Kodakara-jima Is.

Takara-jima Is.

Yokoate-jima Is.

Amami Islands

Io-Tori-shima Is.
(Okinawa Prefecture)

Uke-shima Is.

Yoro-shima Is.

Kikai-jima Is.

Amami-Oshima Is.

Kakeroma-jima Is.

Tokuno-shima Is.

Okinoerabu-jima Is.

Yoron-jima Is.

Kyushu

32° N

31° N

30° N

29° N

28° N

27° N

Map of the Islands in Kagoshima

ix

Right Photos: Various Views in the Tokara Islands.

A–F: Various landscapes in the Tokara Islands; **A**, A view of Kuchino-shima Island from the rocky shore in Nakano-shima Island; **B**, Gaja-jima (top) and Kogaja-jima (bottom) Islands; **C**, Taira-jima Island; **D**, Takara-jima Island; **E**, Kodakara-jima (left) and Ko-jima Island; **F**, Nakano-shima Island, the largest island in the Tokara Islands. .

G–K: Nature in the Tokara Islands. **G**, .Mt. Megami at Takara-jima Island and the *Quercus phillyreoides* community; **H**, Volcanic vegetation in Suwanose-jima Island; **I**, A windswept shrub forest in Takara-jima Island; **J**, Coastal vegetation in Takara-jima Island; **K**, A Chinese banyan tree, *Ficus microcarpa* in Taira-jima Island.

L–N: Public transortation and facilities in the Tokara Islands; **L**, A municipal ferry boat, *Ferry Toshima*, in Nakano-shima Island; **M**, Community Center in Takara-jima Island; **N**, A freshwater spring, *Kou*, in Kuchino-shima Island.

Photos: Ryuta TERADA (B–F, L), Yasushi OTSUKA (A, M, N), Motohiro KAWANISHI (G–K),

Various Views in the Tokara Islands

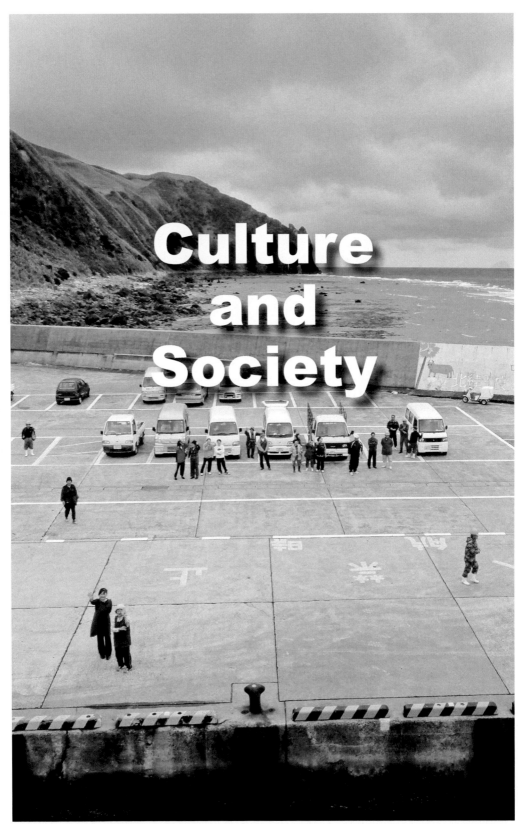

Culture and Society

Kuchino-shima Island. Photo: Ryuta TERADA

Chapter 1
Tokara's Past and Present

Sueo KUWAHARA

1. Introduction

The Tokara Islands are located in the northern part of the Southwest Islands (between mainland Kagoshima and the Amami Islands). The Tokara Islands belong to Toshima Municipal Village, which consists of seven inhabited islands (from north to south: Kuchino-shima, Nakano-shima, Taira-jima, Suwanose-jima, Akuseki-jima, Kodakara-jima and Takara-jima), five uninhabited islands (Gaja-jima, Kogaja-jima, Ko-jima, Kaminone-jima and Yokoate-jima), and twelve small islands within a total area of 101 km². The Tokara Islands make a chain of islands, which stretches from north to south about 160 km and are often referred as "the longest village in Japan" (NAGASHIMA 2009a: 4).

The population of the Tokara Islands is 709 people in 390 households (as of December 2017), and the most populous island is Takara-jima with 137 people. The least populated island is Kodakara-jima with 56 people[1]. A recent feature is the increase of migrants to the islands. The number of migrants in 2012 was 36 people in 20 households, and the number of the migrants for the five years from 2008 to 2012 was 114 people in 69 households. Out of the seven islands, Nakano-shima is the most populous with 29 people in 16 households, followed by Takara-jima with 28 people in 17 households. The population in 1950 was 2,938 people, which declined to 601 people in 2011, but it started to increase from 2012[2].

The overall topographic features of the Tokara Islands are their high elavation. The largest,

Nakano-shima, is 27.5 km², but its altitude is 979 m, which is the second highest next to Yaku-shima in the whole of the Nansei Islands, and the third and the fourth are Suwananose-jima (799 m) and Kuchino-shima (628 m) respectively. All of the islands except Kodakara-jima are mountain over 200 m, with few flat areas, and they have sheer cliffs of more than 100 m suddenly from the coast (TSUKADA 1991: 1–2).

Volcanos also form the Tokara Islands, and their line starts from the Kirishima mountain range in the north and uninhabited Yokoate-jima in the south, and reach to Iwo-tori-shima of Okinawa Prefecture (about 65 km west of Tokuno-shima). Out of the seven inhabited islands, there are volcanos on three islands, among which Mt. Otake of Suwanose-jima continues active volcanic activity (Asahi Shinbunsha 1969: 69, NAGASHIMA 2009b: 26). The chain of islands from Satsuma-Iwo-jima to Kuchino-shima, Suwanose-jima, and to the further south of Iwo-tori-shima were an archipelago producing sulfur. Here, sulfur mining started in 1868 and closed in 1964, and it reached 1,000 tons per month at its peak (NAGASHIMA 2009b: 28–29).

As the industry of the Toakra Islands, the productions of dried bonito and the rush used for tatami mat were once known, but in recent years the production of early loquat and sansevieria, and the beef livestock industry producing "Tokara cattle" are known.

As the main culture of the Tokara Islands, the legends of Heike and pirates, and the annual autumn festival of the masked deity Boze of Akuseki-jima are especially well known. Also, the event that was particularly in the limelight in recent years was the total solar eclipse of 22nd July 2009. As such, the Tokara Islands drew national and international attention as the place to be able to see the total solar eclipse the longest, and a lot of tourists came.

Many of the studies on the Tokara Islands are folkloristic ones (HAYAKAWA 1936, SHIMONO 1966, 2005, 2009, INAGAKI 1973, 1976, 1983, 1995, NAKANO1982, OGO1994, ITAI 2014), among which the earliest article is Hayakawa's study on pre-war Akuseki-jima's New Year's events (HAYAKAWA 1936). There are also some studies on individual themes such as Akuseki-jima's Boze (KREINER 1965, SHIMIZU 2005, ENDO 2014) and Tokara's rituals (OGO 1994, TANAKA 2005, KAWASAKI 2008). Also there are a number of studies overviewing Tokara's nature and culture (SAITO *et al*. 1980, Minaminihon Shinbunsha 1981, Toshima Son-shi Hensan-iinkai 1995, HIDAKA1985, 2005, TOKUNAGA 2002). Also, anthropological studies were conducted on the islands on egalitarianism and leveling (KAKEYA 1972, KONAKA 1989), on the kinship and the age-grade system (TORIGOE 1982, KIMURA 1987, OGO 1987), and on social change (NOGUCHI 1967, OGO 1999, HABARA 2008, MINAMURA 2006). As a recent theme, there are studies on solar eclipse tourism (OTA 2012) and broadband (MASUYA 2013).

2. History of Tokara

Tokara first appeared in the oldest historical document *Nihonshoki* in 654 (NAGASHIMA 2009a: 5). There are various theories about the origin of the name Tokara, one of which meaning volcanic island (Asahi Shinbunsha 1969: 69). Besides this, there are theories of Tohara and Tokabu. In Tohara theory, the offshore sea is called "tohara" in Amami and Okinawa, which means an island in the middle of the Kuroshio Current (Black Current). Tokafu theory is derived from Megamiyama (Mt. Goddess) of Takara-jima, which is a mountain that resembles a woman's breasts, and the breast in Ainu culture is called "tokafu". Also, in the modern era, geographers began to call the seven islands as "Tokara" after calling Takara-jima "Tokara" and this name has taken root (SHIMONO 2005: 335–336).

The tradition of Heike's descendant remains in the Tokara Islands. And it is recorded that the

people of Tokara were active as pirates during the 16th century and Shimazu's invasion of Ryukyu in 1609 (NAGASHIMA 2009a: 5).

In the modern ear, the Tokara Islands became under direct control of the Satsuma Domain. In July 1824 of the late Edo period, a major incident related to Japanese history occurred in Tokara. A British whaling ship which came off Takara-jima sought cattle for food, but an official of the Satsuma Domain declined the request because trade with foreigners was prohibited due to the isolation policy of the Edo government. The British side pulled up once but later they re-landed again, attacked the guardhouse and snatched the cattle. In this gunfight, one Englishman was killed. Triggered by this incident, the Edo government announced the decree for expelling foreign ships the next year in 1825 (Toshima Son-shi Henshu-iinkai 1995, NAGASHIMA 2009a: 6).

3. Two pirate legends

Legends about pirates have been told in Kuchino-shima, Kodakara-jima and Takara-jiam of the Tokara Islands. According to Kodakara-jima's follklore, in the old days, three pirates, Yosuke, Yotaro and Jin'nosuke, came over to the island and plundered it, but the islanders were said to have hidden in the cave at Mt. Unegamiyama and were saved. Yosuke was seen as a pirate, and in *Shimazuke Reccho Seido*[3] and *Sangoku Meisho Zue*[4], Yosuke and others are said to have come over to Nakanoshiam every year from Hyuga-koku (Miyazaki Prefecture), but Yosuke was killed there (HARADA 2015). According to the legend of Nakano-shima, a district governor of the island had a spree with a beautiful girl as a decoy and caught Yosuke and his group and they were killed. Then, Yosuke's soul is said to have become a rock called Yosuke Iwa, and his body was scattered as ashes and became a blood-sacking black fly called

---

3) Satsuma Domain's legal regulations (60 volumes) which were aggregated in 1826.

4) Documents compiled by Satsuma Domain in late Edo period which describe local topography and famous places such as shrines and temples in Kagoshima and a part of Miyazaki Prefecture.

Buyu (or Buto). However, in Kodakara-jima, he was dropped into a pit and buried alive (HARADA 2017).

There is another legend in Takara-jima that the British Pirate Captain Kid hid his treasure on the island in the late 17th century (Fig. 1). News that the island map drawn by Pirate Captain Kid around 1700 was found in the US and that the island might be Tokara's Takara-jima was reported extensively by Tokyo *Nichinichi Shinbun* (present-day *Mainichi Shinbun*) on the 4th February 1937. In August 2006, the full-scale treasure hunt using heavy machinery and detectors was broadcast live from Takara-jima on the 24-hour Television show "Love saves the earth" by Nippon Television Network (HAYWARD and KUWAHARA 2014).

4. Emigration and Immigration

The history of Tokara is one of migration. Above all, Suwanose-jima is known as an island that experienced both island-wide evacuation due to a volcanic eruption, and subsequent resettlement. At the time of this major volcanic eruption in 1813, the entire island population of 200 people were re-settled on Akuseki-jima and Nakano-shima. After that, the island became uninhabited for 71 years. Then, twenty-seven people from Amami Oshima settled in Nakano-shima and the number of households increased to 36 in 1896. Present-day islanders are the descendants of the migrants and the immigrants from outside the island. In the mid 1960s, the Yamaha Company Group embarked on developing and constructing a hotel and an airport with a 700 metre runway, but were closed down

shortly after (NAGASHIMA 2009b: 37–38).

Gaja-jima is known as an island that was uninhabited by voluntary migration and the first in Japan to do this. As of April 1969, 31 people from 7 households were living on this island, but a critical situation emerged where barge work could not be continued. In August 1963, when the number of households decreased from 7 to 6, and the islanders said that "it's over if you cannot have a funeral", and then an emigration application was submitted by the islanders to Kagoshima Prefecture in December. Thereafter, all households left the island and it became an uninhabited island in July 1970 (MINAMURA 2006, NAGASHIMA *et al.* 2009, SHIMONO 2009).

5. Boundary and division

The Tokara Islands were called "Shimo Shichi-to" (Lower seven islands), which, together with "Kami San-to" (Upper three islands), formed one village and called "Jitto-son" (Ten Islands Village) before World War II. In February 1946 after the end of the war, the area from Shimo Shichi-to south of 30 degrees north latitude to Okinawa was put under the US military administration. At that time, the ten island of Jitto-son were officially divided into two, that is, Mishima-mura ([Upper] three islands village) and Toshima-mura ([Lower] seven islands village), and part of the Tokara Islands became Toshima-mura of Kagoshima Prefecture. In Japanese history, it is only Toshima-mura as a village that was divided at the national border (SAITO 2008: 4).

The Tokara Islands are located at the border

Fig. 1. Cave in Takara-jima.

Fig. 2. Boze and Akuseki-jima.

between the mainland area and the Ryukyu area, and drawing attention as a border area from various viewpoints. According to biological distribution, Tokara is the region from temperate to subtropical. The Tokara Structural Strait is located between Akuseki-jima and Kodakara-jima, and the biogeographically is an important boundary that crosses the area from east to west and known as the "Watase Line", which was named after zoologist Watase Shozaburo in 1924 who found it. The fauna is at the border of the Palaearctic region with a high affinity with Eurasia, and the Oriental region with a high affinity with Taiwan and Southeast Asia, whereas the flora is at the border of Holactic Ecozone and Former Tropical Ecozone (Asahi Shinbunsha 1969: 69, NAGASAWA 1969: 179, FUKUZUMI 2009: 84).

6. Cultural intersection

It can be said that Tanega-shima and Yaku-shima belong to the Kyushu Cultural Area, and the Amami Islands belong to the Ryukyu Cultural Area, whereas the Tokara Islands are located in-between the two areas. The best way to show this is through the folk belief bearers such as Noro (priest) and Yuta (shaman), in which women play a main role. In Tokara, the female priest called "Neshi" holds a festival together with a male priest four times a year. Though this Neshi have similar elements with Noro and Yuta of Amami, what differs from Amami is that she always exists together with a male priest (YAMASHITA 1969: 150–151).

Neshi play important roles, including treating disease, conducting funerals, and acting as a medium on the third day after death. Thus, she is both a priest and shaman, and in this, a difference from Amami can be seen (YAMASHITA 1969: 152–153).

Though the Amami Islands had been under the rule of the Ryukyu dynasty from the 13th to the 16th century, it can be seen in Kuro-shima's mask and Akuseki-jima's Boze similar to Yaeyama's Akamata[5] that the Tokara Islands were also under the influence of Ryukyu culture (NAGASAWA 1969: 167) (Fig. 2). In Akuseki-jima, Bozes, the deities in masks and costumes, appear in Bon dances on 16th July of the lunar calendar, and scare children.

According to folklorist Toshimi Shimono, a Boze is a demon wearing a scary mask and covering the body with Biro (Kuba or Chinese fun palm) and Shuro (hemp palm) leaves, and breaks the circle of Bon dance to terminate the Bon event. In the past, Boze appeared on every Tokara island, but today, they appear only in Akuseki-jima, and represents Japanese visiting deities (SHIMONO 2009: 43).

The deities in the form of a demon appear in the mask dance of Take-shima (Takamen) and Kuro-shima (Onimen), Hassaku dance of Iwo-jima (Mendon), Stick dance and Toshitoidon (visiting deity) of Tanega-shima, Toshidons (visiting deities) of Yaku-shima and Koshikij-ima. Thus, the cultures from the north and south are mixed in the Tokara Islands and they have formed a unique folk culture there (SHIMONO 1986). Shimono also illustrates that the Tokara Islands, which are said to belong to the mainland cultural area, are the contact area of the Yamato and Ryukyu cultural areas by giving examples of agricultural tools and non-material cultures such as festivals and annual events (SHIMONO 2005: 337–359).

As noted above, there is a clear biological border between Tokara and Amami, but culturally, though the main culture of Tokara is Yamato culture, it is thought that there is a mixing of Ryukyu or Amami culture. Thus, the Tokara Islands can be said to be the contact and mixing area of north and south cultures (NAGASAWA 1969: 179–180).

7. Steamship and broadband

Tokara people depend on the village-owned large ferry boat (1,391 tons) called "Ferry Toshima" for their transportation between and beyond the islands, which arrives at Kuchino-shima and then goes south along the islands and finally arrives at Naze Port of Amami Oshima. Early the next morning, the ferry departs Naze Port and goes north along the islands and arrives at Kagoshima Port in the evening (Fig. 3). In April 2018, the new ship "Ferry Toshima Two" (gross tonnage 1950 t)

---

5) Visiting deities that appear in Honesai (good harvest festival) of the Yaeyama islands of Okinawa prefecture.

entered service. The distance connecting the seven islands is 131 km and the distance to Yokoate-jima, the southernmost uninhabited island is 177 km. The distance from the location of the village hall[6], which is actually located in Kagoshima city, to the southernmost island, Takara-jima, is 335 km. The route connecting Naze and Kagoshima that is operated directly by the village is 425 km, which is the longest in Japan (Nagashima 2009a: 7–8). The first service of the village ship was in 1933, and the island where liners could berth first was at Nakano-shima in October 1968, and the last was at Kodakara-jima in April 1990 (Nagashima 2009c: 60).

Akira Fumizono who became the first principal of Nakano-shima elementary school in 1930 and later became a village head and dedicated to opening the sea route, said that the "Steamship is also the road" (Nagashima 2009c: 55, 64–65). This century in Toshima village, the development of broadband began, and the trial class of broadband internet between the elementary schools of Nakano-shima and Sendai of Satsuma-Sendai City was carried out for the first time in May 2005, and Akuseki-jima and Suwanose-jima were connected by wireless LAN (Masuya 2009: 75–79). Today, Toshima Village advocates that "Broadband (information) is also the road" (Nagashima 2009c: 65, Masuya 2009: 69).

8. Conclusion

As seen above, Tokara's individuality can be said to lie in the cultural continuity and biological division of north and south. Though in the past, there were uninhabited islands and islands that experienced marginal settlement because of delays in the development of infrastructure such as transportation and communication. However, today, transportation and communication have been greatly improved. With the narrow information gap with the mainland as a result of the internet, along with the increase in I-turn migrants, the day might come for the first time in Japan when

humans and nature can coexist comfortably in a small ecosystem.

References

Asahi Shinbunsha 1969. *Satsunan Shoto no Sshima-jima* (The Satsunan Islands). Asahi Shinbunsha, Tokyo.

Endo, K. 2014. *Tokara Retto ni okeru Bon to Kamen-shin* (Bon Festival and Masked God in the Tokara Islands). Ajia Bunka-shi Kenkyu, 14: 59–65.

Fukuzumi, T. 2009. *Seimei no Michi: Watase-sen wo koete* (Beyond Watase Line). In: *Nihon Ichi Nagai Mura Tokara* (The Longest Village in Japan, Tokara) (eds. Nagashima, S., Takahiro, F., Norimasa, K. and Masuya, H.), Azusa-shoin, Fukuoka.

Habara, K. 2008. *Tokara / Toshima-mura no "Kakusa" to Chiiki no Seiji: Dounaru Nanatsu ni Bunsan suru Rito-son no Tatakai* (Disparity in Tokara Toshima-mura and Local Politics: What It Will Be? The Struggle of Remote Islands Dispersing into Seven). Teikyo Shakaigaku, 21: 1–50.

Harada, N. 2015. *Tokara Retto Kodakarajima no Kaizoku Densetsu* (Pirate Legend of Kodakarajima Island of the Tokara Islands). Niimi Koritsu Daigaku Kiyo, 36: 182–192.

Harada, N. 2017. *Tokara-retto Nakanoshima no Kaizoku Densetsu: Yosuke Iwa to Buto no Kigen* (Pirate Legend of Nakanoshima Island of the Tokara Islands: the Origin of Yosuke rock and But). Amami Okinawa Minkan Bungeigaku, 15: 3–18.

Hayakawa, K. 1936. *Akusekijima Shogatsu Gyouji Kikigaki: Kagoshima-ken Oshima-gun Toshima-mura* (An Interview Record of New Year Event of Akusekijima: Toshima Village of Oshima District, Kagoshima Prefecture). Minzokugaku Kenkyu, 2(1): 70–81.

Hayward, P. and S. Kuwahara, 2014. Takarajima: A Treasured Island Exogeneity, Folkloric Identity and Local Branding. Journal of Marine and Island Cultures, 3(1): 20–30.

Hidaka, U. 1985. *Kuroshio no Foukuroa* (Folklore of the Black current). Miraisha, Tokyo.

Hidaka, U. 2005. *Kuroshio no Bunka-shi* (Cultural Monograph of the Black Current). Nanpo-shinsha, Kagoshiama.

Fig. 3. Ferry Toshima.

---

6) The village halls of Toshima-mura and Mishima-mura are located in Kagoshima City.

INAGAKI, N. 1973. *Tokara no Chimei to Minzoku* (The Place Names and Folkways of Tokara). Bon-kobou, Tokyo.

INAGAKI, N. 1976. *Tokara-koku* (Tokara State). Yaedake Shobou, Tokyo.

INAGAKI, N. 1983. *Kimin Retto: Tokara-jin Koku-ki* (The Islands of Deserted People: The Record of the Tokara Islands). Miraisha, Tokyo.

INAGAKI, N. 1995. *Junana-nen-me no Tokara, Tairajima* (Seventeenth Year Tokara, Tairajima). Fukurosha, Tokyo.

ITAI, H. 2014. *Kyokai no Hensen: Tokara, Amami, Okinawa ni okeru Maruki-bune no Henka* (Transition of Border: The Change of Log Boat in Tokara, Amami and Okinawa). Kokusai Jomin Bunka Kenkyu Sosho, 5:59–83

KAKEYA, M. 1972. Sho Rito Jumin no Seikatsu no Hikaku Kenkyu: Tokara Retto, Tairajima to Akusekijima (A Comparative Study on the Lives of Small Islands: Tairajima and Akusekijima of the Tokara Islands). Minzokugaku Kenkyu, 37(1): 52–65.

KAWASAKI, F. 2008. *Gendai wo Ikiru Nesi: Shima to Tokai no Hazama de* (A Contemporary Neshi (Shaman): Between the Island and the City). Kokuritsu Rekishi Minzoku Hakubutsukan Kenkyu Hokoku, 142: 413–441.

KIMURA, D. 1987. *Sho Shudan Shakai ni okeru "Atsumari" no Kosei: Tokara Retto no Jirei* (The Constitution of "Gathering" in Small Group Society: A Case of the Tokara Islands). Kikan Jinruigaku, 18(2): 172–216.

KONAKA, M. 1989. *Byodo-shugi Shakai no "Ritoku to Daika: Tokara Retto K Shima no Jirei* (The Gain and the Price of Egalitarian Society: A Case of K Isalnd of the Tokara Islands). Nihon Minzokugaku, 179: 1–46.

KREINER, J. 1965. Tokara, Akusekijima no Kamen Gyoji (The Masked Events of Tokara's Akusekijima). Minzokugaku Kenkyku, 30(3): 255–256.

MASUYA, M. 2009. *Joho no Michi* (The Rode of Information). In: *Nihon Ichi Nagai Mura Tokara* (The longest village in Japan, Tokara) (eds. NAGASHIMA, S., TAKAHIRO F., NORIMASA, K. and MASUYA, H.), pp. 67–82, Azusa-shoin, Fukuoka.

MASUYA, M. 2013. Tokubetsu Shotai Koen: Sho Kibo Rito ni okeru Burodo Bando no Seibi to Rikatsuyo (Special invited lecture: The Maintenance, utilization and application of Broadband in small islands). Denshi Joho Tsushin Gakkai Gijutsu Kenyu Hokoku, 113(114): 69–74.

Minaminihon Shinbunsha (ed.) 1981. *Tokara: Umi to Hito to* (Tokara: The Sea and the People). Minami Nihon Shinbun Shuppan-sha, Kagoshima.

MINAMURA, T. 2006, *Sonraku Kyodotai no Hokai: Tokara no shima-jima to Gajajima, Mujinto heno Rekishi* (The Collapse of Village Community: The Islands of Tokara and Gajajima toward the History of Uninhabited Island). Nanpo-shinsha, Kagoshima.

NAGASAWA, K. 1969. *Satsunan-shoto no Shizen to Bunka* (Nature and Culture of the Satsunan Islands). In: Satsunan no Shima-jima (The Satsunan Islands) (ed. Asahai Shinbunsha), pp. 157–183, Asahi Shinbunsha, Tokyo.

NAGASHIMA, S. 2009a. *Josho* (Preface). In: Nihon Ichi Nagai Mura Tokara (The Longest Village in Japan, Tokara) (eds. NAGASHIMA, S., TAKAHIRO F., NORIMASA, K. and MASUYA, H.), pp. 4–8, Azusa-shoin, Fukuoka.

NAGASHIMA, S. 2009b. *Hi no Michi* (The Way of Fire). In: *Nihon Ichi Nagai Mura Tokara* (The Longest Village in Japan, Tokara) (eds. NAGASHIMA, S., TAKAHIRO F., NORIMASA, K. and MASUYA, H.), pp. 25–38, Azusa-shoin, Fukuoka.

NAGASHIMA, S. 2009c, *Kuroshio to Kotsu* (Black Current and Transportation). In: *Nihon Ichi Nagai Mura Tokara* (The Longest Village in Japan, Tokara) (eds. NAGASHIMA, S., TAKAHIRO F., NORIMASA, K. and MASUYA, H.), pp. 53–65, Azusa-shoin, Fukuoka.

NAGASHIMA, S., TAKAHIRO F., NORIMASA, K. and MASUYA, H. 2009. *Nihon Ichi Nagai Mura Tokara* (The Longest Village in Japan, Tokara). Azusa-shoin, Fukuoka.

NAKANO, T. 1982. *Rito Tokara ni Ikita Otoko* (A Man Who Lived in the Remote Island Tokara). Ochanomizu-shobo, Tokyo.

NOGUCHI, T. 1967. *Sho rito shakai no sonraku seikatsu to henka: Tokara Retto Gajajima* (The Village Life of Small Island and its Change: Gajajima of the Tokara Islands). Minzokugaku Kenkyu, 32(2): 126–143.

OGO, O. 1987. A Study of the Family Organization and Kinship in Tokara, Southern Kyushu. Seikei Ronso, 55(5/6): 49–78.

OGO, O. 1994. The Annual Festival of Tokara Society: A Case Study in Takara-Jima. Kagoshima. Seikei Ronso, 62(3): 1–42.

OGO, O. 1999. *Dento Bunka to Shakai Henka ni kansuru Kenkyu (1) Kagoshima-ken Tokara Retto no Jirei wo chushin tosite* (A Study on Traditional Culture and Social Change (1) A Case of the Tokara Islands, Kagoshima Prefecture). Meiji Daigaku Shakai Kagaku Kenkyusho Kiyo, 38(1): 197–239.

OTA, R. 2012. *Rito Kanko Moderu kara mita 2009 nen Toshima-mura Kaiki Nisshoku Tsua* (The 2009 Solar Eclipse Tour to Toshima Village from the Perspective of Island Tourism). Chiiki Seisaku Kagaku Kenkkyu, 9: 1–16.

SAITO, J. 2008. *Tokara Retto: Zekkai no Shimajima no Yutaka na Kurashi* (The Tokara Islands: Rich Life of Solitary Islands in the Distant Sea). Kobunsha, Tokyo.

SAITO, T., TSUKADA. K. and YAMAUCHI, H. (eds.) 1980. *Tokara: Sono Shizen to Bunka* (Tokara: Its Nature and Culture). Kokon-shoin, Tokyo.

SHIMIZU, K. 2005. *Retto Tanbo (No.4) Nihon-jin no Matsuri: Kagoshima-ken Toshima-mura Akusekijima, Boze Kuroshio ga motarasita kisai* (Visit the Archipelago (No.4) Japanese Festival: Boze, a Strange Festival Brought by the Black Current). National Geographic, 11(7): 30–33.

SHIMONO, T. 1966. *Tokara Retto Minzoku-shi Dai 1 kan* (The Monograph of the Tokara Islands Vouume1), Private edition.

SHIMONO, T. 1986. *Yamato Bunka to Ryukyu Bunka* (Japanese Culture and Ryukyu culture). PHP Kenkyu-sho, Kyoto.

SHIMONO, T. 2005. *Amami, Tokara no Dento Bunka: Matsuri to Noro, Seikatsu* (Traditional Cultures of Amami and Tokara: Festival and Noro, life). Nanpo-shinsha, Kagoshima.

SHIMONO, T. 2009. *Minami Nihon no Minzoku Bunka-shi 3: Tokara Retto* (Folk-cultural Monograph of Southern Japan 3: The Tokara Islands). Nanpo-shinsha, Kagoshima.

TANAKA, M. 2005. *Chiiki Shakai ni oekru Saishi no Jizoku to Henka wo meguru Ichi Kosatsu: Tokara Retto no Jirei kara* (A Study of the Continuation and Change of Ritual in Regional Society: from a Case of the Tokara Islands), Nihon Minzokugaku, 242: 1–34.

TOKUNAGA, K. 2002. *Tokara Retto, sono Kaiyo Bunka* (The Tokara Islands, its Marine Culture). Tohokugaku, 6: 110–119.

TORIGOE, H. 1982 *Tokara Retto Shakai no Kenkyu* (A Study of the Tokara Islands Society), Ochanomizu-shobo, Tokyo.

Toshima Son-shi Henshu-iinkai (ed.) 1995. *Toshima Son-shi* (Toshima Village Monograph). Toshima-mura, Kagoshima.

TSUKADA, K. 1991. *Tokara Retto no Shizen-kan* (Nature-views of the Tokara Islands). In: *Tokara Retto Gakujutsu Chosa Hokoku* (The Tokara Islands Academic Research Report) (ed. Kagoshima-ken Hoken-kankyo-bu Kankyo Seisaku-ka), pp. 1–16, Kagoshima Prefecture.

YAMASHITA, K. 1969. *Minkan Shiko. In: Satsunan no Shima-jima* (The Satsunan Islands) (ed. Asahi Shinbunssha). pp. 150–153, Asahi Shinbunsha, Tokyo.

OTSUKA, Y., TERADA, R. and NISHIMURA, S. (eds.), *The Tokara Islands*
Kagoshima University International Center for Island Studies; Hokuto Shobo Publishing, Tokyo. 10 March 2020.

Chapter 2

Ceramic Distribution in the Tokara Islands in the Early Modern Period

Yoshiro WATANABE

1. Introduction

Southern Kyushu historically functioned as the gateway to and from the south via the Nansei Islands. In the Yayoi period (8BC–3AD), shell-rings from the southern sea were brought to the Japanese mainland, and in ancient times (9th–11th centuries), turban shell (*Lunica marmorata*, Japanese: yakogai) was requested as a material for mother-of-pearl work by nobles in Kyoto. In the medieval period (12th–16th centuries), merchants from China and Hakata expanded their sphere of activity to the Nansei Islands, and in the 15th century, the Ryukyu Kingdom became the center of trade activities. In the 16th century, Europeans first arrived in southern Kyushu. The Shimadzu clan (島津氏), the feudal lords of the region, invaded the Ryukyu Kingdom at the beginning of the 17th century, and ruled it throughout the Early-Modern period, all the while trading with China. The Tokara Islands, which lie between the main island of Kyushu and the Amami islands, played an important role as a transit point for north-south distribution. To reveal part of the material distribution and cultural exchange, this paper examines the distribution of the early-modern (17th–19th century) ceramics in the Tokara Islands from an archaeological viewpoint.

2. Historical background

Human settlement in the Tokara Islands began in the Jomon period, and sites dating from the Yayoi period to ancient times have been found thereafter (MITSUTOMO and KAWAGUCHI 1962, Kumamoto University Archaeological Laboratory 1979, 1980, NISHITANI *et al.* 1995, 1997, ITO 2011, SHINTO 2005, 2019, SHINZATO and ITO 2019, etc.). On the other hand, in historical documents, words such as "Tokara" (吐火羅)" are found in Nihon Shoki (日本書紀) of the 8th century, and "Tokamu-jin"(渡感人) is found in an article in 699 of Shoku Nihongi (続日本紀). So far, these have not been considered to indicate the Tokara Islands, and it seems that in ancient times Tokara was collectively called "South Islands"(南島) and was at least not individually recognized by the people in the center on the mainland (Toshima Sonshi Editorial Committee 1995).

Moving into the medieval period, the Shimadzu, in 1227, became the stewards (jitoshiki, 地頭職) of Junishima (十二嶋, Twelve islands) including Kuchino-shima, Nakano-shima, Taira-jima, Suwanose-jima, Akuseki-jima, Gajya-jima, and Takara-jima Islands (Toshima Sonshi Editorial Committee 1995). In addition, trading ships connecting East and Southeast Asia will pass through the sea area including the Tokara Islands. In 1443, when Sin Sukju (申叔舟) came to Japan as an envoy of the Joseon Dynasty. After

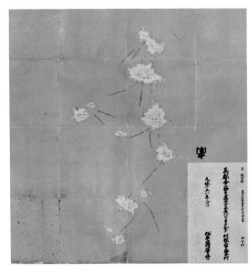

Fig. 1. Tokara Islands drawn in "Genroku Kuni Edzu" (National Archives of Japan Digital Archive).

returning to Joseon, he wrote a history of Japan and the Ryukyu Islands called Kaito-Shokoku-ki (海東諸国記) in 1471. The names of Tokara islands such as "Kuchi-jima (口島)", "Naka-jima (中島)", "Akuseki (悪石)" "Gajya-jima (臥蛇島)", "Kogajya-jima (小臥蛇島)" "Taira (多伊羅)", and "Tokara (渡賀羅)" are found in this book (Sin (trans. by Tanaka) 1991), which shows that the existence of Tokara was recognized in the Joseon Dynasty. Furthermore, in the latter half of the 16th century, the people of Tokara, who were called "Shichito-shu (七島衆)" came under the rule of the Shimadzu clan and took part in trade and military activities (Fukase 2004). It is known from the records of the early 17th century that "Shichito-shu" were deeply involved in the trade between Japan and the Ming Dynasty in China and made a great profit (Tomiyama 2004: 34).

Ceramic materials showing the trade activities in those days include Chinese ceramics being brought to all the Tokara Islands (Kamei 1993), Chinese and Vietnamese ceramics excavated from the Suwanose-jima Kiriishi (切石) site (Kumamoto University Archaeological Laboratory 1994, Ohashi and Yamada 1995), and Kamuiyaki from Tokuno-shima Island found in Taira-jima island (Ito 2009, 2011, Shinto 2019). On Akuseki-

jima Island, a Hokyointo (宝篋印塔) pagoda made of Yamakawa-ishi (山川石) (stone produced near Yamakawa, Ibusuki City, Kagoshima Prefecture) from the 15th century has been confirmed (Hashiguchi and Matsuda 2012, 2013).

In 1609, the Shimadzu clan invaded the Ryukyu Kingdom, which had been independent until then. After that, the area up to the Amami Islands came under the direct control of the Satsuma domain (薩摩藩), and the Ryukyu Kingdom fell under the Satsuma domain's strong political influence. The Tokara Islands also came under the control of the funa-bugyo (船奉行), the naval magistrate of the domain, and zaiban-sho (在番所) administration offices were established on Kuchino-shima, Nakano-shima, and Takara-jima, and officers were dispatched from the domain. There were the islands officers as gunji (郡司) district adiministators, yokome (横目) inspectors and myoshu (名主) village chiefs, and the common islanders such as myoko (名子) tenant farmers and genin (下人) peasants and servants were under them. The Shichito-shu played a role as shipping agents that connected Kagoshima with Amami and Okinawa (Toshima Sonshi Editorial Committee 1995). According to the records of 1709, of the 230 big ships in the Satsuma domain at that time, 40

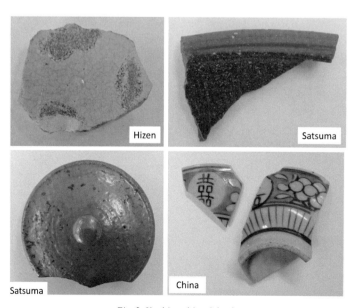

Fig. 2. Kuchino-shima Island.

Fig. 3. Nakano-shima Island.

ships (about 16%) were Shichito ships (Tomiyama 2004: 35). According to the Genroku-kuni-ezu (元禄国絵図) map of Satsuma Province and Ōsumi Province at the beginning of the 18th century, it is clear that the islands are connected by several routes (Fig.1). However, since the map was submitted to the Tokugawa bakufu government, it is considered to have been an official route for the domain, and it is assumed that there was various other private traffic. Also, Shichito dried bonito flakes (七島鰹節) made from bonito taken from Tokara was paid to the domain as tribute and also presented to the bakufu every year in cold weather (寒中) (Around December in the lunar calendar) .

In modern times, today's Mishima and Toshima villages were combined into Toshima in Kawanabe County and incorporated into Oshima County in 1897. It officially became Jitto-son (十島村) in 1920. When WWII ended in 1945, the present Toshima Village came under the military administration of the United States and was separated from Mishima Village. Although it was returned to Japan in 1952, it remained separate from Mishima Village and became Toshima Village, and was changed from Oshima County to Kagoshima County in 1953 which is still the case today (Toshima Sonshi Editorial Committee 1995).

3. Archaeological survey of Tokara Islands
The author has conducted archaeological surveys and excavations of the Tokara Islands since 2011 (Watanabe 2015, 2016, 2018, 2019). This chapter summarizes the early modern ceramics that were identified in the islands. Distribution surveys are conducted mainly in villages on each island. This is because the communities of the Early-Modern period basically overlap with the present-day communities.

3.1. Kuchino-shima Island (Fig.2)
Pottery and porcelain made in the 17th century includes early 17th century Hizen (肥前) bowls, Naeshirogawa (苗代川) Satsuma-ware jars, and Chinese blue-and-white bowls. From the 18th century onwards, Hizen porcelain, Naeshirogawa pottery mortar, pots and jars, and Ryumonji (龍門司) bowls and Satsuma porcelain bowls were seen. In addition, White Satsuma (白薩摩) bowls produced at the Tateno (竪野) kiln, which was directly controlled by Satsuma domain, were also found around the graveyard. In addition, 18th century Qing dynasty colored porcelain bowls have been found.

In August 2017, the front garden of the small Amida-do (阿弥陀堂) shrine on the island was excavated, and ceramic ware from medieval to modern times was found. Among early modern

11

ceramics, a 17th century Hizen pottery mortar, Hizen porcelain plates, and a small cup from China were excavated. From the 18th century onwards, Naeshirogawa pottery jars, teapots and mortars, Hizen porcelain, and Satsuma porcelain bowls (19th century) were also used.

3.2. Nakano-shima Island (Fig. 3)

Many pieces of early-modern ceramics were collected in the old villages, Satomura (里村) and Kusunoki (楠木), and many pieces of ceramics were scattered around the small Shimanaka-don (島

中どん) shrine in Satomura.

Examples of ceramics from the 17th century include a Hizen pottery bowl (late 17th century – early 18th century), a Chinese blue-and-white bowl (early 17th century), and a small bowl (17th century). A Chinese blue-and-white bowl, Naeshirogawa pottery mortars and teapots, and Kajiki and Aira (加治木・姶良) pottery bowls were made in the 18th century. Hizen and Satsuma porcelain from the 19th century were also found. An unglazed bottle from Tsuboya (壺屋) kiln in Okinawa has also been found. This bottle was

Fig. 4. Gajya-jima Island (Toshima Village History and Folklore Museum in Nakano-shima Island).

Fig. 5. Taira-jima Island (* Pi Pi donburi).

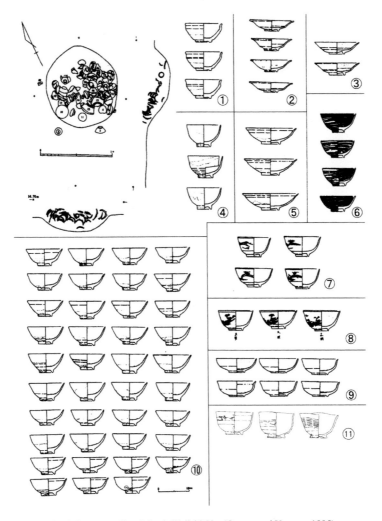

Fig. 6. Suwanose-jima Island, Kiriishi Site (OHASHI and YAMADA 1995).

mainly used as a container for awamori (泡盛), the strong Okinawan liquor.

3.3. Gajya-jima Island (Fig. 4)

Gajya-jima Island has been uninhabited island since 1970. The author has not yet had an opportunity to go there. However, in the Toshima Village History and Folklore Museum on Nakano-shima, pottery that was introduced to Gajya-jima Island is stored and exhibited. They were cataloged in 2013.

There are a total of 40 pieces of ceramics that have been brought from Gajya-jima Island on display at that museum. Of these, 18 are from overseas such as China and Southeast Asia, 21 are early modern Japanese ceramics, and 1 is unknown, but only early modern ceramic ware is mentioned here. KAMEI (1993) reported about the ceramics from overseas.

There are Hizen pottery and porcelain, and the white-slipped Ryumonji bowls, dating from the 17th century to the 19th century. Other than two bottles, all of them are bowls, characterized by two or four bowls of the same production area, shape and pattern. There are very few damaged items. If we look more closely, we can see that the small ash that fell from the kiln still remains on the inner bottom of the bowl. Such ash wears out during use, but there is a possibility that the

13

Gajya-jima imported product did not wear out and was therefore not used. These characteristics are common to the ceramics excavated from the Suwanose-jima Kiriishi site described later, and are important in considering their characteristics.

3.4. Taira-jima Island (Fig. 5)

Early 17th century blue-and-white Hizen porcelain plates were recovered. There are Hizen pottery bowls and plates from the Uchinoyama (内野山) kiln from the latter half of the 17th century to the first half of the 18th century, Naeshirogawa pottery mortars and pots from the 18th century onwards, and Kajiki and Aira pottery bowls and plates. In addition, many blue-and-white Qing dynasty porcelain bowls with rough patterns have been found. The same type of porcelain has also been found on other islands, but Taira-jima has the largest number and they are called "pi pi donburi" there. These are presumed to have been mounted on unmanned ships that drifted ashore on Taira-jima in 1894 (SHINZATO 2016).

3.5. Suwanose-jima Island

Following evacuation due to the 1813 eruption of Mt. Ontake, the island remained uninhabited until 1883. The settlements from before the eruption are covered with a thick layer of volcanic ash, so the early modern layer is buried deep underground. Therefore, only a few materials have been found and the distribution of ceramics in the Early-Modern period cannot be understood.

However, the Kiriishi site on the island was excavated and researched by Kumamoto University Archaeological Laboratory in 1992,

and a total of 148 pieces of ceramic ware and 16 pieces of earthenware were unearthed from the inside of the pit and its surroundings (Fig. 6). The pit was covered with the volcanic ash of 1813 and is thought to have been buried before that. Fragments of nails were also excavated from the underground part, and it is assumed that ceramic ware was buried in a wooden box (Kumamoto University Archaeological Laboratory 1994, OHASHI and YAMADA 1995).

The unearthed ceramics were from China, Vietnam, and Japan from the latter half of the 14th century to the 18th century, and were classified into 6 periods. Among them, ceramics corresponding to the Early-Modern period from the latter half of the third period to the sixth period have several characteristics. One of them is limited to tableware such as bowls and plates because there are no storage or cooking utensils such as jars, pots and mortars. It is also characterized by very little damage. Several bowls and plates with the same shape, the same size and the same glaze and pattern were excavated. In particular, 40 Ryumonji bowls from the 18th century have been unearthed, but they are almost the same size and shape. There is no wear or defect caused by use, and it is highly possible that it was buried without being used. There are many common points with the materials brought from Gajya-jima (see above).

3.6. Akuseki-jima Island (Fig. 7)

Early-modern ceramics include Naeshirogawa pottery jars from the 18th century onwards and 19th century blue-and-white Qing dynasty porcelain. A relatively large number of ceramics

Satsuma

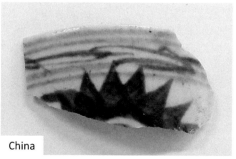

China

Fig. 7. Akuseki-jima Island..

were found in the center of the village, where there is a small shrine.

3.7. Takara-jima Island (Fig. 8)

The Uenotera (上の寺) graveyard is where the most pottery has been found on this island. It is considered that the ceramic ware originally offered at the graves was discarded there. There are also cases in which ceramics are scattered under the banyan trees, or are entangled between the widely stretched roots.

Examples of ceramics from the 17th century include small blue-and-white Chinese cups, from the 18th century are Naeshirogawa pottery pots and teapots, blue-and-white Hizen porcelain lids, and blue-and-white Satsuma porcelain bowls and lids from 19th century. Fragments of a color painted Kyoto-ware (京焼) bowl believed to be from the 19th century were also found.

3.8. Kodakara-jima Island (Fig. 9)

Kodakara-jima Island is the smallest inhabited island. The harbor is small, and a barge was used until 1990. Excluding Suwanose-jima Island, which was buried in volcanic ash, the number of materials found is the smallest, with only Hizen

porcelain bowls from the end of the 17th century to the first half of the 18th century as the early modern ones. However, at a former shrine on the island, a Hizen pottery bowl (late 17th century to early 18th century) and a Ryumonji pottery bottle (19th century?) as well as a black-glazed Kajiki and Aira pottery bottle (18th–19th century) were identified.

4. Three layers of distribution of early modern ceramics

A summary of early-modern ceramics in the Tokara Islands reported in the previous chapter follows (Table 1).

First, porcelain and pottery were used for tableware such as bowls and plates in early-modern Tokara. Hizen porcelain circulated throughout the Early-Modern period and Hizen pottery from the 17th century to the first half of the 18th century. In Hizen, the production of pottery tableware declined around the middle of the 18th century, and pottery pots were the main products, reflecting that production situation. On the other hand, regarding Satsuma ware, products made in Ryumonji kiln in the first half of the 18th century can be found from Gajya-jima, and there

Fig. 8. Takara-jima Island.

15

are also mass-produced products with white slip from the latter half of the 18th century. After the end of the 18th century, Satsuma porcelain also began to circulate. In addition, a small number of pieces of Kyoto-ware with colored pictures were found on Takara-jima Island. Although the amount of Chinese porcelain is small, blue-and-white porcelain from the 17th to 19th centuries can be seen. Also, the same kind of colored 18th century Qing dynasty porcelain bowls found on Kuchino-shima have been unearthed from the Madama-michi (真珠道) site at Shuri Castle (首里城) in Okinawa (Chinen *et al.* 2006), which suggests that these Chinese porcelain bowls were brought to Japan via Okinawa.

Next, most of the jars and pots as storage and mortars as cooking utensils are Naeshirogawa. Although 17th century Naeshirogawa jars were found, they only increased in the 18th century, especially in the latter half of the 18th century. From this period, Naeshirogawa pottery teapots began to be seen.

For Ryukyu pottery, there were unglazed pottery such as big bottles and mortars, and glazed pottery such as teapots. You can also see many

large Tsuboya pots in the garden of private houses throughout the Tokara Islands. It is difficult to tell whether these were made in the Early-modern period or after, but there is a possibility that they were in circulation to some extent because bottles which have been estimated to date back to the Early-Modern period have been found.

The distribution pattern of early-modern ceramics in Tokara Islands can be summarized as follows. That is to say, Hizen pottery and porcelain were used for eating utensils, Kajiki and Aira Satsuma ware and products of Ryumonji were used, Satsuma porcelain was used in the 19th century, storage and cooking utensils were mainly Naeshirogawa products, and glazed and unglazed Tsuboya pottery from Okinawa were in also circulation. This aspect is very similar to that of the mainland area of early-modern Kagoshima (HASHIGUCHI 2002, WATANABE 2010). In other words, it is highly possible that the source of these Japanese ceramics in Tokara was the mainland of Kagoshima. In addition, it is presumed that the owner of the high quality Hizen porcelain and colored Kyoto ware may have been influential people on the islands.

As described above, the distribution of ceramics in Tokara Islands in the Early-Modern period includes the flow of Hizen ceramics and Satsuma ware from the mainland of Kagoshima and the flow from Okinawa in the south. There are two types of streams from the south: a stream of Chinese porcelain from China via Okinawa, and a stream of pottery produced in Tsuboya on Okinawa. Such a trend extended not only to Tokara Islands but also to the entire Nansei islands including Amami and Okinawa, and it can be said

Hizen

Fig. 9. Kodakara-jima Island.

Table 1. A summary of early-modern ceramics in the Tokara Islands.

	Hizen	Satsuma	Ryukyu	China	Others
Tableware (Bowl, plate, teapot)	Porcelain (17c~19c) Pottery (17c~the first half of 18c)	Kajiki and Aira, Ryumonji pottery (18c~) Porcelain (the end of 18c~) Naeshirogawa pottery teapot (the late half of 18c~)	Glazed pottery (Modern?)	Blue and White Porcelain (17c~19c) Colored Porcelain (18c)	Kyoto colored pottery (19c)
Storageware (Vase, bottle)		"Naeshirogawa pottery (17c ~ 19c) Ryumonji pottery (19c)	No glazed pottery (19c)		
Cookware (mortar)		Naeshirogawa pottery (17c ~ 19c)	No glazed pottery		

that there were three layers of flows of ceramic distribution: from the north, from the south and within the islands (Fig. 10) (HASHIGUCHI 2001, 2009, WATANABE 2016, 2018).

5. Opportunity and purpose of obtaining ceramics

How did the people of Tokara Islands get the pottery? Unfortunately, there are few historical records on the distribution of goods in early modern Tokara. Here, we will consider the records of visits to the Mishima and Tokara Islands known as Jitto-Jokyoroku (拾島状況録) by Gisuke SASAMORI (笹森儀助), who was the governor of Amami Island in 1895, as a clue (SASAMORI 1968).

According to the report, there were no shops in the Tokara Islands except on Suwanose-jima Island, and it is said that itinerant merchants did not come. Some islands individually described the visits of merchants, but this shows that such visits to the islands were rare. In other words, people in the Tokara Islands had few opportunities to buy household goods including ceramics on a daily basis. On the other hand, it says that the islanders bought household goods at the places where they sold their local produce (seafood, sugar, turban shells etc.). Most of the products were shipped to Kagoshima, but Taira-jima, Suwanose-jima, Akuseki-jima, and Takara-jima Islands also shipped to the Amami-Oshima Islands. It is also said that, in the Early-Modern period, they made commercial transactions with fishing boats at the port, or they bought when they visited Kagoshima once a year. In other words, goods were purchased as part of various social activities, and it is assumed that ceramics and other items were included in them.

What kinds of ships were there to connect Kagoshima, Amami-Oshima and Okinawa? In the Early-Modern period, there were official ships operated by domain officials. Traveling to Kagoshima once a year to pay tax is also thought to have been an important opportunity to obtain ceramics. It is seen in the diaries of the officers on Yoron-to Island in the Early-Modern period that various goods were distributed as gifts and ordered goods along with the travel of official

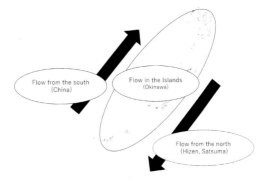

Fig. 10. Three Layers of distribution of Early Modern Ceramics in the Nansei Islands.

ships (SAKITA 2012).

The Tokara sailors of the Early-Modern period were heavily involved in the transportation of goods between Satsuma and Ryukyu, and it is thought that they were actively engaged in commercial transactions at that time (TAKARA 2004). Although the records of the transport of ceramics so far are not mentioned, it can be assumed that these early modern ceramics found in the Tokara Islands, from the Japanese mainland, Okinawa and China were brought by the people of Tokara, who served as the sailors and the owners of the ships between the Satsuma and Ryukyu islands.

For what purpose did the people of Tokara acquire the pottery? Needless to say, the biggest reason is their acquisition for everyday use. For example, bowls, plates and pottery teapots are used as daily tableware. Also, jars and pots were indispensable as containers to store various things such as water and grain. Mortars for pounding miso (bean paste) and potatoes were also used as a cooking tool every day. However, it seems that the people of Tokara obtained ceramics for the purpose of dedicating them to shrines.

According to Sasamori's Jitto-Jokyoroku visit reports, ceramic ware was placed in shrines such as Hachiman-gu (八幡宮) Shrine on Gajya-jima Island, Hachiman-gu Shrine on Akuseki-jima Island, and Chinju-jinja (鎮守神社) Shrine on Takara-jima Island. Among them, Chinju-jinja Shrine on Takara-jima Island had a custom of dedicating vases to shrines in appreciation of their safe return to the island from their voyage to Kagoshima, and it is said that the number of vases reached several hundred as the custom was repeated. As it is unlikely that the household goods that had been used until then were diverted, it is assumed that the dedication articles were newly obtained in Kagoshima. This indicates that ceramics were brought to Tokara for dedication, not for everyday use.

What comes to mind here are the early modern ceramics unearthed from the Kiriishi site on Suwanose-jima Island and the ceramics from Gajya-jima Island in the possession of the Toshima Village History and Folklore Museum. As mentioned above, these two types of ceramic ware have some similarities, such as the number of bowls and plates (the absence of pots and jars), the number of same-sized ceramic ware with the same pattern, many of which are not damaged, and there is a high possibility that they were unused because there are no signs of wear or other damage. The artefacts from Gajya-jima Island are regarded as cultural properties related to Hachiman-jinja (八幡神社) Shrine on the island. Judging from the description in the Jitto-Jokyoroku reports, it is possible that these ceramics were brought into the island not for everyday use but as gifts in advance.

Even though they were used to the sea, it was extremely dangerous for the people of Tokara to cross the open sea of the Shichito-nada (七島灘), where the current is strong, so when they were able to cross the sea and return to their home islands, they must have offered the ceramics they obtained at their destination to the gods with gratitude.

6. Conclusion

Before planes were invented, the only way to cross the sea was by ship. Before precise charts were drawn, the islands were a clue to the destination and a place of rest for the voyage. Long ago, people, goods and information were transported through the sea and islands. Some of this was given in historical records, but much not. However, even if it was not recorded, the material traces of the circulation of goods remain. Ceramics, in particular, do not decay even after having been in the ground for a long time, providing a valuable clue to understanding past exchanges. Pieces of

pottery found in the Tokara Islands, which have no history of pottery production themselves, were all imported from outside. These are therefore a source of information on access to the outside world and the distribution of goods.

It can be said that by carefully collecting the fragments of pottery that remain on each of the Tokara Islands and accumulating estimates of their ages and localities, it is possible to reveal the history of material distribution in Tokara Islands that has not been documented yet.

Acknowledgment

I would like to thank Professor Steve COTHER (Kagoshima University) who helped me write this article. However, all the responsibility for the text lies with WATANABE.

References

CHINEN, T. *et al.* 2006. *Madama-michi ato* (Madama-michi Site). Okinawa Prefectural Archaeological Center, Nishibaru.

FUKASE, K. 2004. *Kan shinakaiikiken ni okeru Tokara retto* (Tokara Islands in the China sea). In: *Ryukyu to Nihonhondo no sen'i tiiki toshiteno Tokara retto no rekishiteki ichidzuke wo meguru Sougou teki kenkyu* (Comprehensive Study on the Historical Position of the Tokara Islands as a Transition Region between Ryukyu and Mainland Japan) (ed. TAKARA, Y.), pp. 87–100, Ryukyu University, Nishibaru.

HASHIGUCHI, W. 2001. *Nansei shoto ni motarasareta Kinsei Satsuma yaki* (Early Modern Satsuma Ware Brought to Nansei Islands). Karakara, 10: 9–16.

HASHIGUCHI, W. 2002. *Kagoshimakenchiiki ni okeru 16-19 seiki no Toujiki no Shutsudo yoso* (The Excavation of Ceramics in the 16-19th Century in Kagoshima Prefecture). Kagoshima Chiikishi Kenkyu, 1: 3–14.

HASHIGUCHI, W. 2009. *Kinsei satsuma ni okeru Chugoku jiki no ryunyu* (The Inflow of Chinese Ceramics in Early-modern Satsuma). In: *Karafune ourai* (Traffic of Chinese Ships) (ed. East Asia Interregional Exchange Study Group), pp. 53–66, Chugoku Shoten, Fukuoka.

HASHIGUCHI, W. and MATSUDA, T. 2012. *Tokararetto no chusei sekito (1)* (Medieval Stone Pagoda in the Tokara Islands (1)). MinamiNihon Bunkazai Kenkyu, 14: 6–9.

HASHIGUCHI, W. and MATSUDA, T. 2013. *Tokararetto no chusei sekito (2)* (Medieval Stone Pagoda in the Tokara Islands (2)). MinamiNihon Bunkazai Kenkyu, 15: 1–5.

ITO, S. 2009. *10-13seikizengo no Ryukyu retto: Taigai koryu to bunkateki shutai* (The Ryukyu Islands around the 10-13 Century: Foreign Exchanges and Cultural Entities). Koukogaku Journal, 591: 11–14.

ITO, S. 2011. *Ryukyu Bunkaken no hokugen ni kansuru Koukogaku teki kisokenkyu (Chukan houkoku)* (Basic Archaeological Study of the Northern Limit of the

Ryukyu Culture (Interim Report)). Kokugakuin University Kenkyu kaihatu kikou, Tokyo.

KAMEI, A. 1993. *Nanseishoto ni okeru bouekitouji no Ryutsu keiro* (Trade and Distribution Channels of Ceramics in Nansei Islands). Jochi Asiagaku, 11: 11–45.

Kumamoto University Archaeological Laboratory (ed.) 1979. *Tachibana Iseki* (Tachibana Site). Kumamoto

Kumamoto University Archaeological Laboratory (ed.) 1980. *Tachibana Iseki (2)* (Tachibana Site (2)). Kumamoto.

Kumamoto University Archaeological Laboratory (ed.) 1994. *Tokara retto no koukogaku teki chousa* (Archaeological Surveys of the Tokara Islands). Toshimamura.

MITSUTOMO, K. and KAWAGUCHI, S. 1962. *Takarajima Hamasaka kaidzuka no chosagaiyo* (Outline of the Excavation of Hamasaka Shell Mound in Takarajima Island). Bulletin of Saitama University 11: 39–46.

NISHITANI, H. SHITARA, H. and HARUNARI, H. 1995. *Tokara retto Takarajima Ohike iseki* (Ohike Site in Takarajima Island of Tokara Islands). Bulletin of the National Museum of Japanese History, 60: 261–282.

NISHITANI, H. SHITARA, H. and HARUNARI, H. 1997. *Tokara Takarajima Ohike iseki* (Ohike Site in Takarajima Island of Tokara Islands). Bulletin of the National Museum of Japanese History, 70: 219–251.

OHASHI, K. and YAMADA, Y. 1995. *Kagoshimaken Kagoshimagun Toshimamura Suwanosejima iseki shutudo no toujiki* (Ceramics Unearthed from the Site in Suwanosejima Island, Toshimamura Village, Kagoshima County, Kagoshima Prefecture). Boekitouji Kenkyu, 15: 141–164.

SAKITA, M. (ed.) 2012. *Yoron-to no komonjo wo yomu* (Read the Ancient Documents of Yoron Island). Nanpo Shinsha, Kagoshima.

SASAMORI, G. 1968. *Jitto Jokyoroku* (Report of Circumstances of Mishima and Tokara Islands) In: *Nihon Shomin Seikatushiryo Shusei* 1, pp. 117–299, Sanichi Shobo, Tokyo.

SHINTO, K. 2005. *Ohike iseki* (Ohike site). In: *Senshi Kodai no Kagoshima*, pp. 725–726, Kagoshima Prefecturem, Kagoshima.

SHINTO, K. 2019. *Toshima mura Tairajima no shinhakken no Kamuiyaki tsubo nitsuite* (Kamuiyaki Ware Newly Discovered in Tairajima Island of Toshima Village). In: *Nakayama Kiyomi to Amamigaku*, pp. 361–366, Amami Archaeology Society, Setouchi.

SHINZATO, T. 2016. *Pi Pi donburi kou* (Study of Pi Pi donburi (Big Bowl)). Kagoshima Kouko, 46: 77–92.

SHINZATO, T. and ITO, S. 2019. *Tokara retto Gajajima no Senshijidai Ibutsu* (Prehistoric relics of the Gajajima Island of Tokara Islands). In: *Nakayamakiyomi to Amamigaku*, pp. 349–360, Amami Koukogakkai,

Setouchi.

SIN S. (Tr. by TANAKA, T.) 1991. *Kaito- Shokoku-ki* (A History of Japan and the Ryukyu Islands). Iwanami Shoten, Tokyo.

TAKARA, Y. 2004. *Ryusatsu kankei niokeru Tokara* (Position of Tokara in the relation between Satsuma and Ryukyu). In: *Ryukyu to Nihonhondo no sen'i tiiki toshiteno Tokara retto no rekishiteki ichidzuke wo meguru Sougou teki kenkyu* (Comprehensive Study on the Historical Position of the Tokara Islands as a Transition Region between Ryukyu and Mainland Japan) (ed. TAKARA, Y.), pp. 187–199, University of the Ryukyus, Nishihara.

TOMIYAMA, K. 2004. *Kyozo to jitsuzo no sakusousuru shima, Tokara* (Tokara, a mixture of fiction and reality). In: *Ryukyu to Nihonhondo no sen'i tiiki toshiteno Tokara retto no rekishiteki ichidzuke wo meguru Sougou teki kenkyu* (Comprehensive Study on the Historical Position of the Tokara Islands as a Transition Region between Ryukyu and Mainland Japan) (ed. TAKARA, Y.), pp. 30–40, University of the Ryukyus, Nishihara.

Toshima Sonshi Editorial Committee (ed.) 1995. *Toshima Sonshi* (History and Folklore of Toshima village). Toshima Village, Kagoshima.

WATANABE, M. 2004. *Kinsei Tokara to hyoryu, hyochaku (Drifting of Tokara in the Early-Modern period). In: Ryukyu to Nihonhondo no sen'i tiiki toshiteno Tokara retto no rekishiteki ichidzuke wo meguru Sougou teki kenkyu* (Comprehensive Study on the Historical Position of the Tokara Islands as a Transition Region between Ryukyu and Mainland Japan) (ed. TAKARA, Y.), pp. 101–138, University of the Ryukyus, Nishihara.

WATANABE, Y. 2010. *Kagoshima joka shutsudo no tojiki to Satsuma yaki* (Ceramics and Satsuma ware excavated from Kagoshima castle town). Kikan Kokogaku, 110: 48–51.

WATANABE, Y. (ed.) 2015. *Kinsei Nihon kokkaryoiki kyokaiiki niokeru busshiryutsu no hikaku kokogaku teki kenkyu* (A Comparative Archaeological Study on Circulation in Marginal Area of Early-Modern Japan). Kagoshima University, Kagoshima.

WATANABE, Y. 2016. *Shima no tojiki* (Ceramics in Islands). In: *Chukinsei tojiki no Kokogaku*, 2: 13–32. Yuzankaku, Tokyo.

WATANABE, Y. 2018. *Kinsei Tokara no busshiryutu* (Distribution in Tokara Islands of Early-Modern period). Hokuto shobo, Tokyo.

WATANABE, Y. 2019. *Tokara retto Kodakara-jima no kinsei toujiki ryutsu ni tsuite* (Early Modern Ceramics Distribution in Kodakarajima Island of Tokara Islands). In: *Nakayama Kiyomi to Amamigaku*, pp. 339–346, Amami Archaeology Society, Setouchi.

19

Otsuka, Y., Terada, R. and Nishimura, S. (eds.), *The Tokara Islands*
Kagoshima University International Center for Island Studies; Hokuto Shobo Publishing, Tokyo. 10 March 2020.

Chapter 3

Discarded Ceramics which had been Stored in Ji-nushi Shrine, Nakano-shima Island, in the Tokara Archipelago

Takayuki SHINZATO

1. Introduction

In September 2017, when Ji-nushi (地主) Shinto Shrine in Nakano-shima Island was renovated, many ceramics were discarded. They were almost complete shaped ceramics belonging from the Medieval to the Pre-modern periods. They were thought to be extremely important artifacts for studying ceramic exchange or trade in the Ryukyu Archipelago.

2. Location of Ji-nushi Shinto Shrine in Nakano-shima Island

Nakano-shima Island is the largest inhabited island in the Toshima village, which consists of the islands in the Tokara archipelago. The Toshima village in turn belongs to Kagoshima-County in Kagoshima Prefecture (Fig. 1). The circumference of the island is approximately 32 km with the area of about 34.5 km². The highest peak is Mt. Otake whose elevation is approximately 979 m high. While the island is located in the subtropical climate, it sometimes snows on the mountain. Among the islands of the Tokara Archipelago, Nakano-shima Island has the largest population with 159 people as of 2018 (Fig. 2).

Ji-nushi Shinto Shrine is located on a gentle slope of the south side of Miyago river (宮川) near the Nakano-shima Port which is the gateway to the island (Figs. 2 and 3). In 2008, Shinji Ito from Kokugakuin University (then, now at Seinan Gakuin University) successfully collected prehistoric pottery shards from Ji-nushi Shrine for the first time. In 2015, I conducted surface survey which resulted in a finding of

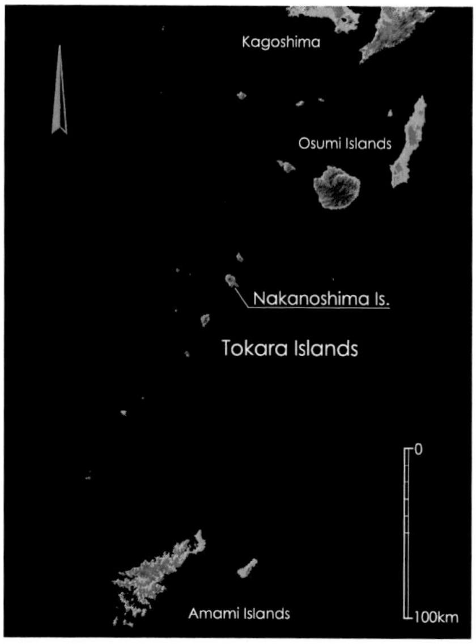

Fig. 1. Nakano-shima Is. in Tokara archipelago. This map is made of the Kashimier 3D and 50 m mesh data published by Geospatial Information Authority of Japan.

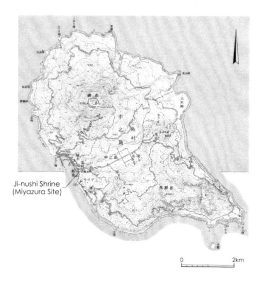

Fig. 2. Location of Ji-nushi Shrine. This map is based on the Nakano-shima (25,000) published by Geospatial Information Authority of Japan.

Fig. 3. Location of Ji-nushi Shrine. a: Entrance of Ji-nushi Shrine on Nakano-shima Island (▽); b: Before the renovation of front shrine (2016); c: After the renovation, only a shrine (2018), d: Discarded ceramics from front shrine (2018).

possible archaeological site. In 2016 and 2018 we excavated here and successfully identified archaeological site, now known as the Miyazura site (宮水流遺跡), dating mainly to the Yayoi and the Heian periods (about 2,000 years ago and 1,000 years ago, respectively). In addition we unearthed artifacts belonging to the Jomon (about 3,500 years ago) and the Kamakura period (about 800 years ago) (SHINZATO 2017).

3. Background Information on Collected Ceramics at Ji-nushi Shrine

In July, 2018, when I revisited Ji-nushi Shrine for the preliminary survey for the excavation of the Miyazura site, I realized that the Shrine was largely renovated since 2016 when I conducted my first excavation at the site. That is, there were two shrines first, the Front and Main Shrines. Now only a new Shrine is built. At the same time, I found numerous ceramics exposed in the open area around the Shrine (Fig. 3). While these ceramics had become filthy because of dirty water with rotten leaves, I was certain that some remains would belong to the Baisong and the Ming Eras in China. Importantly, most of them were complete in their shapes. Because of the importance of the

findings, I interviewed Mr. M. Hidaka, the head of the west ward (西区) on the island, about what happened to the Shrine since 2016. Accordingly I was able to gather following pieces of information. 1) The Shinto Shrine was renovated in September, 2017. 2) The Shinto Shrine had been severely damaged by white ants and mold from leaking. In addition, the roofs were considerably damaged by typhoon in 2017. 3) The renovation of the Shinto Shrine was carried out by a company in Kagoshima city. 4) The west ward, who manages the Shinto Shrine, renovated it with 1 million yen of the reserved fund. 5) The ward members buried ceramics from the new Shrine under its floor so that they would not be stolen. 6) The members of the ward discarded the ceramics from the Front Shrine (which I will describe below) in the Shrine ground. Based on the interview with Mr. Hidaka, three points became evident. a) The abandoned ceramics had been stored in the Front Shrine until 2017. b) Since they were considered as unnecessary ceramics among the ward people, they were discarded around the Shrine ground. c) The Front Shrine has become a part of the new Shrine (front and main shrines were combined after the renovation).

Scale 1:3

Fig. 4. Discarded ceramics from Ji-nushi Shrine (1). 1: Celadon small plate (China), middle to latter half of 12C; 2: Celadon bowl (China), middle of 14C to first of 15C; 3-4: White porcelain bowl (China), latter half of 14C to first half of 15C; 5: White porcelain bowl (China), about 14C.

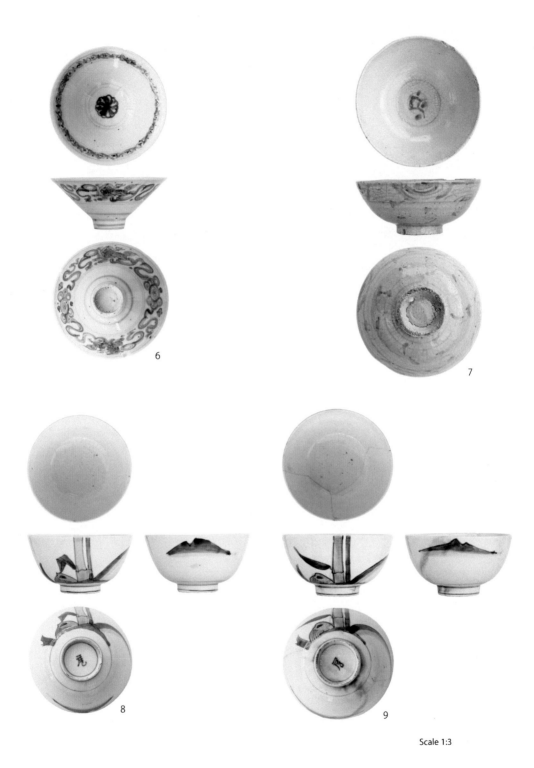

Scale 1:3

Fig. 5. Discarded ceramics from Ji-nushi Shrine (2). 6: Blue-and-white porcelain bowl (China), latter half of 15C to first half of 16C; 7: Blue-and-white porcelain bowl (China), latter half of 16C to first half of 17C; 8–9: Japan porcelain bowl, latter half of 17C.

Scale 1:3

Fig. 6. Discarded ceramics from Ji-nushi Shrine (3). 10: Japan glazed stoneware bowl, about 18C; 11: White porcelain bowl (China), latter half of 18C to first half of 19C; 12: Blue-and-white porcelain bowl (China), latter half of 18C to first half of 19C.

Fig. 7. Chinese ceramics discovered from the Miyazura Site in the Ji-nushi Shrine Area. 13: White porcelain bowl, latter half of 11C to first half of 12C; 14: Yuezhou kiln (越州窯系) celadon pot, latter half of 11C to first half of 12C; 15: White porcelain bowl, middle to latter half of 12C; 16: White porcelain pot, middle to latter half of 12C; 17: Brown glazed China ware, 13C; 18–19: China ware, about 13C.

4. The Discarded Ceramics from The Front Shrine

The traded ceramics discarded around the Front Shrine include Chinese and Japanese wares. They belong from the Medieval to Pre-Modern periods. I will briefly explain these ceramics and mention some interesting aspects of the Medieval period ceramics inferred from them (Figs. 4–6; also see Table 1).

Fig. 4-1: This is a small plate of celadon porcelain with comb marks made in the Pútián zhuāng biān kiln(莆田庄辺窯系), dating from the middle to the latter half of 12th century. This is complete shape and the oldest ceramic collected from the Shrine.

Fig. 4-2: A celadon porcelain bowl without decoration, and the rime is everted. It is made in the Longquan kiln (竜泉窯系), dating from the middle of 14th century to the first half of the 15th century. While a small part of rim is lacking, probably it had been complete shape until recently.

Figs. 4-3, 4-4: These are white porcelain with everted rim (in Okinawa, it is called Biro-suku III

[ビロースクⅢ類] bowl), made in Fujian Nanpin Chayo kiln (南平茶洋窯系), dating from the latter half of 14th century to the first of 15th century. Both of them are complete shape.

Fig. 4-5: This is white porcelain bowl. While the kiln is difficult to identify, it was made in Fujian region. It belongs to the 14th century. It has complete shape. The most characteristic part is the incised double circles, within which glaze was removed, at the bottom of the inside of the bowl.

Fig. 5-6: This is a blue-and-white porcelain bowl shaped like an umbrella (斗笠碗) made in Jingdezhen kiln (景徳鎮窯) in the Ming Era. The Shihou Tasukimon (四方襷文; This is featured by a consecutively drawn multiple –mostly three– lines of X-like shape. In this case, several dots are drawn between 'X' s and one dot above the space where multiple lines overlap) is drawn on the inside of the mouth rim, and the flower pattern is drawn at the center of the inside. Furthermore, the lion, flower and ticklish vine scroll patterns are drawn on the outside of the ware. This is also perfect shape, belongs to the 16th century.

25

Fig. 5-7: This is a blue-and-white bowl with straight mouth made in the Zhangzhou kiln (漳州窯系). The apricot pattern is drawn at the center of the inside, half apricot pattern, and vine scroll pattern are drawn on the outside of the ware, but color is not well development because it was burnt in poor condition. This dates from the latter half of the 16th century to the first half of the 17th century, and it is complete shape.

Figs. 5-8, 5-9: These are Japan porcelain (染付) bowl made in Hizen (肥前). The mountain and bamboo pattern (山水文) are drawn on the outside of the mid-section, and 'Kotobuki (寿–meaning long life)' is written inside of the foot-ring on the outside of ware. Both of them date to the latter half of the 17th century, and complete in shape.

Fig. 6-10: The Japanese glazed stoneware bowl strongly everted at the rim. It was made in Seto region (瀬戸). This one possibility dates to the 18th century. There are four spur marks at the center of the inside. The most outstanding characteristic is the grated lines carved on the inside of the foot-ring. The most outstanding characteristic is the latticed pattern carved on the inside of the foot-ring.

Fig. 6-11: This is white porcelain bowl with no decoration made in Dehua kiln (徳化窯系) dating

from the latter half of the 18th century to the 19th century, and complete in shape.

Fig. 6-12: A blue-and-white bowl made in Dehua kiln (徳化窯系). The flower and tree patterns are drawn on the mid-section, and 'Chengmei (成美–meaning to become beautiful)' is written on the inside of foot-ring. It is complete shape.

5. Discussion and Conclusion

These traded ceramics date wide range from the Medieval period to the Pre-Modern period (from the 12th century to the 19th century). As they have almost complete shape, it is clear that they must have been dedicated ceramics to the Shinto Shrine. Ceramics date to the Medieval period are only Chinese. On the other hand, all Japanese domestic Hizen and Seto ceramics and some Chinese ceramics date to the Pre-modern period. Based on the studies of the traded ceramics (SETO 2007, WATANABE 2015), we can infer followings. 1) The Chinese ceramics of the 12th century were imported from Hakata (today's Fukuoka, Kyushu) via the trade between Japan and the Sung Dynasty. 2) The Chinese ceramics of the 14th to 19th centuries were imported from the Ryukyu Kingdom via the trade between the Ryukyu Kingdom and the Ming

Fig. 8. Chinese ceramics of surface collection from west ward on Nakano-shima Island. 20: Longquan celadon bowl, first half of 13C; 21–23: Longquan celadon bowl, first harf to middle of 15C.

Table 1. Discarded Celamics from Ji-nushi Shrine, Nakano-shima Island.

No.	Type	Size	Place of production	Date	Condition
1	Celadon small plate	Caliber: 11.4–11.7cm Height: 2.4–2.7cm Bottom: 5.2–5.5cm	China/Pútián zhuāng biān kiln (莆田庄辺窯)	Middle to latter harf of 12C	Complete
2	Celadon bowl	Caliber: 14.7cm Height: 5.6cm Bottom: 5.2–5.5cm	China/Longquan kiln (竜泉窯系)	Middle of 14C to first half of 15C	Almost complete
3	White porcelain bowl	Caliber: 16.4–17.3cm Height: 5.8–6.0cm Bottom: 5.4cm	China/Nanpin Chayo kiln (南平茶洋窯系)	Latter half of 14C to first of 15C	Complete
4	White porcelain bowl	Caliber: 17.6–18.0cm Height: 6.8–7.2cm Bottom: 6.8cm	China/Nanpin Chayo kiln (南平茶洋窯系)	Latter half of 14C to first of 15C	Complete
5	White porcelain bowl	Caliber: 17.2–17.6cm Height: 6.4–7.0cm Bottom: 6.8cm	China/Fujian (福建省系)	14C	Complete
6	Blue-and-white porcelain bowl	Caliber: 12.6cm Height: 5.4cm Bottom: 3.2cm	China/Jingdezhen kiln (景徳鎮窯)	Latter half of 15C to first half of 16C	Complete
7	Blue-and-white porcelain bowl	Caliber: 13.8–13.9cm Height: 5.6–5.7cm Bottom: 5.1cm	China/Zhangzhou kiln (漳州窯系)	Latter half of 16C to first half of 17C	Complete
8	Japan porcelain bowl	Caliber: 11.5–11.7cm Height: 6.2cm Bottom: 4.4cm	Japan/Hizen (肥前系)	Latter half of 17C	Complete
9	Japan porcelain bowl	Caliber: 11.6–11.8cm Height: 6.3cm Bottom: 4.5cm	Japan/Hizen (肥前系)	Latter half of 17C	Complete
10	Japan glazed stonware bowl	Caliber: 16.9–17.0cm Height: 7.0-7.1cm Bottom: 7.6cm	Japan/Seto (瀬戸系)	18C	Almost complete
11	White porcelain bowl	Caliber: 10.3–10.4cm Height: 5.2-5.3cm Bottom: 4.4cm	China/Dehua kiln (徳化窯系)	Latter half of 18C to 19C	Complete
12	Blue-and-white porcelain bowl	Caliber: 14.5–14.6cm Height: 6.3–6.4cm Bottom: 6.9cm	China/Dehua kiln (徳化窯系)	Latter half of 18C to 19C	Complete

to the Qing Dynasty. 3) The Japanese ceramics of the 17th to 18th centuries were brought to the island from Satsuma (now Kagoshima Prefecture) after Satsuma's invasion of the Ryukyu Kingdom.

While the aforementioned ceramics have complete shape and dedicated to the Shinto Shrine, we were not able to identify ceramics dating to the 11th century, the 13th century and the first half of the 15th century. Interestingly, we have discovered other artifacts dating not only the dates of the dedicated ceramics, but also the 11th, 13th and the first half of the 15th centuries. For example, the latter were unearthed from the Miyazura site, which is located within the Shinto Shrine ground (Fig. 7) and from the surface survey conducted at the present day the west ward (Fig. 8). Thus, it is considered that the traded Chinese ceramics

had not been continuously imported in order to especially dedicate to the Shine. It is also thought that these imported ceramics were used by the islanders and some of them were dedicated to Ji-nushi Shrine.

Notes and Acknowledgements

After the analysis of the artifacts, these ceramics will be donated (returned?) to the Toshima Museum of History and Folklore in Nakano-shima Island.

I would like to thank Professor Yoshiro WATANABE (Kagoshima University) and the members of Japan Society for Southeast Asian Archaeology for their valuable comments on ceramics, and to Professor Hiroto TAKAMIYA (Kagoshima University) for improving this manuscript.

References

SETO, T., NIOU, K., TAMASHIRO, Y., MIYAGI, H., AZAMA, M. and MATSUBARA, S. 2007. *Okinawa ni okeru Boueki Touji Kenkyu: 14-16 Seiki wo Tyushinni* (The Trade Ceramics Study in Okinawa: Focusing on the 14th to 16th Century). Bulletin of the Archaeological Study on Okinawa, 5: 55–76. (in Japanese)

SHINZATO, T. 2017. *Tokara Rettou no Yayoi Jidai to Heian Jidai: Nakanoshima Ji-nushi Jinzya Shikichi Nai Hakkutsu Chosa Seika kara* (The Yayoi Period and Heian Period in Tokara Islands: from the Result of Excavation in the Nakanoshima Ji-nushi Shrine Site). The 83rd General Meeting and Presentation Abstract of the Japanese Archaeological Association, pp. 178–179. (in Japanese)

WATANABE, Y. 2015. *Kinsei Nihon Kokka Ryouiki Kyoukai Iki ni okeru Busshi Ryutsu no Hikaku Koukogaku Teki Kenkyu* (Archeological Comparative Study of the Supplies Circulation of Japan National Territory Border Area in the Pre-modern Period). pp. 1–144, Kagoshima University, Kagoshima. (in Japanese with English summary)

Chapter 4
Population History of the Tokara Islands

Hiroto TAKAMIYA

1. Introduction

Population history has become one of the most crucial factors in recent years for our understanding of prehistoric culture. For example, KIRCH, P. states that "since the degree of adaptedness of a (human) group means how they successfully reproduce, it is clear that in order to understand adaptedness of the group, one must know population decrease, stability, and increase of this group" (KIRCH 1980: 143). This statement is applicable not only to prehistory but also to today's world. How have groups of people adapted to their environments? A small island is an ideal space for understanding human population adaptedness as it has clear boundaries with a less complicated environment as compared to a continent or a large island.

Among the world's islands, the Tokara Islands were considered to be an adequate collection of islands to study population history due to their small sizes and the fact that the population on each of its islands has been recorded since the 1870s. This study attempts to examine the population history of the Tokara Islands in order to understand how the islands' inhabitants adapted to life there. There are three main sections: The first section describes various population models that evaluate adaptedness of human groups to their island environments; the second section reconstructs the population history of the Tokara Islands; and the third section examines the adaptedness of islanders over approximately 100 years.

2. Population Models

KIRCH (1984) and KEEGAN AND DIAMOND (1987) described five models relating to the fate of human groups colonizing island environments. In the extinction model (Fig. 1), a group of humans enter an island but are unable to successfully colonize it, leading to a complete deterioration in population numbers, eventually becoming zero. In the crush model (Fig. 2), a colonizing human group is initially successful at adapting to an island and accordingly, the population rapidly increases. However, the number of people somehow increases beyond the island's carrying capacity, resulting in rapid population decline. In the oscillation model (Fig. 3), similar to the crush model, the population is initially successful at adapting to the island's environment and grows rapidly, increasing beyond the island's carrying capacity. However, unlike the crush model, the population oscillates around the

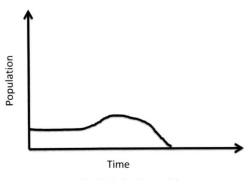

Fig. 1. Extinction model.

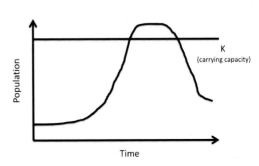

Fig. 2. Crush model.

island's carrying capacity. In the logistic model (Fig. 4), a group of humans adapt to an island's environment and the population grows rapidly toward carrying capacity, but as the capacity is reached, growth rate decreases. In the step model (Fig. 5), a group of people successfully adapt to the island's environment and population grows logistically. Due to certain changes, such as technological innovations or climate changes, this model assumes an increase in carrying capacity and predicts that population will once again increase logistically towards a new carrying capacity. According to KIRCH (1984), the logistic and step models are expected when human populations adapt to an island's environment.

3. The Tokara Islands

The Tokara Islands is an archipelago of seven habited islands and five uninhabited islands, located between Kyushu Island and Amami-Oshima Island, stretching over approximately 160 km. Table 1 lists these islands and their areas. The largest habited island is Nakano-shima Island

(34.5 km^2), while the smallest habited island is Kodakara-jima Island (1 km^2).

While *Homo sapiens* inhabited both Kyushu Island and Amami-Oshima Island during the Paleolithic period, no site has been reported on the Tokara Islands (ITOH 2011). SANO (2019 pers. comm.), a Paleolithic specialist, studied Paleolithic stone tools recovered from the Amangusuku site on Tokuno-shima Island and commented on their resemblance with those unearthed on Kyushu. This implies that a Paleolithic site might be discovered in the future on the Tokara Islands. The earliest Holocene site reported is on the Takara-jima Island, dating to ca. 5,000 to 6,000 years ago. This period is known among archaeologists as Early 2 of the Shellmidden period. According to ITOH (2011),

Table 1. Area of each island in the Tokara Islands.

Habited Islands	Area (km^2)
Kuchino-shima	13.3
Nakano-shima	34.5
Taira-jima	2.1
Suwanose-jima	27.8
Akuseki-jima	7.5
Kodakara-jima	1.0
Takara-jima	7.1

Uninhabited Islands	Area (km^2)
Gajya-jima	4.1
Kogajya-jima	0.5
Ko-jima	0.36
Uenone-jima	0.54
Yokoate-jima	2.76

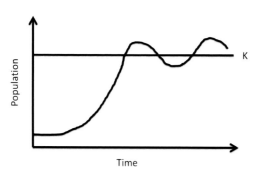

Fig. 3. Oscillation model.

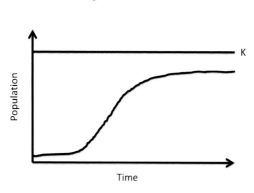

Fig. 4. Logistic model.

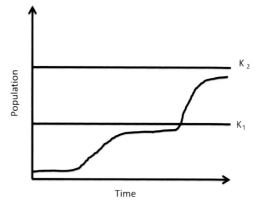

Fig. 5. Step model.

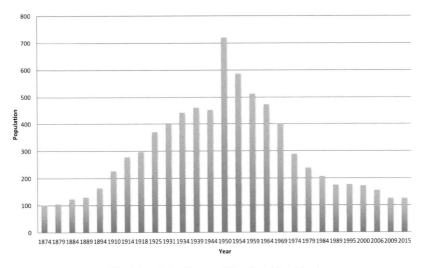

Fig. 6. Population History of Kuchino-shima Island.

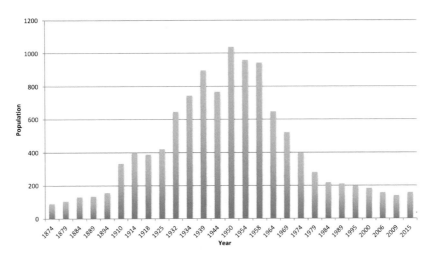

Fig. 7. Population History of Nakano-shima Island.

MOTOYAMA (1995), SHINZATO (2015), SHINZATO and ITOH (2019), and WATANABE (2019), archaeological investigations revealed that these islands have been occupied over the Early 2, Medieval, and Recent periods, and is still even today (also see Toshima-mura Shi Henshu Iinkai 1995).

However, archaeological data as well as written documents do not provide adequate data to reconstruct population history from ca. 6,000 years ago until the 1880s. MOTOYAMA (1995) explains that while population records were maintained between 1626 and 1885, they were of the total

number of people living on all of the Tokara Islands combined. The total populations of the Tokara Islands in the years of 1626, 1627–1763, and 1818, were 1,159, 1,169, and 1,009 people, respectively (MOTOYAMA 1995: 311), indicating that the population was more or less stable. According to MOTOYAMA (1995: 311), this tendency is the initial step of population growth. MOTOYAMA (1995: 311) also says that during this period, medicines were not widely available in Japan, especially in rural areas such as the Tokara Islands, resulting in high birth and death rates. Thus, unfortunately, this

31

makes it difficult to evaluate how people adapted to the islands during this extended period of time.

However, since the 1870s, the population of each island was recorded. The next section demonstrates the population history of each island.

4. Population History of the Tokara Islands
4.1. Kuchino-shima Island (Fig. 6)
Population records for this island date back to 1874, when the island was occupied by 101 people. Until 1944, the population seemed to grow logistically. Notably, the population jumped from 450 people in 1944 and peaked at 720 people in 1950. Since then, it gradually decreased, numbering 126 people in 2015.

4.2. Nakano-shima Island (Fig. 7)
Population records on this island date back to 1874, and the initial population recorded was 90 people. The population gradually increased between 1874 and 1894 and then twice increased like a step model; first, between 1910 and 1925, and then in 1932 and 1944. The third step might be recognized around the 1950s. On Nakano-shima Island, the population hit its peak in 1950 with 1,039 people, which was followed by gradual decreases between 1954 and 1958, and then sharp decreases after 1964. As of 2015, the population was 158.

4.3. Gajya-jima Island (Fig. 8)
At present, Gajya-jima Island is uninhabited. It was

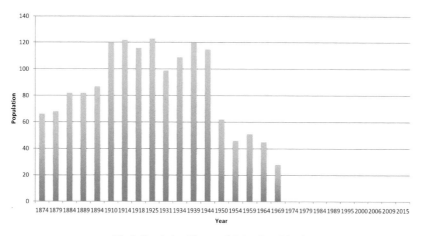

Fig. 8. Population History of Gajya-jima Island.

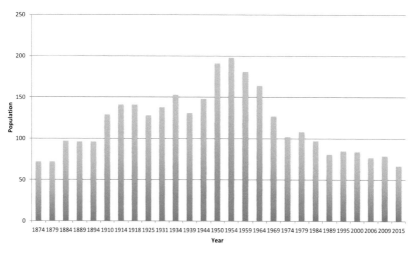

Fig. 9. Population History of Taira-jima Island.

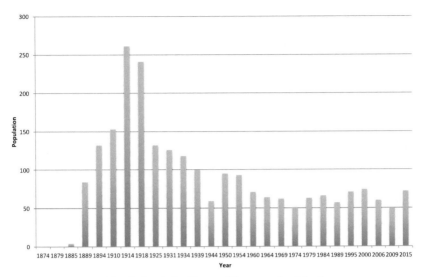

Fig. 10. Population History of Suwanose-jima Island.

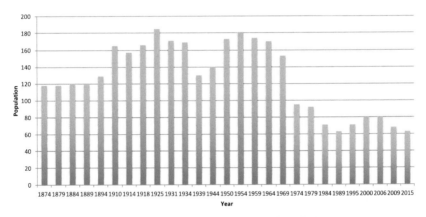

Fig. 11. Population History of Akuseki-jima Island.

deserted in 1970 as all islanders (28 in 1969) were forced to relocate. The first recorded population was 66 people in 1874. The population gradually grew until 1894. Between 1910 and 1944, the population reached its first peak—particularly in 1925 with 123 people. During this period, the population was more or less stable ranging between 109 (in 1934) and 123 (in 1925). In 1950, population decreased by more than 50% compared to that of 1944, further dramatically decreasing until 1969.

4.4. Taira-jima Island (Fig. 9)

The population recorded in 1874 was 72 and did

not change until 1879. It rapidly grew in the periods between 1884 and 1894 (95 people) and 1910 and 1944 (130 to 150 people). The population also increased between 1950 and 1954 (190 people) but since then, it decreased slowly until 1964 (160 people). As of 1970, it has continued to decrease steadily, recording 67 people in 2015.

4.5. Suwanose-jima Island (Fig. 10)

Prehistoric sites have been identified on the island, suggesting that it was occupied for a long time. However, the island witnessed a large volcanic eruption of Mount Otake in 1817, forcing all inhabitants to flee to islands such as Amami-

33

Oshima Island. After approximately seven decades, people began to recolonize Suwanose-jima Island, starting with 4 people in 1885, and growing to 84 in 1889. Two decades later, the population reached 130 to 150 people. During 1914 and 1918, the population count was 261 and 241 people, respectively. However, after that, the population dramatically decreased; 72 people lived on the island as of 2015.

4.6. Akuseki-jima Island (Fig. 11)

In 1874, the recorded number of islanders was 118. Between 1874 and 1894, the population appears to have been more or less stable (approximately 120 people). In 1919, the population increased to 160 and by 1934, it fluctuated between 160 and 180 people. Between 1939 and 1944, it decreased to nearly 130 or 140, but jumped to approximately 170 in 1950 and remained at that number until 1969. As of 1974, the population fell to 95 and failed to increase until recently. As of 2015, its population was recorded at 63 people.

4.7. Kodakara-jima and Takara-jima Islands (Fig.12)

The population on these two islands was combined and recorded in 1874, with the earliest records showing a population of 299. As seen in Fig. 12, the population gradually increased until 1934. It began with 299 people in 1874, reached 400 to 500 in the period between 1894 and 1914, and then in 1934, increased to 690. It dropped to approximately 570 people in 1939 but recovered and grew to between 600 to 650 people during 1944 to1954. However, in 1959, the population decreased once again—to nearly 500. Like other islands, populations of these islands also failed to recover. During the 1970s and 1980s, the population fell to 200, and since the year 2000, it had fallen further to between 160 and 170 people. In 2015, an increase in population was recorded with 196 people.

While we do not have separate population histories for Kodakara-jima and Takara-jima Islands for this study, the former was on the verge of becoming an inhabited island. According to KAWASAKI (1995: 785), in 1955, the population of the Kodakara-jima Island was 90. By the 1970s, it had decreased to 48. Notably in 1979, after three junior high school students graduated, only one junior high school student and one prospective elementary grade 1 student remained on the island. The Toshima Village Board of Education decided to shut down the branch school on the island, compelling the two students to leave the island for further education. In 1981, the island's population numbered less than 20 people, and many thought

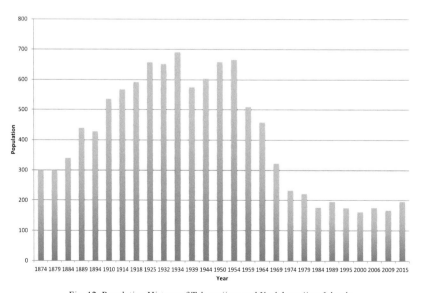

Fig. 12. Population History of Takara-jima and Kodakara-jima Islands.

Fig. 13. Population History of the Tokara Islands.

that Kodakara-jima Island would witness the same fate as Gajya-jima Island. However, in 1987, a family with young children moved back to Kodakara-jima Island, enabling the branch school on the island to restart. Since then, the island's population has remained stable.

5. Discussion and Conclusions

In the "Population Models" section, five population trajectories were introduced on possible outcomes when a human population colonizes an island. The following comments are general statements based on Figs. 6–12. The extinct model appears to apply to Gajya-jima Island which became a no-man's island in 1970. While this island became uninhabited in 1970, between 1874 and the 1950s, a similar population trend can be observed between Gajya-jima and Akuseki-jima Islands, both showing population numbers peak twice: around the 1910s and 1940s for Gajya-jima Island; and in 1910s–1930s and the 1950s for Akuseki-jima Island. Moreover, the population history of Takara-jima and Kodakara-jima Islands also witnessed double peaks–around the 1920s and 1950s. The population of Suwanose-jima Island, which was recolonized during the early Meiji era, spurred around the early 1910s but decreased rapidly by the late 1910s. From a broader perspective, Suwanose-

jima Island's population pattern proceeded Kuchino-shima, Nakano-shima, Taira-jima, and Takara-jima / Kodakara-jima Islands. The latter four reached their peak populations in the 1950s and populations decline rapidly afterwards. While the extinction model seems applicable to Gajya-jima Island, the population histories of Kuchino-shima, Nakano-shima, Taira-jima, Suwanose-jima, Akuseki-jima, Takara-jima / Kodakara-jima islands appear to be more complicated than the models provided. Further examination is needed to understand the population histories of these islands.

Fig. 13 compares the population histories of seven islands. From this figure, it appears to be obvious that three islands, Kuchino-shima, Nakano-shima, and Takara-jima / Kodakara-jima Islands are major islands in terms of carrying capacity. In other words, these three islands possess higher carrying capacity than the others. Two general trends are observed on the population history of the Tokara Islands. First, most islands experienced a population peak around the 1950s. Second, there was rapid population decrease since the 1960s. As of 2015, populations on these islands totaled between 60 and 200. Since the 1960s, islanders immigrated to Kagoshima and other prefectures on mainland Japan. According to

MOTOYAMA (1995: 319), the maximum population recorded in the Tokara Islands was 3394 in 1952. As of 2015, the total population on the archipelago was 670, less than 20% of its maximum number. While population has sharply decreased since the 1950s, Toshima Village (Kagoshima ken Toshima-mura 2015) expects to see a rise in population over the next three decades. While living on small islands is challenging, the population history of the Tokara Islands reveals that people have successfully lived on these islands and conquered any challenges they faced.

Acknowledgments

Mr. Shoji FUKUZAWA, the Director of the General Affairs Division from Toshima Village Office, provided me with important sources of population history of the Tokara Islands. I am extremely grateful for his kindness.

References

ITOH, S. 2011. *Ryukyu-bunkaken no hokugen ni kansuru kokogakuteki kisokenkyu* (The Basic Archaeological Studies on the Northern Limit of the Ryukyu Culture). 100 pp., Kokugakuin University, Tokyo. (in Japanese).

Kagoshima ken Toshima-mura. 2015. *Toshima-mura Machi/ Hito/Shigoto Sousei "Jinko Bishon/Sogo Senryaku"* (Toshima Village: An Area, People, Employments, Creation of Jobs. Population Visions and Overall Strategies). 54 pp., Toshima-mura, Kagoshima. (in Japanese)

KAWASAKI, K. 1997. *Kin/Gendai no Tokara* (The Tokara Islands in the Modern Era). In: Toshima-mura Shi (ed. Toshima-mura Shi Henshu Iinkai), pp. 677–792, Toshima-mura Shi Henshu Iinkai, Kagoshima. (in Japanese)

KEEGAN, W. F. and DIAMOND, J. 1987. Colonization of Islands by Humans: A Biogeographical Perspective. In: Advances in Archaeological Method and Theory 10 (ed. SCHIFFER, M. B.), pp. 49–92, Academic Press, New York.

KIRCH, P. V. 1980. The Archaeological Study of Adaptation: Theoretical and Methodological Issues. In: Advances in Archaeological Method and Theory 3 (ed. SCHIFFER, M. B.), pp. 101–156, Academic Press, New York.

KIRCH, P. V. 1984. The Evolution of the Polynesian Chiefdoms. 314 pp., Cambridge University Press, Cambridge.

MOTOYAMA, F. 1995. *Jinko, shuraku, chimei* (Population, Communities, and Place Names). In: Toshima-mura Shi (ed. Toshima-mura Shi Henshu Iinkai), pp. 310–359, Toshima-mura Shi Henshu Iinkai, Kagoshima. (in Japanese)

SHINZATO, T. 2015. *Tokara retto/ Yokoatejima no Tsuboya yaki* (The Tsuboya ware Recovered from Yokoatejima Island in the Tokara archipelago). In Archaeology from the South III (ed. Honda Michiteru Sensei Taishoku Kinen Jigyokai), pp. 317–330, Honda Michiteru Sensei Taishoku Kinen Jigyokai, Kagoshima. (in Japanese)

SHINZATO, T. and ITO, S. 2019. *Tokara retto/ Gajyajima no senshi jidai ibutu* (Prehistoric Artifacts Recovered from Gajyajima Island in Tokara archipelago). In: Nakayama Kiyomi to Amamigaku (ed. Amami Koko Gakkai), pp. 349–360, Amami Koko Gakkai, Kagoshima. (in Japanese)

Toshima-mura Shi Henshu Iinkai (ed.) 1995. *Toshima-mura Shi* (History of Toshima Village). 1763 pp., Toshima-mura, Kagoshima. (in Japanese)

WATANABE, Y. 2019. *Tokara retto/ Kodakarajima no Kinsei Tojiki ni tsuite* (On the Recent Porcelain Recovered from Kodakarajima Island in Tokara Archipelago). In: *Nakayama Kiyomi to Amamigaku* (ed. Amami Koko Gakkai), pp. 339–346, Amami Koko Gakkai, Kagoshima. (in Japanese)

Chapter 5

Migration from Urban to Remote Islands:
A Case Study of Suwanose-jima Island

Satoru NISHIMURA

1. Introduction

The paper discusses a broader issue focusing on the Japanese case of Japanese migration. Migration from urban to rural is necessarily to tackle with the problems of ageing and decreasing population in rural areas. Population growth in urban in Japan is basically higher than in rural areas at the moment. However, the trend will change under some conditions. The chapter describes the emerging change of migration and the reasons behind. The paper explains other factors by showing an example of Suwanose-jima Island in Kagoshima prefecture in Japan. It also discusses a provisional theoretical approach to grasp the mechanism of migration from urban to rural, which the author names as 'reverse migration' by the several discussion of early development economics.

2. Internal Migration Trend in Japan

People are moving from the rural area to the cities looking for employment with higher wages and modern life style in Japan. Lewis model (LEWIS 1954) explains the reason behind. The gap in income between rural and urban areas pushed the people from the former to the latter. Figure 1 shows the population of immigration to Metro Tokyo and that of emigration from Metro Tokyo. After Plaza Agreement in 1985 which caused appreciation of yen and acceleration of overseas transfer of Japanese companies, many employments have been lost in the urban area such as Metro Tokyo.

Figure 1 shows that the number of emigrations increased and that of immigration decreased during 1986 to 1993 in Metro Tokyo. And the number increased also from 2008 to 2011 after the world economic recession caused by Lehman

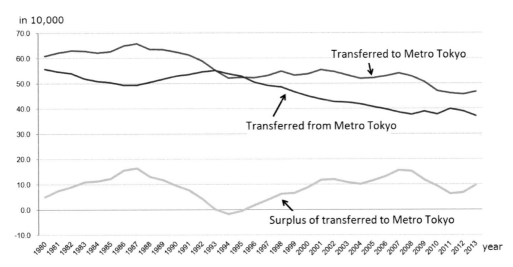

Fig. 1. Migration trend in metro Tokyo from1980-2013. Red: transferred to metro Tokyo (IN), blue: transferred from metro Tokyo (OUT), *green: balance (IN-OUT). Source: Ministry of Internal Affairs and Communications.

Shock. Besides the two periods, the number of emigrations has been going down, and the number of immigrations has been almost the same. It was only in 1994 when the number of emigrations exceeded that of immigration.

However, if the numbers are examined by age group, a different picture will be seen. Figure 2 shows the number of migrations in metro Tokyo in 2013, it shows that the numbers of immigration

exceed a lot in the age group between 18 and 34, but the numbers of immigration and emigration are almost balanced in other age group. It should be noted that the numbers of emigration exceed those of immigration in the age group between 55 to 69. It means a lot of young people move to Tokyo to study in the high-quality university and to better jobs. However, there are a lot of people who exit from metro Tokyo especially among those who are

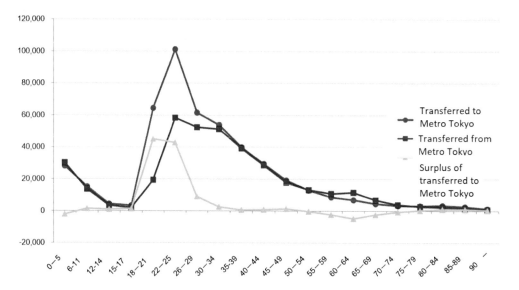

Fig. 2 Migration in metro Tokyo in 2013 by age group. Red: transferred to metro Tokyo (IN), blue: transferred from metro Tokyo (OUT), *green: balance (IN-OUT). Source: Ministry of Internal Affairs and Communications.

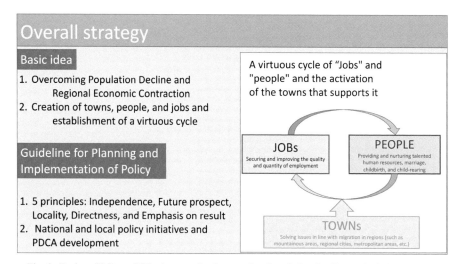

Fig. 3. Basic guideline of 'Headquarter for Overcoming Population Decline and Vitalizing Local Economy in Japan'. Source: http://www.kantei.go.jp/jp/singi/sousei/mahishi_index.html

close to age of retirement.

There are several reasons why people leave urban area such as metro Tokyo. One of them is deteriorating infrastructure. MATSUTANI (2015) says that some parts of metro Tokyo will become slums because some of the infrastructure will become out of use. He also says that the area will get short of the home for the aged in spite of accelerating aging population.

3. Japanese Government Policy for rural revitalization: Town / People / Jobs

Japanese government has launched country side revitalization act (地方再生法) been active in tackling the problem of decreasing and aging population in rural areas in Japan. Below is the

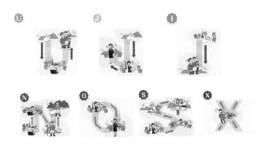

Fig. 4. Various types of internal migration in Japan. Source; home page of JOIN, https://www.iju-join.jp/feature_cont/guide/003/

translation from the web site of the government. Figure 3 shows the basic concept of the policy.

The government will work together with local communities to deal with the major challenges facing Japan, such as rapid population decline and super-aging population, and aim to create an autonomous and sustainable society that takes advantage of the characteristics of each region. In order to overcome population decline, secure growth potential in the future, and maintain a vital Japanese society, "make local work and work with peace of mind", "create a new flow of people to the region", "give the hope of younger generations for marriage, childbirth and child-rearing", "creating a region that fits the times, protecting safe living, and linking the region with the region". The Japanese government is proceeding with policies aimed at the four basic goals.

4. New trend of migration from big cities to rural areas and small islands: various patterns

Thanks to the government policy and ICT, people are starting to migrate from big cities to rural areas and small islands. According to JOIN, or Japan Organization for Internal Migration, the patterns of migration from big cities to countryside are becoming more diversified.

The Overall Picture of Work Style Reform

Basic Approach to Work Style Reform

Work style reform is a reform that enables working people to choose their own diverse and flexible way of working according to their individual circumstances.

In order to meet the challenges facing Japan, such as "a decline in the working-age population due to the declining birthrate and aging population", and "diversification of the needs of working people," It is necessary to create an environment in which employees can fully demonstrate their motivation and abilities, as well as improve productivity through investment and innovation.

We aim to build a virtuous cycle of growth and distribution by realizing a society in which employees can choose a variety of work styles according to their individual circumstances, and to ensure that each and every worker has a better outlook for the future.

Fig. 5. Image of 'Work-Style Reforms' by Japanese government. Source; home page of Ministry of Health, Labour and Welfare, https://www.mhlw.go.jp/content/000474499.pdf

Figure 4 shows the variation of internal migration in Japan. The variation used to be limited to I-turn and U turn before. I-turn means that people in the urban areas go directly to rural areas where they are not from. On the other hand, U-turn means that the people move back to their home towns. According to JOIN, there are several more new turns added such as J-turn, X-turn, O-turn and Z turn. J turn means that one migrates to the place near his or her home town which has more employment. O-turn means that one moves between an urban area and a rural area regularly after staying at each place for a while. X turn means that one moves to several remote areas after a while based on a city. One moves several cities and rural areas without having a fixed base in the case Z turn. Nowadays, people don't always needed to stay in a place to work, even some jobs which relate ICT don't require people to go to an office, people can work at home. Those workers will choose their place and duration of stay in a place more freely than before. The Japanese government policy on work-style reforms will also accelerate the trend. The government is also promoting various styles of work, which help the people move to rural areas. Figure 5 shows the basic picture of the policy.

5. A case of population growth in a small island

Suwanose-jima Island is located in the south of Kagoshima city in Kyushu island (Fig. 6). Figure 7 depicts the transition of the population of Suwanose-jima Island and Toshima Village from 2000 and 2016. The graph indicates that since 2010, the population has kept increasing in the village and Suwanose-jima Island. The population on Suwanose-jima Island increased from 42 in 2010 to 79 in 2016, an increase rate of 88.1%,

Fig. 6. Location of Suwanose-jima Island.

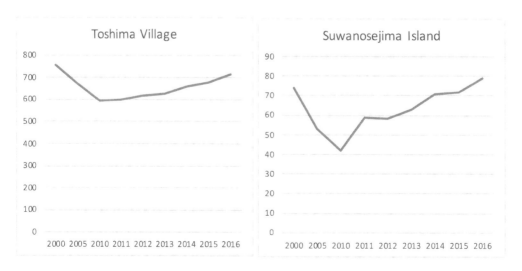

Fig. 7. Population transition of Toshima Village and Suwanose-jima Island (2000–2016). Source: Toshima Village Office. Note: Excluding teachers and study abroad students.

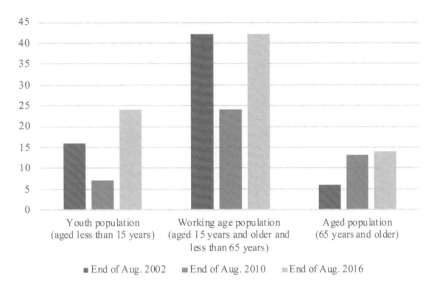

■ End of Aug. 2002   ■ End of Aug. 2010   ■ End of Aug. 2016

Fig. 8. Population transition by age group (at the end of August 2002, 2010, and 2016). Source: Toshima Village Office. Note: Excluding teachers and study abroad students.

Table 1. Number of U/I-turners and U/I-turning households in Suwanose Island by year.

	2009	2010	2011	2012	2013	2014	2015	2016	Total (2009-2016)
U/I-Turning Households	1	4	3	1	5	2	1	3	20
Number of U/I-turners	1	6	7	3	11	4	1	5	38
I-Turning Households	1	2	2	0	5	1	1	3	15
Number of I-turners	1	4	6	0	11	3	1	5	31

Source: Toshima Village Office. Note: Excludes teachers and foreign study students.

greatly surpassing the population increase rate of 20% (594 to 713) in Toshima Village during the same period. Figure 8 shows the transition of the population of Suwanose-jima Island by age group in 2002, 2010, and 2016: the youth population (aged less than 15 years), working age population (15 or older, but under 65 years), and the aged population (65 years and older). The graph shows that the youth and working age populations have decreased, while the aged population increased between 2000 and 2010.

On the other hand, the youth and working age populations greatly increased between 2010 and 2016, while the aged population plateaued. The youth population increased greatly from 7 people in 2010 to 24 in 2016. On Suwanose-jima Island, the population increase and rejuvenation of the population occurred simultaneously. Table 1 shows

the number of migrants to Suwanose-jima Island, categorizing people who have U/I-turned and the number of I-turning households according to the years from 2009 to 2016. Here, U-turn refers to the movement where people return to their original area of residence from urban area. Examining the total for this period, there are 20 U/I-turning households and 15 I-turn households, accounting for 75% of the total number. In terms of the number of people, the former account for 38 and the latter 31, meaning that I-turners account for 81.6% of the total. This shows that I-turners have brought about the population increase/rejuvenation.

The major reason Suwanose-jima Island has many I-turners is the series of resident settlement promotion policies initiated by Toshima Village in 2010. In 2010, the Village conducted measures such as the Employment Training Bonus Program and restoration of vacant housing. In 2012, the Resident Settlement Promotion counter of the village office was unified. From 2013, the Village Office started participating in relocation events in urban areas, and in 2014, it secured places of employment. From 2015, it started recruiting volunteers to help in community building activities, and opened a nursery. In addition to these policies, the island provides education in small classes and assistance toward childcare expenses.

Mr. A (male, 36 years old), who was interviewed for the purposes of this study, applied for the publicly advertised position of an employee at the Kyudenko Corporation Power Plant located on the island. He was hired, and with his wife and two children, moved to the island in 2017. While living on the island, he had two more children, so his family currently comprises six members. The reason he decided to relocate to the island was strongly influenced by one factor, namely that he wanted to live in the countryside. However, having a stable job and being able to take time off to raise his children were also important factors. The island has an elementary and middle school, although there are only one to three students per grade, allowing children to receive better education in a small class.

In addition, the village grants a monthly childcare allowance of 10,000 JPY (93.90 USD) to the first and second children, and 20,000 JPY (187.80 USD) for the third child onward. According to Mr. A, unlike Osaka, where they lived previously, he can secure sufficient time to play with his children. He is planning to continue living on Suwanose-jima Island until the youngest child graduates from middle school, because of the excellent

Table 2. 2017 Residents' association events (Suwanose-jima Island).

Month	Date	Residents' association events	School events	Notes
4	6	New transfer welcoming party	Entrance ceremony	
	26	General Residents' Association Assembly		
5	31			Fishing festival
7	1	Roads repair (cleaning activity)		
	2	″		
8	13	Bon dance for welcoming		Lantern Festival (Bon Festival)
	15	Bon dance for parting		″
	16			Mountain festival
	29	Summer festival		
9	16			
	25	Arasetsu Dance	Athletic meets	
	26	″		
10	1	Shibasashi Dance		
	2	″		
	4	Full moon night		
	8	Old water resource cleaning task		
	14			Festival for praying
11	4		Cultural festival	
12	2	Roads repair (cleaning activity)		
	7		Long distance relay race	
1	1	New Year's celebration		
	2			Boat celebration (ship owners)
	11			Fishing festival
	14			Nari mochi
2	23		Farewell excursion trip	
3	10		Graduation ceremony	
	Undecided	Transfer farewell party		

Resource: Suwanose Island Residents' Association.

environment in which to raise children.

The second reason there are many I-turners is the existence of senior I-turners who support the island. Mr. B (male, 72 years old), an interviewee in the study, is one such member. After graduating from university, he embarked on a long trip around the world and then moved to the island aged 26 years to visit Banyan Ashram, a commune on the island that practiced communal living. This commune housed a group referred to as "hippies" by the media, but according to him, it was a "group sustaining themselves to matched human sensibilities through Hinduism or Buddhism." The commune started when Suwanose-jima elders begged Nanao Sakaki, who was visiting the island, to bring more young people there to live at the onset of the population decline. This was consequent to the island having to close, because of a lack of young people to perform boat-related jobs such as loading and unloading shipments. He belonged to a group called Buzoku in Japan, and contacted his peers and created a commune in 1967 along with members such as the American poet Gary Snyder. Many young people visited the commune and collaborative living had commenced by 1977 / 1978.

Thereafter, many members of the commune left the island, but some remained and lived in a household unit. Those who remained became island residents and supported the island by participating in its activities and events (Table 2). Currently, five households play a central role in running various events as the elders of the island. Events include festivals held by the shrine and those run by the residents' association and schools. Events held at the shrine include the fishing festival (January and May), ship-launching festival (January), O-bon Lantern Festival (August), and festival for praying (October). Events held by the residents' association include road repair (July and December), Bon dance (August), Arasetu and Shibasashi dances (September and October) that originated in the Amami Islands, and welcoming and farewell parties for transferring members (April and March). School events are important activities in which children and adults participate, including the athletics meeting (September), cultural festival (November), and long-distance

relay race (January). As seen, events on Suwanose-jima Island seamlessly take place throughout the year. Senior I-turners serve as the organizers of this series of events.

Although Suwanose-jima Island still has various tasks to tackle in the future, such as the lack of vacant housing and settlement of I-turners after their allowance has been cut, currently, the vitalization of the island via I-turners has been successful. The factors for this success are explained by the following two points from the perspective of "diversity." The first is the diversity of the island residents. The island became isolated after a major volcanic eruption in 1813, with Tomiden Fujii from the Amami Islands settling 70 years later in the 1880s. Thereafter, the establishment of a commune in the late 1960s formed the island residents' group mentioned earlier. The descendants of the settlers from Amami islands and island residents from the commune overcame their differences and created a community. This is believed to have created a culture that approved of I-turners, who have diverse values. The second factor is the collaborative relationship between various organizational bodies. Island residents work towards receiving I-turners by collaborating with the village office and NPOs. An NPO organization, namely Takara Interface, also plans and runs island visit tours for those wishing to I-turn.

The results of interviews with Mr. A and Mr. B revealed important points regarding the future prospects of the island. From a financial efficiency viewpoint, it is difficult for public or private institutions to provide higher education and advanced medical treatment based on the population size of Suwanose-jima Island. As such, once the children graduate middle school, they must leave the island to advance to high school. There is the option of the parents staying on the island until the youngest of their children graduates from middle school, for which primary education is subsidized, and send an allowance to their children living outside the island, as Mr. A is planning to do. However, many people likely leave the island as a family when their oldest child advances to high school. Furthermore, as they age, many people like Mr. B will be forced to move to an urban area equipped with advanced medical institutions to receive medical treatment for their spouse or themselves. In other words, the discrepancy in education and medical service between the island and the city creates a structure that generates a certain percentage of people regularly emigrating from the island.

Therefore, more people moving to the island than those leaving are needed. To do so, it is necessary to enhance and provide support for primary education, and to create industries that are high in productivity and can make a good living, both of which are currently possible in Toshima Village. This will probably center on the agriculture and fishery as well as tourism industries. Furthermore, public relations for the islands must be conducted by hosting events in the cities to promote resident settlement. An island that has many people leaving and many moving in at the same time will signify that the island residents will have diverse ways of thinking, leading to a strong likelihood of creating a flexible and vital economy and society. In addition, information on vacant housing and the repair thereof must be available

to attract settlers. Toshima Village effectively executed such policies and activities.

Table 3 summarizes the various activities implemented by Toshima Village to promote residents' settlement in the village (Toshima Village 2017). The chart indicates the Employment Training Bonus Program as the basis for the creation of industry. Public relations events are vigorously conducted in the local Kagoshima Prefecture, Kanto region, and urban regions, with the smooth renovation of vacant housing and provision thereof to new migrants. However, as mentioned, the lack of vacant housing may become an obstacle in accepting migrants in the future.

5. Economic theory to approach the issue of migration from urban to rural

As explained above, people will move from urban to rural under some conditions. If the social and economic mechanism or system of the migration, government, local government, Non-Profit Orga-nization (NPO) are able to know what they should and how much cost they should prepare.

The author considers that the discussion of

Table 3. Resident settlement policies in Toshima Village.

	Major policies / activities	Notes
2010	The Employment Training Bonus Program (which serves as the basis of the relocation policy) is initiated The vacant housing usage program is started	By 2016, 24 vacant houses are prepared
2011	Briefing seminars are hosted locally	
2012	Community Promotion Section is newly established (Resident Settlement Promotion counter unified into one counter) The Settlement Project Team is launched Comprises each island's residents' association chief, local politicians, and dispatched agents	
2013	Participated in a relocation event in urban areas	
2014	The Site Operations Work Program is started A solo event is held in Tokyo.	
2015	Recruitment of volunteers to participate in community building activities begins Conferences on the Settlement Project are held on all islands	According to the national census, Suwanose Island ranks second in Japan in terms of the population increase rate by municipality Increased from 69 in 2010 to 132 in 2015
2016	The two volunteers for community building activities (stockbreeding assistants) start their activities Event held only by the Village is held in Tokyo	

Resource: Created based on Toshima Village (2017) Takara Islands; full of fascinating islands <Resource Edition>.

dual economy which started way back in 1950's to 1970's by several eminent development economists such as Sir William Arthur Lewis. His economic development theory is based on dual economy of urban sector under industrialization and rural sector under limited supply of labor (Lewis 1954). He points out that the wage level in the rural area is so low at subsistence level because the production level is quite low in the rural areas. Then the capitalists can hire the worker in the rural areas for their industrial production at the extremely low level.

Thus, migration of the rural people leads 'rosy' economic development thanks to low wage in urban areas which make the profit bigger than otherwise. The work of Fei and Ranis (1970) discusses the point when the migration starts. It says that the migration will end when the shortage of labor in the rural areas increase the wage increase to the level of that in urban. Harris and Todaro (1970) analysis how the rural people decide to migrate to the urban. The discussion of growing 'informal sector' is also helpful in understating the reverse migration. In the discussion, informal sector in urban is considered as a sector where the migrated people collect information on formal sector and they adjust themselves to the urban life. It is important that the urban economy itself is considered to be dual. This dualism is actually happening in big cities such as Tokyo and Osaka in Japan. There are people with high income and those with low income. The patterns of reserve migration differ between the two groups. The upper class who doesn't need to stick to a single work place will migrate to rural searching for extra benefits to live there. On the other hand, the lower class whose wage level is almost the same or less seek for the job in rural and extra benefits.

It explains that the rural people calculate the expected life time income between the home town and the urban area to head for, if the former is bigger, he or she make the action. Otherwise, he or she stays where he or she lives.

These discussions point out dual economy, turning point and decision-making process of the migrants from economic viewpoints. We can ally the approach to understand the process of

migration from urban to rural in Japan and other countries in the same situation. Firstly, it can be said that the rural economy and urban economy in Japan are very different. It is very difficult to get the average profit in rural areas. But the situation which differs from that of developing countries is that there are no affluent labor and the population is decreasing and aging on the contrary. It is necessary to come up with a new theory of dual economy in Japan. Secondly, the discussion of the turning point also needs to be modified to clarify why people in Japan migrate from urban to rural. One assumption is the accelerating dual economy in urban areas. The income gap between rich and poor is increasing there, so the gap of income between rural and urban shrink if only the low-income class dwellers in urban is focused.

Second assumption is that some people don't need to choose the place to stay thanks to ICT, and considering the benefit of healthy life surrounded by nature and good education in some areas. The mutual helping system in some rural areas are considered to be benefits for the migrant. There is a social problem especially in urban areas called 'lone death' in Japan. In some rural areas, there are still strong community ties going on which help 'the excluded people from the society'. It should be noted that it is not be always the case in rural areas. Even in the theory of Lewis, rural people cannot automatically migrate and help industrialize the country or a region. He says that the rural people need to be educated enough to be employed in a modern economic sector. People in urban areas cannot calculate the expected income and additional benefits in the rural area to migrate for a certain period time, and if it is bigger than staying in the urban area where they live. Basically, the turning point is up to the individual, but there could be several groups depending on the age, job and other attributes.

6. Conclusion

Migration in japan is basically happening from rural to urban at the moment. However, the trend may change after the infrastructure in urban areas become old and income gap grows. ICT is enabling the people to work in rural areas and the people in rural areas can buy almost all which those in urban are buying by using online shopping. On the contrary, the positive features such as the richness of culture, community tie, and rather inexpensive education cost are attracting attention of the people in urban. It is not easy but possible to make a model of the 'reverse migration' by borrowing the classic development theories. One important thing is that the economy in urban now in Japan is dual between urban and rural. And the urban economy is also dual, or high-income economy and low-income economy. In the development economic theory, the dual economic sectors in urban, or formal and informal sector are considered to be closely connected. In a simple way, the informal sector is considered to a steeping sector to the formal. In the present Japanese economy, the two groups should be considered as divided. Thus, the mechanism of the migration with high income should be considered in different ways each other.

Acknowledgements

I would like to extend my gratitude to Mr. KUMAMOTO from the Toshima Village Office, Mr. ITO and all the people from the Island for cooperating in the research and investigation conducted to write this paper.

References

FEI, J. C. H. and RANIS, G. 1961. A Theory of Economic Development. The American Economic Review, 51: 533–565.

HARRIS, J. R. and TODARO, M. P. 1970. Migration, Unemployment and Development: A Two-Sector Analysis. The American Economic Review, 60(1): 126–142.

LEWIS, W. A. 1954. Economic Development with Unlimited Supplies of Labour. The Manchester School, 22(2): 139–191.

MATSUTANI, A. 2015. Tokyo Rekka. PHP Shinsyo, Tokyo.

Toshima Village 2017. Miwakunoshimajima Tokara Retto, Shiryohen. Kagoshima Prefecture Toshima Village Tourist Information Magazine, Toshima Village.

Chapter 6
Regional Revitalization in Toshima Village: Population Growth & Regeneration

Kei KAWAI

1. Introduction

Toshima Village is situated in the north of the Satsunan Islands and extends about 160km from north to south. The village consists of seven populated and five uninhabited islands. The main inhabited island is Nakano-shima Island, and the other six are Kuchino-shima, Taira-jima, Suwanose-jima, Akuseki-jima, Kodakara-jima, and Takara-jima Islands. There is not town hall on the islands, and it has been situated in Kagoshima City since 1956.

The only way to get to the village is by a village-run ferry (Fig. 1) which runs twice a week. The ferry leaves from Kagoshima and passes through each island in Toshima Village before docking at Amami Oshima Island, after which it returns to Kagoshima. This frequency of the ferry limits the circulation of people and goods, making human movement and shipping of goods expensive. Getting to Toshima's central island of Nakano-shima from Kagoshima takes 7 hours 10 minutes and costs 6,290 yen for a one-way fare.

The population of Toshima Village was around 2,600 in 1953. However, the current population is 688 (as of March 2018). According to a report by the National Institute of Population and Security Research (IPSS), the population will fall to 466 by 2040. If the population keeps on declining, the village's survival will be under threat.

Population decline is affecting not just Toshima Village but all over Japan as well. Because of this, the Japanese government has come up with a regional revitalization strategy to encourage regeneration in rural areas. In December 2015, Toshima Village formulated "Population Vision & Comprehensive Strategy for Township, People, and Job Creation in Toshima Village" as a regional revitalization strategy (Fig. 2). This chapter will explain the current status and outlook regarding the population in Toshima Village, followed by an introduction of its revitalization strategy.

2. Current Status and Outlook regarding Population

The population of Toshima Village in 2015 was 678. When the "Population Vision & Comprehensive Strategy" was formulated, a questionnaire survey was carried out to discover what the island inhabitants thought about their current and future lives.

In a question regarding population, 53% answered that "the population should grow from its current level," while 32% responded that they "did not want the population to fall and that the current population levels should be maintained." Moreover, a question regarding intent to stay revealed that 56% of the island inhabitants wanted to carry on living there while only 10% wanted to live elsewhere, demonstrating that most of the island inhabitants wanted to continue living on the islands.

Based on these results, Toshima Village's town hall summarized "five basic perspectives as seen

Fig. 1. A village-run ferry "*Ferry Toshima*".

from the current status and issues concerning the population."

1. Maintaining and regenerating the population size in accordance with island characteristics
2. A sustained trajectory away from population decline and toward population growth through migration measures
3. Overcoming natural decline
4. Strengthening weaknesses and creating new human flows
5. Ensuring safety and security in daily life

Based on these perspectives, the future population outlook in the Comprehensive Strategy aimed to achieve a population count of 680 in 2020, 720 in 2040, and 750 in 2060. A variety of policies have been formulated and implemented to achieve this population outlook.

The next section introduces some of these policies and the basic principles behind them.

3. Comprehensive Strategy

Fig. 2. "Population Vision & Comprehensive Strategy for Township, People, and Job Creation in Toshima Village" as a regional revitalization strategy.

The four basic principles for rural community development detailed below were chosen as the basis for the formulation of the measures.

1. Value people
Value all people associated with the village, whether they are currently living there, returning there, moving there, tourists, or friends of the island.

2. Coexist with nature
Everyone from residents to island visitors should coexist with nature to protect, enjoy, and get the most out of it.

3. Create things
Capitalize on and create using the great treasure of nature's resources through sectors like agriculture, livestock, marine products, forestry, commerce, and tourism.

4. Everyone contributes
It is everyone's responsibility to make decisions and implement them together.

Four basic goals were set in accordance with the above-mentioned principles, with specific measures decided for each goal to be carried out by FY2019. The goals and their specific measures are outlined below:

Basic Goal 1: Strengthen the basic industries that coexist with nature and create stable employment
We will develop initiatives in addition to previously implemented industrial development policies in which people explore and utilize Tokara Islands' great natural resources, and endeavor to establish healthy agriculture and marine products industries and create new business. Moreover, we will create stable employment through initiatives to strengthen education and employ talented people to take on the challenges presented by the location and established companies.

Measures have been formulated and implemented to achieve this goal in the form of the promotion of industries resilient to changes in the business environment, the expansion of sales channels and the development of production bases for superior agricultural products, and the development of businesses that capitalize on the diversity of natural resources. For example, grants and barn maintenance are being provided to the livestock industry, which is one of the island's important industries.

Basic Goal 2: Create new flows of people to the island

In coexistence with the harsh environment of the island, we aim to build a healing place for people by focusing on tourism operating in a slow life style. We will also create value by having tourism unique to the islands where tourists can feel "the spirit of OMOTENASHI (hospitality)" in every corner and will proactively develop tourism exchanges. We will also expand the Mountain and Seas Study Program from outside the islands and work to nurture children who represent the next generation. We will endeavor to provide and make the most of transport and information infrastructure – that is, the convenience of the ferry as the only public transport facility in Toshima Village and the broadband sector – in order to encourage these types of new flows of people.

Measures have been formulated and implemented to bring this goal to life, in the form of the promotion of tourism exchanges, the expansion of the Mountain and Seas Study Program, and improvements in the convenience of the Toshima ferry along with the provision and utilization of information communication infrastructure. For example, we are carrying out a project aimed at travelers which has been widely reported in the media to provide a long-term village settlement support program and discount ferry tickets.

Basic Goal 3: Satisfy the younger generation's hopes for moving, marriage, childbirth and child raising

Initiatives to encourage immigration have resulted in younger generations moving here in recent years and creating new life on the islands, increasing support needs for childbirth and child rearing. We will promote initiatives to satisfy the hopes of the younger generations concerning moving, marriage, childbirth and child raising in order to maintain this inward flow.

Measures have been formulated and are being implemented to bring this goal to life in the form of settlement support projects and marriage, childbirth and child raising support projects. For example, we are establishing institutions to support child raising, multi-generational exchanges, and the elderly.

Basic Goal 4: For everyone to play a leading role in rural community development, protecting safe living and linking the islands within the region

We will promote rural community development so people will want to continue living on the islands, satisfying the common desire among residents to be able to always stay on the islands to which they have grown accustomed. We will promote ferry fare reductions, community development, and professional development. We will also work to improve living standards by using renewable energy, with a view to building lives that coexist with nature and eco-friendly, clean islands. The seven islands will cooperate as a body sharing a common destiny, and we will also promote regional cooperation with Kagoshima City and Amami-Oshima Island, with whom we are connected by the sea route, and with the World Heritage island of Yaku-shima.

Measures have been formulated and are being implemented to bring this goal to life in the form of establishing secure living through the use of ICT, improving living standards using clean energy and the promotion of regional cooperation projects. For example, we are moving ahead with the introduction of eco-cars on the islands.

4. Conclusion

The implementation of the various policies outlined in this chapter resulted in an upwards trend in immigration in recent years, as can be seen from the fact that population growth rose to fifth place nationwide in the 2015 census. However, the population is on a downward trend in 2019 because of the death of elderly inhabitants. While previous measures can be said to have been somewhat effective, it can't be said that they have completely solved the population challenges facing Toshima Village.

The first stage of regional revitalization ended in FY2019, and the second will begin in FY2020. Therefore, there is a need to revisit the measures previously implemented to bring about changes and implement even better policies for Toshima Village's development.

Industry

A municipal ferry boat, *Ferry Toshima*. Photo: Ryuta TERADA

OTSUKA, Y., TERADA, R. and NISHIMURA, S. (eds.), *The Tokara Islands*
Kagoshima University International Center for Island Studies; Hokuto Shobo Publishing, Tokyo. 10 March 2020.

Chapter 7

Present Situation and Prospects in Sustaining Fishery in Takara-jima Is. and Kodakara-jima Is.

Remote, Inhabited Islands Establishing Japan's Territorial Seas

Takashi TORII

1. Introduction

Areas of remote islands in Japan have drawn increasing attention in recent years. Despite its small land area, Japan has the world's sixth largest exclusive economic zone thanks to a number of islands scattered across the territory. Although there are diverse biological resources and rich mineral resources, fishery is the major industry supporting the economy of the remote islands. In particular, islands with smaller areas under cultivation tend to show higher ratios of the overall labor force aged 15 or over engaged in fishery. Fisheries of remote islands once represented more than 10% of the gross domestic fishery production value, showing their role as the nation's food providers (YAMAO 2009). However, both the volume and value of fishery production of remote islands decreased rapidly after 2000 and they now represent less than 8% of the gross domestic fishery production value (OKUNO 2013). The shrinkage of fishery, which is the major industry of remote islands, may not only lead to a decline in their role as food providers, but also result in weakening of their economy (TORII 2012a).

Also in recent years, illegal fishing by foreign boats and intrusion by foreign government vessels in Japan's territorial waters widely signaled that a decline in fishery and local economy in inhabited islands in border areas may directly affect Japan's national security. When focusing on the correlation between "the land area of an island" and "the ratio of labor force engaged in fishery to overall labor force aged 15 or over," islands with smaller land areas often show higher ratios of the labor force engaged in fishery (TORII 2012b). This indicates that, in terms of industrial development of an island, the importance of fishery is higher in islands with limited areas of cultivation. Thus

promotion of fishery operations in islands will contribute to development of their economy, as well as developing their role as food providers, and, in turn, possibly enhancing national security.

Accordingly, this paper focuses on Takara-jima Is. and Kodakara-jima Is., two islands in an area of remote, inhabited islands establishing territorial seas in Kagoshima Prefecture, to demonstrate the present situation and future prospects of fishery for the two islands. Both islands have very limited areas of cultivated land. Although surrounded by supposedly rich fishery resources, fishery production is not thriving in either island. Although disadvantage in distribution conditions is often mentioned regarding fishery in the islands, is it the only obstructive factor hindering fishery development? The following discussion examines the present situations, issues to be solved, and future prospects of fishery in Takara-jima Is. and Kodakara-jima Is. based on interviews with persons actively engaged in fishery operations.

2. Overview of Toshima Village

Toshima Village in Kagoshima Prefecture has seven inhabited islands. Of the village population totaling 688, Takara-jima Is. and Kodakara-jima Is. represent 131 and 53, respectively. There are ferry services operated by the village twice a week between the islands and the mainland Kagoshima and Amami-Oshima Is. It is a 13-hour trip from Kagoshima Port to Takara-jima Is. or Kodakara-jima Is.

There were almost 3000 people in Toshima Village in the 1950s. During and after the 1960s, however, the population sharply declined. Following an active effort to attract internal migrants, the population recovered from 601 in 2011 to 688 at the end of March 2018.

A breakdown of the industrial structure of Toshima Village by sector follows: primary (28.2%), secondary (20.8%), and tertiary industries (51.0%) (at the end of March 2018). Of the number of persons engaged in primary industries, 75% are mainly engaged in agriculture and 25% are in fishery. In recent years, some internal migrants have engaged in fishery as a part of combined means of income.

Toshima Village has a fishery cooperative (headquartered in Kagoshima City) consisting of 38 regular and 102 associate members. The annual business volume of this cooperative totals 32.61 million yen (in fiscal year 2017). Flyingfish, lobsters, Japanese butterfish, alfonsinos, and wahoos are among the catch from the sea around the village. Fish are shipped from the islands by ferry, but this is available only twice a week and it takes many hours before arriving at its destinations. This results in deterioration in freshness of fishery products and a decrease in their market prices – a substantial disadvantage in terms of distribution conditions. Amid these situations, Toshima Village introduced rapid freezers in Takara-jima Is. and Nakano-shima Is. in 2011 and 2012, respectively, with the purpose to improve distribution conditions (Torii 2017, 2018). Accordingly, with cooperation from private wholesale stores of fishery products, Nakano-shima Is. started shipping of frozen products. In Takara-jima Is., a group of fishery operators developed frozen processed foods aimed at shipment to markets outside the island.

3. Situations of Fishery in Takara-jima Is.
3.1. Overview of Takara-jima Is.

Takara-jima Is. comprises raised coral reefs with a land area totaling 7.14 km². The ferry enters the Maegomori Fishing Port located in the northern part of the island. The port was built by excavating the coral reefs, and has a ferry dock on the western side and a boat basin on the eastern side. The population of the island is 131 and the number of households is 68, of which around 15% have migrated from outside the village.

The industries of Takara-jima Is. are traditionally centered on agriculture. There are ferry services to connect the island and mainland Kagoshima twice

Fig. 1. Fishing Port in Takara-jima Is.

weekly. Although the surrounding sea has resources such as flyingfish, shipment of fresh products is subject to restraints of the ferry service and, without an appropriate facility on the island, it is not possible to improve their shelf lives through processing. These significant problems with shipping conditions have long deterred the islanders from effectively utilizing their fishery resources.

As a result, fishery operations are not very active in Takara-jima Is. The island has nine regular and 16 associate members of the fishery cooperative but there are only eight fishing boats, all of small size. The catch of operators includes flyingfish, Japanese snapper, wahoos, Japanese ruby fish, lobsters, and turbo marmoratus, using fishing techniques such as gill netting, trolling, and trawling. However, only two of them catch a volume of fish sufficient to regularly ship outside the island.

Amid the significant restraints in shipping conditions, a rapid freezer was introduced to Takara-jima Is. in 2011 with a subsidy from Toshima Village. This backed up the fishery operators on the island to start fishery processing. The following section analyzes the present situations and issues to be solved based on the case of Person A, who is actively engaged in fishery operations in Takara-jima Is. (Fig. 1).

3.2. Person A

Person A is male, in his 40s, and migrated from outside Takara-jima Is. Finding that Toshima Village was recruiting internal migrants, he applied in 2009. The requirement for candidate migrants then was to submit a plan for revitalization of the islands, which the village would evaluate. The plan by Person A included engagement in a primary industry, processing and selling of his products, acceptance of volunteers, and operation of a guesthouse, and this was approved.

After migrating to the island, Person A engaged in agriculture. He rented about eight tans of former farmland (1 tan = 991.736 m²) which had turned into a thicket (for annual rent of about 1000 yen per tan) and cultivated the land by himself. Now he crops "shima-rakkyos" or small Japanese scullions, which are less susceptible to diseases, pests, and typhoons, on half of the lot. The cultivation method was learned from elderly people on the islands. Usually he plants the seedlings in October, harvests and ships them during February–May for eating raw, and later, for processing, such as pickling. The annual production volume is around two tonnes. Of the scullions shipped outside the island, 90% are bound for Tokyo areas and 10% are for Amami-Oshima Is.

In the third year, Person A started trawling for flyingfish with another fishery operator on Takara-jima Is., targeting a rich amount of flyingfish in the surrounding sea. During the peak fishing season of May to late June, several kinds of fish are caught, including flyingfish, coast flyingfish, and blotchwing flyingfish. During March–November, wahoos are also caught.

The flyingfish they catch are treated at the facility on the island before being rapidly frozen and processed to such items as fried foods and sashimi. Because the flyingfish are smaller than those caught around Yaku-shima, they have low ratings in the market, and so are all sent to the processing facility. However, the fishing season for flyingfish is short and only two people, including Person A, catch flyingfish. Accordingly, the operation rate of the processing facility is low and so it also purchases flyingfish from Kodakara-jima Is. The facility purchases other fish such as wahoos, pomfrets, bonitos, and Japanese butterfish from neighboring islands to process them into such products as fried food, cold-smoked roasted sashimi, and sashimi. For wood chips used in the smoking process, Machilus thunbergii native to the island was used originally. However, the scent was weak and so cherry trees purchased from outside are used now.

In 2015, a general incorporated association named the Takara-jima Cooperative was established (with four board members and eight part-timers) for the purpose of local revitalization and its fishery processing and marketing division was named Hanamimaru Store. The processed products are sold to restaurants and consumers, some through the Internet. In addition to these activities, Person A undertakes product development utilizing banana fibers and construction works (Fig. 2).

Selling of processed fishery products involves many difficulties. Since the post office in Takara-jima Is. is not equipped with a freezer, the products are shipped to Kagoshima City in boxes provided by a non-profit organization Tokara Interface (Kagoshima City). From the base in the city, products are delivered as ordered.

One of the problems facing the business is

Fig. 2. The Appearance of the Hanamimaru Store.

Fig. 3. Specialty of Hanamimaru Store.

unstable supply of raw materials. Because there are very few fishery operators in Takara-jima Is., it is difficult to supply a stable volume of raw materials. Although the Hanamimaru Store also purchases fishery products from neighboring islands, they are insufficient to compensate the unstable supply. For this reason, expansion of the procurement area is being examined. Another problem is securing sales channels for processed products. Despite successful development of unique products such as cold-smoked foods, they are yet to make significant sales – some are shipped to Tokyo areas but high shipping costs hamper active trading.

In addition to fishery operation, Person A engages in loading and unloading of ferry cargo and raising dwarf bananas. The income from fishery operations represents only 20% of his total income, but he regards this as an important source (Fig. 3).

4. Situations of Fishery in Kodakara-jima Is.

4.1. Overview of Kodakara-jima Is.

Kodakara-jima Is. is the smallest of the inhabited islands of the Tokara Archipelago, with a land area totaling 0.98 km². As for Takara-jima Is., Kodakara-jima Is. is an island of raised coral reefs. The population is 53 with 32 households. During the 1970s and 1980s, the population dropped below 30 and the island was on the verge of being deserted. After Toshima Village started accepting internal migrants and launched a program to accept students from outside to study at a school on one of its islands, the population of the island is showing an upward trend.

Kodakara-jima Is. has three regular and eight associate members of the Toshima Fishery Cooperative. Among them, however, only Person B operates fishery for more than 100 days a year. The other members fish seasonally and mostly for self-consumption and to give to acquaintances on the island (Fig. 4).

4.2. Person B

Person B is a male in his 50s and is native to Kodakara-jima Is. He first went trolling for wahoos with his father when he was a third grader

Fig. 4. Fishing Port in Kodakara-jima Is.

in elementary school. There was no freezer then and the capacity of their refrigerator was small, and so his family salted the wahoos they caught and dried them in the sun before preserving them. The dried wahoos were taken to neighboring Takara-jima Is. to barter for other commodities, including rice. Later, Person B entered high school in Kagoshima City, before graduating from the school and finding a job in the city. Person B returned to the island when he was 22 years old. The population of Kodakara-jima Is. was 21 at that time and it was a major concern that the island might become deserted; when asked by his friends, Person B decided to return.

After coming back to the island, Person B started dive fishing for turbo marmoratus, gill netting for lobsters, harpooning for wahoos, and trolling for wahoos, yellowfin tunas, toothed tunas, and giant trevallies. Turbo marmoratus were sold at high prices then, as were lobsters shipped to the Kagoshima Federation of Fishery Cooperatives. However, it was difficult to keep the catch alive when the ferry services were cancelled. In particular, lobsters were thinned in just a few days, significantly losing market value. Despite the difficulty of a lack of secured shipping measures, turbo marmoratus and lobsters were sold at prices high enough for Person B to produce sufficient income from fishery operation to maintain his livelihood (Fig. 5).

At that time, several people were engaged in fishery in Kodakara-jima Is. other than Person B, and there were five or six fishing boats in service. The rice fields on the island were small and many islanders earned their livelihood from the sea. Because the fishing port was not properly developed, fishery operators used a small cove as a boat dock and winched their boats up a ramp. In the neighboring sea, visiting operators from Itoman City, Okinawa, performed drive fishing for double-lined fusiliers.

Later on, Person B started trolling for wahoos during April–October while still mainly performing dive fishing. After catching wahoos, he directly sailed to Takara-jima Is. and sold the catch to the islanders. The catch was also shipped to Kagoshima Federation of Fishery Cooperatives if the volume was large enough. Person B maintained this style of fishery operation for a while.

His boat was damaged by typhoons in 1990 and 1991 and then he purchased a newly built boat (2.8 t). Its size was constrained by the capacity of the crane facility at Kodakara-jima Is., and so he purchased the largest boat that could be handled by the facility. However, the new boat was too long to be winched up the ramp at the existing facility, making it necessary to take refuge at a port in Takara-jima Is. or Amami-Oshima Is. during typhoons. In addition, the so-called "burst of the bubble economy" in the 1990s triggered a drop in turbo shell prices, pressuring Person B to change his operation style.

Around 2002, Person B switched his fishery style to pole-and-line fishing targeting deep-sea fish and this continues. The principal targets are Japanese ruby fish, Japanese snapper, and ruby snapper. For bait, he uses bullet mackerels, sardines, and others purchased from Kagoshima.

Fig. 5. Abundant Marine Resources (*Turbo Marmoratus*).

His fishing grounds are scattered in the area within 15 min to 3 h from the homeport.

Usually Person B leaves the port around 2 am and operates fishery until sunset, before coming back to the port. After returning, he sorts his catch based on size and kind, before shipping them to Kyushu Chuou Uoichi (the central fishery market) in Kagoshima City or to Amami-Oshima Is. depending on market prices at the time. Taking into account the long hours to ship the catch by ferry, which operates only twice a week between Takara-jima Is. and Kagoshima Is., he pays special attention to post-processing of his catch, such as how to kill and ice the fishery products in order to maintain their freshness – the freshness can be maintained for about ten days at the longest. When a cancellation of ferry service is expected, he processes the catch all the more carefully.

The total number of days that Person B operates annually remains low at around 130. When winds blow from northwest, north, or northeast, it is difficult for a boat to enter the Jounomae Fishing Port, thus often forcing him to give up the day's operation. On other occasions, he must stay in the offshore area due to rough waves at the port mouth at the time of his return.

However, there are large fishing boats (19 t class) from Amami-Oshima Is. and other prefectures operating in the neighboring sea all year round and Person B considers that he could go fishing more often if there was a port with proper facilities in Kodakara-jima Is. In other words, people of Kodakara-jima Is. cannot purchase large-scale fishing boats because they lack a proper port and crane facility. This means that they cannot exploit the rich fishery resources in the surrounding sea and so fishery production does not develop on Kodakara-jima Is.

Person B also operates stock farming and a guest house, but a large portion of his income is attributed to fishery.

5. Present Situations and Future Prospects of Fishery in Takara-jima Is. and Kodakara-jima Is.

Although there is more than one regular member of the fishery cooperative both in Takara-jima Is. and Kodakara-jima Is., only few of them ship their catch to outside the respective islands. Most fishery operators in the islands operate for self-consumption and for acquaintances on the island. The interviews revealed the situations that insufficiencies of not only distribution conditions but also production-related facilities serve as preventive factors against fishery development for both islands. The limited number of operators and limited volume of catch means the importance of fishery in these islands in terms of production is low.

Is it important to sustain fishery operation in these islands at all? The answer is yes, and for two reasons.

5.1. Livelihood of Islanders

There is significance for fishery in terms of islanders' livelihoods. Person A of Takara-jima Is. earns his income year round from both agriculture and fishery. Fishery represents about 20% of his total income, indicating an important source of income. Additionally, the Takara-jima Cooperative processes fishery products caught by the islanders and provides several part-time jobs, which are rare employment opportunities on the islands. Their products are also valuable as local specialties and souvenirs. In the case of Person B of Kodakara-jima Is., fishery operation is the main source of his income. Considering that he provides some of his catch to Takara-jima Is., he also serves as a fishery provider within the islands. For people who live in the two islands, fishery and fishery processing are necessities. As Toshima Village actively accepts internal migrants, it is possible that these migrants will incorporate fishery in their job combination to maintain their livelihoods.

5.2. National Security

Fishery is significant for national security. Because Takara-jima Is. and Kodakara-jima Is. are in the areas of remote, inhabited islands establishing territorial seas, they are indispensable for preservation of Japan's territorial waters as well as its exclusive economic zone. It is likely that disappearance of the islands' societies as a result of a decline in their industry may cause problems for national security. When the rich fishery resources surrounding the islands are taken into account,

sustention of fishery production in these islands is very important from the perspective of the livelihood of the nation.

The restrictive conditions for fishery development of the two islands are the poor facilities for fishery production such as cranes and breakwaters in their ports, in addition to the disadvantage in distribution due to limited ferry services. Of these two restrictive conditions, the disadvantage in distribution has been compensated somewhat by the introduction of a rapid freezer in Takara-jima Is., which led to development of frozen and processed foods. Since Takara-jima Is. is a short distance from Kodakara-jima Is., it is possible that fishery operators of Kodakara-jima Is. could perform similar practices using the same facility. Regarding production-related facilities, construction of breakwaters for Kodakara-jima Is. will require a large expense. Because there is only one fishery operator on the island, there is no choice but that the operator takes early refuge at the port in Takara-jima Is., which is equipped with proper facilities, on occasions of a prospective disaster such as a typhoon.

Considering the current situation, improvement in the crane facility is a more probable option in terms of development of production facilities. However, in addition to the fact there is only one fishery operator on the island, there is no prospective successor to sustain the operation. In these situations, how should this kind of investment be evaluated? Should it be regarded as excessive because of the situation of only a single fishery operator and no prospective successor? Or should it be considered worthwhile based on an expectation that an improved crane facility and resulting improvement in the production environment will bring about future successors in fishery? If the latter is the case, measures will have to be examined in a context combined with the program to accept internal migrants, as actively promoted by Toshima Village.

Another option is to let those from other areas take roles in terms of national security. Luckily, aside from Amami-Oshima Is., fishery operators from Okinawa and Kumamoto Prefectures visit this area, targeting its rich fishery resources. Thanks to these visiting operators, the function of border patrolling, one of many functions performed through fishery operations, is fulfilled to some degree.

References

OKUNO, K. 2013. Marine Product Industry of the Remote Islands in Japan: On the Fisheries Outputs and Fishing Boats Powers, Marine Production Types. The Journal of Island Studies, 14: 75–112. (in Japanese)

TORII, T. 2012a. The Present Conditions and Problems of Fishery in Isolated Islands. Journal of Regional Fisheries, 52(3): 1–6. (in Japanese)

TORII, T. 2012b. Official Support for Fishery in Isolated Islands and Changes in Fishery Structure. Journal of Regional Fisheries, 52(3): 29–46. (in Japanese)

TORII, T. 2017. Efforts for Improving the Distribution of Fishery Products in Toshima, Kagoshima Prefecture. Kagoshima University Research Center for the Pacific Islands Occasional Papers 58: 17–22.

TORII, T. 2018. Efforts and Problems of Improving the Distribution of Fishery Products through the Introduction of Refrigeration Technology, A Case study of Nakanoshima Island in Toshima Village Kagoshima. Japanese Journal of Island and Community Studies, 5: 1–19. (in Japanese)

YAMAO, M. *et al.* 2009. The Multiple Functions of the Fishing Industry and Fishing Villages. 248 pp., Hokuto Shobou, Tokyo. (in Japanese)

OTSUKA, Y., TERADA, R. and NISHIMURA, S. (eds.), *The Tokara Islands*
Kagoshima University International Center for Island Studies; Hokuto Shobo Publishing, Tokyo. 10 March 2020.

Chapter 8
Current Status, Problems and Perspective of Native Goats in the Tokara Archipelago and its Neighboring Islands

Yoshitaka NAKANISHI

1. Introduction

There are a variety of native domestic and feral animals as well as wildlife indigenous to Japan on the Satsunan Islands comprising Osumi, Tokara and Amami islands in Kagoshima Prefecture, which suggests a high level of biodiversity has been conserved. Thus, native domestic animals are regarded as important and the rarest animal genetic resources from an academic point of view. In the early 1960s, morphology and genetics of native domestic animals on small islands located in the southern and western margins of Japan were investigated by many researchers of Kagoshima University, Tokyo University of Agriculture and Nagoya University, so that cattle, horses and goats which had not been exposed to crossbreeding or artificial selection due to geographical and economical isolation were found in the Tokara Archipelago (The Research Group on the Native Farm Animals in Japan and its Adjacent Localities 1964). In contrast, extraneous animals have been introduced in some islands, and it is suggested that the animals have a harmful impact on the species indigenous to each island, agriculture and environment together with some of feral animals (Ministry of the Environment 2019).

Kuchino-shima feral cattle and Tokara native horses are preserved on Kuchino-shima Is. and Nakano-shima Is. of the Tokara Archipelago, respectively, but Tokara native goats and their hybrid with another breed (Japanese Saanen) inhabit all of the islands (SAITO and KISANUKI 1980, MINEZAWA 2004). Kuchino-shima feral cattle and Tokara native horses are free-ranged on native pasture or woodland under artificial conservation, whilst Tokara native goats are fed by stockpersons or become feral due to abandonment of feeding.

Of all the native domestic animals in the Tokara

Archipelago, Tokara native goats are one of two Japanese indigenous breeds for meat production together with Shiba goats in Nagasaki Prefecture (NOZAWA *et al.* 1978, PORTER 1996). The former breed is mostly hybridized on the Tokara and Amami Islands, so that the purebred population has declined sharply in recent years (MANDA 1986). There exists a traditional dietary culture of consuming goat meat on the Nansei Islands including the Tokara Islands, where goat meat is considered to be a medicinal cooking ingredient for nutrients and tonics.

Since feral goats, which have been abandoned and free-ranged by stockpersons, often overgraze on wild plants and browse field crop on some islands, the animals are popularly referred to as "*Noyagi*" (stray goats) by islanders. Overgrazing by feral goats induces vegetation destruction and subsequent soil erosion. Therefore, it is urgent that we prevent damage caused by feral goats. However, there is a scarcity of detailed information on the current status of goat farming and the damage derived from feral goats.

In this paper, a couple of case studies on the present situation of goat farming and some problems related to native goats on the Tokara Archipelago and its neighboring islands were reviewed. The paper also alludes to the perspectives of local households regarding feral goats to overcome the problems and to improve livelihoods of islanders.

2. Actual damage from feral goats in Taira-jima Is., Tokara Archipelago

2.1. Background

According to the Toshima Village Government Office (2019), Taira-jima Is., which is in the Tokara Archipelago, has the area of 2.08 km^2 (7.23 km in circumference) and an active volcano (secondary sedimentary rocks in the Neogene Pliocene). About 80% of the island's vegetation is Ryukyuchiku (*Pleioblastus linearis* Nakai). The island has a population of 78 (43 families), and basic industries are animal husbandry (beef cattle production) and fishery. It is said that Tokara native goats also live on Taira-jima Is., and islander's life and vegetation are often hampered by feral goats (Fukuzawa pers. com.). However, feeding of domestic goats and the ecology of the feral goats are not clarified in detail. Therefore, the objective of this investigation was to examine the ecological aspect of feral goats and the damage to agricultural fields on Taira-jima Is.

2.2. Study site and methods

The present study was carried out on Taira-jima Is., Toshima Village, Kagoshima Prefecture during 5–30 November in 2018. It is located at long. 129°32′E. and lat. 29°40′N.

2.2.1. Ecological aspect of feral goats

Field signs of feral goats, such as dung-deposited areas and their eating marks on wild plants were monitored by driving a car or by walking along the road to elucidate the animals' natural habitat on November 6th. Whenever feral goats were found, the location of the discovery site, the number of groups and group sizes were recorded.

In addition to sex and growth stage of each goat, morphological characteristics such as coat color, horn and beard were identified using binoculars (×10).

2.2.2. Problems derived from feral goats

A questionnaire and oral survey of islanders (37% of total families) was taken on gender, age, damage from feral goats, injury to the crop, damage to the site, provisions taken against the animals, impression of the animals, and whether people keep household goats or not.

2.3. Results and discussion
2.3.1. Ecological aspect of feral goats

Habitat and population of feral goats identified on Taira-jima Is. are shown in Fig. 1. A total of 27 feral goats were identified throughout the daytime observational period, and they were present as solitary animals (3 individuals) or as flocks of four to five animals (2–8 herdmates) in southern (around Minami-no-hama Ranch) or eastern area (around Higashi-no-hama Ranch and Oura Ranch) of the island. It was found that some feral goats invaded the pasture which beef breeding cows were grazed, suggesting that they consumed the grass intended for cows (Fig. 2).

Tokara native goats have two types of coat

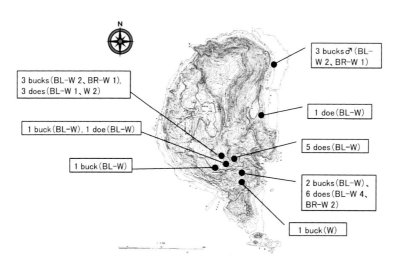

Fig. 1. Habitat and population of 27 feral goats identified on Taira-jima Is. (Nov. 6, 2018). Initials in parenthesis represents coat color of goats. BL-W: black-white pied, BR-W: brown-white pied, W: white.

Fig. 2. Feral goat which invaded the pasture for beef breeding cows on Oura Ranch in Taira-jima Is. (Nov. 6, 2018). A buck with black-white pied coat color is shown in the circle.

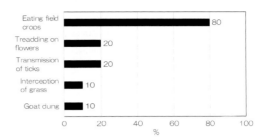

Fig. 3. Types of damage from feral goats in Taira-jima Is. (10 respondents including multiple answers allowed).

color, i.e. black-white pied and brown-white pied (MANDA 1986), but more than 70% of the feral goats had a black and white mottled coat color in this study. Although feral goats free-ranged the pasture and woodland, there was little serious vegetation destruction and soil erosion due to overgrazing. In particular, there was no damage to the ancient trees which is called the 1,000-Year-Old Gajumaru Banyan in Kamiyama (conservation area for wild plants). Therefore, a provision against damage by feral goats is not necessarily urgent. However, further investigation is required on the annual change of the feral goat population because the more the animals, the higher the risk of vegetation destruction and soil erosion in the future.

2.3.2. Problems derived from feral goats

When questionnaires were sent out to the 16 islanders, every single islander answered (recovery rate 100%). According to the survey, half of the respondents were from the over-60 age group. Over 60% of the respondents were damaged by feral goats. The feral goats gave the largest damage to field crops, followed by flowers and ornamental plants, transmission of ticks to cattle, and interception of grass for grazing cattle (Fig. 3). As for field crops damaged by feral goats, 50% of them were vegetables and 12% were crops, such as sweet potatoes and figs. Most respondents (90%) were engaged in preventing damage from the feral

goats, and 75% of them protected the crops or flowers using a net fence. A couple of answerers captured feral goats and shipped live animals to Amami-Oshima Is. in order to sell them. Some people hope to feed the captive feral goats in the pasture and to sell them in the future.

In conclusion, it seems that feral goats are not necessarily harmful to vegetation in Taira-jima Is. at the moment because they have no great impact on plants, but further survey is needed on goat farming and ecology of feral animals in order to avoid the risk of overgrazing, vegetation destruction and soil erosion in the future. It was also shown that no one worked for goat farming all year round, but only a few people temporarily kept the captured and sold the animals. In the future, some people hope to capture the feral goats to prevent vegetation destruction and to sell the animals after a temporary feeding, which may lead to regional revitalization.

3. Current status of goat farming and the related problems in the Amami Islands

3.1. Goat farming and the related problems in Kikai-jima Is.

3.1.1. Background

According to Kikai Neighborhood Government Office (2019), Kikai-jima Is., which is located in the Amami Islands, has an area of 56.82 km² (48.6 km in circumference), and about 40% of the island is arable land while about 19% is occupied by woodland. Most of the island consists of raised coral reef. The island has a population of 6,744 (3,219 families), and basic industries are sugarcane production and animal husbandry (beef cattle production). Kikai-jima Is., of the Satsunan Islands, is one of the major islands where goat farming is popular, and according to Kikai Neighborhood Government Office (pers. com.), about 500 household goats are fed mainly for meat production. This indicates a traditional dietary culture of goat meat consumption on Kikai-jima Is. Unused bioresources such as weeds and tree leaves are offered to household goats as feedstuff, but in some cases byproducts of sweet potato (*Ipomoea batatas* (L.) Lam.) such as leaves and vines are given.

Tsuda (2004) and Nojima (pers. com.) pointed out that feeding the sweet potatoes to goats might lead to the spread of a special pest, especially the sweet potato weevil (*Cylas formicarius*). Therefore, how to use the aboveground sweet potatoes or how to find the alternatives to the plants is a common and urgent issue in the Nansei Islands. Because Kikai-jima Is. is located near the southernmost area of the Tokara Archipelago and those islands are similar in regard to goat farming and the outbreak of sweet potato weevil. In order to promote the eradication and control of sweet potato weevil on Kikai-jima Is., information on types of goat farming and kinds of feed is needed. However, there is little data available on goat farming and the related problems.

Therefore, the aim of this survey was to clarify the present situation of goat farming in an attempt to obtain the basic information for the eradication and control of sweet potato weevil on Kikai-jima Is.

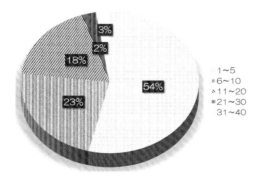

Fig. 4. The number of goats per capita raised by goatkeepers on Kikai-jima Is. (39 respondents).

3.1.2. Study site and methods

The present study was carried out on Kikai-jima Is., Kikai Neighborhood, Kagoshima Prefecture between September 22nd and October 13th in 2017. It is located at long. 130°00′E. and lat. 28°19′N.

A questionnaire survey of 85 goatkeepers was conducted from Sep. 22nd to Oct. 6th, in which 15 items such as age, purpose of goat farming, the number of goats, breed, site, feed, whether sweet potato byproducts are offered or not, measure to get the byproducts and meat production (the number of goats shipped, age, body weight, selling price and customer etc.) were included. An oral survey was also taken when visiting Kikai-jima Is. during 11–13 Oct.

3.1.3. Results and discussion

Thirty-nine goatkeepers in total answered via a questionnaire and oral survey (recovery rate: about 46%), and about 70% of them were over 60 years old. Half of the respondents had 1–5 animals per capita, which are considered smallholders (Fig. 4). More than 90% of the respondents raised the goats for meat production (self-consumption or sale). Most of the respondents were full-time goat farmers, farmers with various side jobs, i.e. sugarcane, sesame seeds or beef cattle production, chevon restaurant, and full-time farmers.

It was shown that about 90% of respondents gave weeds as feedstuff to their goats. Aboveground sweet potatoes were also offered to goats as roughage by about half of the goatkeepers. *Ipomoea indica* and *I. pes-caprae* as well as sweet potato were used as roughage for goats, which are affected by sweet potato weevils because those plants belong to Convolvulaceae (Kuriwada 2017). Therefore, control of feeding the plants to goats in combination with insecticide and setting of pheromone traps may result in a reduction of population of wild strains. Kuriwada (2017) advocated that releasing of sexually sterile males in addition to setting pheromone traps can help to exterminate the wild strains more efficiently. As for whether to feeding sweet potato byproducts in the future, it is difficult for local government to prohibit the use of the byproducts by goatkeepers, because the plants are more palatable to goats than weeds. Nevertheless, some goatkeepers indicate that they are able to substitute other feed resources for the byproducts in order to prevent damage from sweet potato weevils if local government grants them a substitution (e.g. grass hay) or grass seeds. Unless the goatkeepers use sweet potato byproducts on which sweet potato weevils are parasitic, it may contribute to the control of the spread of the insect pests.

Concerning the goats which had been fed for sale, 2–3 animals weighing 30–50 kg were sold to islanders or slaughtered at the age of 12 months or more every year. If the goatkeepers hope to increase their income in the goat sector, goat production should be elevated in scale and a new market should be developed. Okinawa Prefecture is considered to be one of the potential markets, because about 60% of goat meat consumed is imported from Australia and there is not a good domestic supply of goat meat despite expanding demand. Development of the domestic market (e.g. Okinawa Prefecture) for the sale of goats is considered to be a common issue for Taira-jima and Kikai-jima Is. Thus, developing a marketing system for live goats and goat meat is required.

In conclusion, most goatkeepers in Kikai-jima Is. were engaged in full-time goat farming, running both sugarcane, sesame seeds or beef cattle production, chevon restaurants and goat production, and full-time farming. The goatkeepers mainly offered weeds as feedstuff to their animals and about half of them gave the animals aboveground sweet potatoes, suggesting a high possibility of the spread of sweet potato weevils. Local government should not only prevent sweet potato weevils using insecticides, pheromone traps and sexually sterile males but also enlighten the goatkeepers not to use as much sweet potato byproducts as possible, on which the insect pests are parasitic.

3.2. Problems related to feral goats in Amami-Oshima Is.

3.2.1. Background

Amami-Oshima Is. is the largest of the Amami Islands which has the area of 720 km^2 (Amami City Office 2019). The island also has traditional dietary culture of consuming goat meat like other Satsunan Islands, where about 800 goats are fed by small-holders (Amami City Office pers. com.). In contrast, feral goats are also present due to abandonment of feeding, and their population has increased annually. The fact that the feral goats caused vegetation destruction and soil erosion in Setouchi Neighborhood, Amami-Oshima Is. was reported by the mass media in 2006. For that reason, Regulations about Prevention of Free-ranging of Goats were enforced by five communities in 2007, i.e. Tatsugo Neighborhood, Amami City, Yamato Village, Uken Village and Setouchi Neighborhood. However, little extermination of free-ranging goats proceeded because the goats were not categorized as game animals under Wildlife Protection and Hunting Law.

Since the damage from the feral goats became increasingly serious, the Amami City Office applied to the Cabinet Office for authorization as a Structural Reform Special Zone. Following several applications, feral goats were finally authorized as game animals in Structural Reform Special Zone by the Ministry of the Environment in 2010. Owing to the partial amendment of the ministerial ordinance, it seems that hunting and extermination of the feral goats have been conducted more easily by hunters than it was previously and their population has since decreased annually. However, the population of the feral goats was estimated at over 1,200 in 2011 and 2013 according to Amami City Office (pers. com.) which conducted an oral survey with people and hunters in collaboration with other communities. In order to achieve the aim of registering the Amami Islands as a World Natural Heritage Site, it is urgent to promote hunting and extermination of the feral goats. However, it is not known how the feral goats affect the vegetation, and the present situation of the extermination of the animals after authorization is not clear to date.

Therefore, the purpose of this investigation was to elucidate the current status of the extermination of feral goats on Amami-Oshima Is.

3.2.2. Study site and methods

The present study was conducted on Amami-

Oshima Is., Amami City, Kagoshima Prefecture during 14-16 November in 2013. It is located at long. 129°29′E. and lat. 28°22′N.

Observational points were nominated based on the results of the preliminary oral survey with Amami Mammalogical Society, Amami City Hunting Association and Amami City Office. Like the above-mentioned survey on Taira-jima Is., on Nov. 15th and 16th, we monitored field signs such as feral goat dung-deposited areas and their eating marks on wild plants, discovery sites, and the number of groups as well as group sizes were recorded when the animals were found, as described by NAKANISHI (2017). Sex and growth stage of each goat and morphological characteristics were also identified according to the methods of the aforementioned survey.

3.2.3. Results and discussion

Habitat of feral goats identified on Amami-Oshima Is. was shown in Fig. 5 (NAKANISHI 2017). A total of 23 feral goats were identified throughout the daytime observational period, and they consisted of five flocks (2–6 herdmates) in Amami City, Uken Village and Setouchi Neighborhood. There were three flocks (2, 5 and 6 herdmates, respectively) of the feral goats around Sotsukousaki Lighthouse in Setouchi Neighborhood. In a previous investigation in 2010, vegetation destruction and its resultant soil degradation by feral goats were observed on the northeast slope of the heliport attached

to the lighthouse (NAKANISHI unpublished data). Although it seemed that vegetation on the south slope of the heliport had somewhat recovered, heavy soil erosion was found on the northeast slope of the heliport (Fig. 6). This indicates that hunters have difficulty in capturing feral goats in such steep, inaccessible and dangerous area for humans, and consequently goat population around here may not be decreasing contrary to expectation. As areas inaccessible to hunters are considered to be a safe habitat for feral goats, the number of the animals which escape capture may increase due to delayed and insufficient extermination. It seems that the delayed and insufficient extermination is also related to passive hunting, because hunters are not eager to capture feral goats in dangerous areas and they are not permitted to slaughter the captured animals by themselves and to sell the goat meat unlike game animals such as wild deer and boars under the Slaughterhouse Act by the Ministry of Health, Labour and Welfare. Thus, the total population in this island has not changed, even though feral goat population in other areas is reduced by active hunting and extermination.

It is not desirable for feral and free-ranging goats to survive on Amami-Oshima Is. from the viewpoint of the World Natural Heritage Registration. Therefore, further application to the Cabinet Office for authorization as a Structural Reform Special Zone should be made for the deregulation of post-slaughtering treatment for

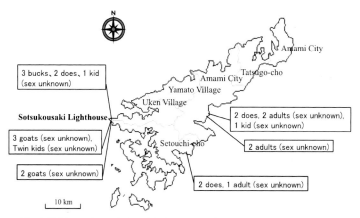

Fig. 5. Habitat and population of 23 feral goats identified on Amami-Oshima Is. (Nov. 15–16, 2013). Adapted from NAKANISHI (2017).

Southwest slope

Japan Coast Guard Heliport

Northeast slope on the side of the heliport

Northeast slope (opposite direction)

Fig. 6. Overgrazing, vegetation destruction and soil degradation caused by feral goats around Sotsukousaki Lighthouse (Nov. 15 in 2013). Reprinted from NAKANISHI (2017)

the captured feral goats which is similar to the treatment of game animal meat according to Food Sanitation Law excluding the Slaughterhouse Act by Ministry of Health, Labour and Welfare. This can lead to more effective utilization of feral goat meat.

It is concluded that a total of 23 feral goats were identified during 15–16 Nov. in 2013, and they consisted of five flocks (2–6 herdmates) on Amami-Oshima Is. Although the heaviest vegetation destruction and soil erosion were observed on the south slope of the heliport at Sotsukousaki Lighthouse in Setouchi Neighborhood among study sites of the island in the previous survey, it seemed that the vegetation had somewhat recovered in the current investigation. However, soil degradation on the north slope of the heliport remained terrible, suggesting delayed hunting and insufficient extermination of feral goats. Live free-ranging feral goats are regarded as game animals under the Wildlife Protection and Hunting Law by Ministry of Environment, whereas slaughtered domestic goats are handled under the Rendering Plant Control Act by Ministry of Health, Labour and Welfare. Therefore, it is impossible to use meat

of slaughtered feral goats like game animals under the Rendering Plant Control Act, even though live feral goats are regarded as game animals. This is a discrepancy in definitions between game animals and domestic animals despite being the same animal. This possibly makes it difficult for hunters to actively shoot feral goats and to use the goat meat effectively.

4. Conclusion

Throughout the Satsunan Islands, including the Tokara Archipelago and Amami Islands, goats are seen as important multipurpose animals whether in positive or negative terms. They play a key role in meat production, healing as companion animals and weeding, whose contribution to meat production is of particular importance, while feral goats cause serious problems associated with overgrazing, vegetation destruction and their resultant soil erosion. Nonetheless, the population of purebred Tokara native goats is declining due to hybridization with other breeds and extermination of feral goats is not always promoted. Further efforts should be made to conserve purebred Tokara native goats, to capture feral animals and to avoid hybridization, because the animals are one of the rarest animal genetic resources as well as one of two important native breeds in Japan academically, socio-economically and culturally.

Acknowledgments

The author is most grateful to Mr. Shouji FUKUZAWA, Deputy Mayor of Toshima Village for his enthusiastic support for the investigation in Taira-jima Is. and Mr. Hidenobu NOJIMA, Counselor of the Oshima Branch, Kagoshima Prefecture for greatly assisting in the initiating of the survey in Kikai-jima Is. Thanks are also due to Mr. Tetsuyori TOMITA who is one of the goat farmers for his kind assistance in the study in Kikai-jima Is., Ms. Yukari HANDA and Mr. Naoshi NAGAE who are members of Amami Mammalogical Society, Mr. Masao Izumi, President of Amami City Hunting Association, and Amami City Office staff for their kind cooperation in the study of Amami-Oshima Is.

References

Amami City Office 2019 Introduction of Amami City. Retrieved on July 17, 2019, from https://www.city.amami.lg.jp/kikaku/shise/gaiyo/shokai/ichi.html

Kikai-cho Neighborhood Government Office 2019 Information of town. Retrieved on July 17, 2019, from http://www.town.kikai.lg.jp.e.aeb.hp.transer.com/densan/machi/index.html

KURIWADA, T. 2017. *Gairaiseibutu to shiteno Satsumaimo no Tokushugaichu Arimodoki-zoumushi to Imozoumushi–Seitai to Boujo ni kansuru Saikin no Kenkyu–*. In: *Amamiguntou no Gairaiseibutsu* (ed. Kagoshima Daigaku Seibutsu Tayousei Kenkyukai), pp. 36–71, Nanpoushinsha, Kagoshima, Japan. (in Japanese)

MANDA, M. 1986. *Tokarayagi no jikkenndoubutsu to shiteno yuyousei* (Availability of Tokara goats for laboratory animals). Soushokukachikuyou Jikkenndoubutsu (Laboratory Animals as Herbivore), 11: 84–95. (in Japanese)

MINEZAWA, M. 2004. Present situation of native animal genetic resources originated in island area of Kagoshima Prefecture. Survey Report for Animal Genetic Resources, 14: 1–20. (in Japanese with English abstract)

Ministry of the Environment. 2019. *Amamishotou no gairaishu* (Introduced Species in Amami Islands). Retrieved on July 17, 2019, from http://kyushu.env.go.jp/okinawa/wildlife/pamph.html

NAKANISHI, Y. 2017. *Satsunanshotou no Noyagi Mondai to Taisaku ni tsuite*. In: *Amamiguntou no Gairaiseibutsu* (ed. Kagoshima Daigaku Seibutsu Tayousei Kenkyukai), pp. 206–214, Nanpoushinsha, Kagoshima, Japan. (in Japanese)

NOZAWA, K., KANO, Y., SAWAZAKI, T., NISHIDA, T., ABE, T., SHOTAKE, T. and MATSUDA, Y. 1978. *Kogatayagi iwayuru Shibayagi no idennshikousei* (Gene constitution of miniature 'Shiba' goats). Experimental Animals, 27(4): 413–422. (in Japanese with English abstract)

PORTER, V. 1996. Goats of the World. 179 pp., Farming Press, Ipswich.

SAITO, T. and KISANUKI, H. 1980. 6. *Tokararettou ni okeru Yagishiiku no Bunka-chirigakutekiigi*. In: *Tokararettou sono Shizenn to Bunka* (eds. SAITO, T., TSUKADA, K. and YAMAUCHI, H.), pp. 247–255, Kokin Shoin, Tokyo, Japan. (in Japanese)

The Research Group on the Native Farm Animals in Japan and its Adjacent Localities 1964. Report of the research group on the native farm animals in Japan and its adjacent localities, 1: 1–92. (in Japanese with English summary)

Toshima Village Government Office 2019. Introduction of Toshima Village. Retrieved on July 17, 2019, from http://www.tokara.jp/english/?id=001

TSUDA, K. 2004. *Arimodokizoumushi no konzetsu ni mukete*. Amami Newsletter, 9: 13–15. (in Japanese)

Otsuka, Y., Terada, R. and Nishimura, S. (eds.), *The Tokara Islands*
Kagoshima University International Center for Island Studies; Hokuto Shobo Publishing, Tokyo. 10 March 2020.

Chapter 9
Medicinal Plants in the Tokara Islands

Sota YAMAMOTO

1. Introduction

Many of the Nansei Islands (including the Tokara Islands) of Japan are distributed like stepping stones from north to south, with several types of habitats, climates, languages, cultures, etc. In such a region, exploring the similarities and dissimilarities of plant usage can elucidate the historical movement of local people, transmission of traditional knowledge, and introduction of new plants. Moreover, plants used for traditional medicine have great potential to provide important compounds for modern medicine to treat specific diseases.

The Tokara Islands have long had limited transportation and poor medical access. Therefore, traditional medicines or remedies, which are based on traditional knowledge transmitted from generation to generation, have been very important for local people to remain healthy. However, there are very few English articles on traditional medicines or remedies in the Tokara Islands. Therefore, the present chapter focuses on medicinal plants and traditional remedies related to plants on seven of the Tokara Islands with comparison to those on other Nansei Islands.

2. Medicinal plants and traditional remedies in the Tokara Islands (from Higashi et al. [1975], Saitou et al. [1980], and Shimono [1966, 2009])

2.1. Kuchino-shima Island

Burns: *Aloe arborescens* (no detailed method of use)

Constipation: *Sambucus chinensis* (no detailed method of use)

Eye injury/disease: a branch of *Lythrum anceps* is tapped on a sty in the eye

Hemostasis: *Centella asiatica* (no detailed method of use)

Neuralgia: a decoction of *Ajuga decumbens* is taken

Otorrhea: *Saxifraga stolonifera* (no detailed method of use)

Skin diseases/ringworm, scabies, etc.: *Cycas revoluta* seeds; *Impatiens balsamina* leaves; *Lycoris radiata* (no detailed method of use); *Plantago asiatica* (no detailed method of use); *Saururus chinensis* (no detailed method of use)

Stomachache/gastrointestinal disorder: *A. arborescens* (no detailed method of use); *P. asiatica* (no detailed method of use)

Swelling/boils: a decoction of bark of *Elaeagnus* spp. (probably *E. pungens*) is taken; toasted *Farfugium japonicum* leaves are applied; *P. asiatica* (no detailed method of use)

Tetanus: a decoction of bark of *Elaeagnus* spp. (probably *E. pungens*) is taken

Wounds: *I. balsamina* leaves

2.2. Nakano-shima Island

Burns: *Cucumis sativus* (no detailed method of use); *F. japonicum* leaves are applied; *I. balsamina* (no detailed method of use)

Common cold: *Ampelopsis glandulosa* (no detailed method of use); *Citrus aurantium* (no detailed method of use)

Cough medicine: a mixture of *Zingiber officinale* roots and brown sugar is taken

Diarrhea: a mixture of *Allium tuberosum* leaves and bonito flakes (*katsuobushi* in Japanese) is taken

Eye injury/disease: *A. glandulosa* (no detailed method of use)

Hemostasis: *Oxalis corniculata* (no detailed method of use)

Ichthyism: a decoction of *Crepidiastrum lanceolatum* is taken

Kidney disease: a decoction of *Lagenaria siceraria* is taken; a decoction of dried *P. asiatica* leaves is taken; a decoction of male inflorescence from *Zea mays* is taken

Liver disease: *Artemisia* spp. (no detailed method of use)

Otorrhea: *S. stolonifera* (no detailed method of use)

Skin diseases/ringworm, scabies, etc.: *C. lanceolatum* leaves are applied; toasted *Crinum asiaticum* leaves are applied; the liquid of squeezed *F. japonicum* leaves is applied; *Houttuynia cordata* (no detailed method of use); *I. balsamina* leaves; toasted *P. asiatica* leaves are applied; *Rumex acetosa* (no detailed method of use)

Sprain/fracture/bruise: *Gardenia jasminoides* fruits for bruises; a decoction of *Morella rubra* bark is taken for sprains and bruises

Stomachache/gastrointestinal disorder: a decoction of *C. lanceolatum* leaves is taken; a decoction (of leaves?) of *Eriobotrya japonica* is taken; a decoction of male inflorescence from *Z. mays* is taken

Swelling/boils: a decoction of bark and leaves of *Elaeagnus* spp. (probably *E. pungens*) is taken; *F. japonicum* leaves are applied

Swollen tonsils: grated *Solanum tuberosum* tubers are applied

Wounds: *Artemisia* spp. (no detailed method of use); *C. revoluta* seeds; the liquid of squeezed *F. japonicum* leaves is applied; *Hydrocotyle sibthorpioides* leaves; *I. balsamina* leaves; *Paederia foetida* leaves; *P. asiatica* leaves

2.3. Suwanose-jima Island

Eye injury/disease: *A. glandulosa* (no detailed method of use)

Skin diseases/ringworm, scabies, etc.: toasted *C. asiaticum* leaves are applied

Swelling/boils: *C. revoluta* seeds; a decoction of bark of *Elaeagnus* spp. (probably *E. pungens*) is taken

Swollen tonsils: *Alocasia odorum* (no detailed method of use)

Wounds: fluff of female *C. revoluta* flower; inner parts of *Miscanthus sinensis* stems; *P. foetida* (no detailed method of use)

2.4. Taira-jima Island

All complaints: *Smilax* spp. roots

Antipyretic: a decoction of *Artemisia* spp. is taken; *Musa basjoo* stems

Eye injury/disease: *A. tuberosum* stems; the sap from *A. glandulosa* stems

Fatigue recovery: the liquid of squeezed, fresh *Artemisia* spp. leaves is taken

Gonorrhea: a decoction of *P. asiatica* is taken

Headaches: the liquid of squeezed, fresh *Artemisia* spp. leaves is taken; *S. chinensis* (no detailed method of use)

Hemostasis: *C. asiatica* leaves

Hypertension: a decoction of *Artemisia* spp. is taken

Liver disease: a decoction of *Oryza sativa* straw is taken

Otorrhea: the liquid (of fruits?) of *Luffa cylindrica*

Skin diseases/ringworm, scabies, etc.: the sap from *A. glandulosa* stems; a decoction of *Coix lacryma-jobi* fruits is taken; *C. lanceolatum* (no detailed method of use); *C. asiaticum* (no detailed method of use); *Lygodium japonicum* (no detailed method of use); *P. asiatica* (no detailed method of use)

Sprain/fracture/bruise: a mixture of *G. jasminoides* fruits, wheat flour, and vinegar (or liquor) is applied to sprains and bruises

Stomachache/gastrointestinal disorder: *Allium bakeri* (no detailed method of use); fresh *A. arborescens* stems and leaves are eaten; moxibustion of dried leaves (and stems) of *Artemisia* spp.; *C. lanceolatum* (no detailed method of use); *Momordica charantia* (no detailed method of use); a decoction of *Swertia japonica* is taken

Swelling/boils: a decoction of fresh *Elaeagnus* spp. branches and shrimp shells is taken; a mixture of sticky rice and roasted shrimp shells is applied; roasted *P. asiatica* leaves are applied

Tetanus: a decoction of *Oenanthe javanica* is taken

Vermifuge: a decoction of *Digenea simplex* is taken

Wounds: a mixture of grated *Allium sativum* bulbs and salt is applied; *A. arborescens* (no detailed method of use); *C. revoluta* fruits; inner parts of *M. sinensis* stems

2.5. Akuseki-jima Island

Abarticulation: a mixture of deep-fried *Prunus* subg. *Cerasus* spp. bark, lime, and starch paste is applied; a mixture of wheat flour (*Triticum aestivum*) and chicken egg is applied

All complaints: a decoction of *H. cordata* leaves is taken; roots of *Smilax* spp. (probably *Smilax bracteata*)

Burns: the liquid of *C. sativus* fruits is applied

Common cold: *Artemisia* spp. (no detailed method of use); a mixture of the liquid from roots of *Z. officinale* and sugar is taken

Constipation: a decoction of *H. cordata* leaves is taken

Diabetes: a decoction of *H. cordata* is taken

Eye injury/disease: pounded *C. revoluta* fruits are applied; the liquid of *Mentha canadensis* leaves is applied

Gynecopathy: *P. asiatica* (no detailed method of use)

Hemostasis: *Artemisia* spp. (no detailed method of use)

Lung disease: a decoction of *C. aurantium* peel (or peeled fruits?) and *Z. officinale* roots is taken

Nasal congestion: *S. stolonifera* (no detailed method of use)

Otorrhea: *S. stolonifera* (no detailed method of use)

Skin diseases/ringworm, scabies, etc.: *A. odorum* roots (tuber?); finely shaved *Cinnamomum camphora* tips are burned and the smoke is applied to affected areas; *F. japonicum* leaves; a mixture of cooked rice and an Onychomycosis ointment is applied to a rash from lacquer

Sprain/fracture/bruise: a decoction of *Ficus superba* bark is taken

Stomachache/gastrointestinal disorder: *A. arborescens* (no detailed method of use); the liquid of squeezed, fresh *Artemisia* spp. leaves is taken; *Clerodendrum trichotomum* (no detailed method of use); a decoction of *C. lanceolatum* is taken; *P. asiatica* (no detailed method of use); a decoction of *S. japonica* is taken

Swelling/boils: roasted *C. asiaticum* leaves are applied; a decoction of *Elaeagnus* spp. bark is taken; squeezed *H. cordata* leaves are applied; roasted fruits and/or bark of *Pittosporum tobira* are applied

Tooth disease: moxibustion of *Artemisia* spp.

Wounds: roasted *Camellia japonica* leaves are applied; a decoction of *Elaeagnus* spp. bark is taken; *F. japonicum* (no detailed method of use); *H. sibthorpioides* (no detailed method of use); *I. balsamina* (no detailed method of use)

2.6. Kodakara-jima Island

Arthritis: *Artemisia* spp. (probably *A. indica*) (no detailed method of use)

Hypertension: a decoction of *Cirsium spinosum* roots is taken

Lung disease: *Peucedanum japonicum* roots

Skin diseases/ringworm, scabies, etc.: roasted *C. asiaticum* stem bark; roasted *F. japonicum* leaves are applied; *P. asiatica* (no detailed method of use)

Stomachache/gastrointestinal disorder: *Artemisia* spp. (probably *A. indica*) (no detailed method of use); a decoction of *C. lanceolatum* roots is taken; *O. javanica* (no detailed method of use); *P. japonicum* roots

Swelling/boils: a mixture of roasted fruits and/or bark of *P. tobira*, shrimp shells, and cooked rice is applied

Tetanus: a decoction of branches of *Elaeagnus* spp. (probably *E. pungens*) is taken; a mixture of roasted fruits and/or bark of *P. tobira*, shrimp shells, and cooked rice is applied

Wounds: *A. arborescens* (no detailed method of use); *Gynura bicolor* leaves

2.7. Takara-jima Island

Antipyretic: a decoction of *Artemisia* spp. (probably *A. indica*) is taken; a decoction of *M. basjoo* shoots is taken

Burns: *A. arborescens* (no detailed method of use)

Common cold: a decoction of *Artemisia* spp. leaves is taken; a decoction of *Diospyros kaki* leaves is taken

Cough medicine: a decoction of *F. japonicum* leaves is taken

Eye injury/disease: *A. glandulosa* (no detailed method of use)

Kidney disease: the liquid of *Benincasa hispida* fruits is taken

Neuralgia: a soak in bathwater with *C. camphora* leaves

Skin diseases/ringworm, scabies, etc.: *C. asiaticum* (no detailed method of use)

Stomachache/gastrointestinal disorder: *A. arborescens* (no detailed method of use); a decoction of *Artemisia* spp. (probably *A. indica*) is taken; a decoction of *O. javanica* leaves is taken

69

Swelling/boils: a decoction of *Elaeagnus* spp. (probably *E. pungens*) is taken; a decoction of *O. javanica* leaves is taken; roasted fruits and/or bark of *P. tobira*

Tetanus: a decoction of bark of *Elaeagnus* spp. (probably *E. macrophylla*) is taken; a decoction of *F. japonicum* leaves is taken; a decoction of *O. javanica* leaves is taken; roasted *Osmanthus insularis* leaves; a decoction of fruits and/or bark of *P. tobira* is taken

Vermifuge: *Melia azedarach* roots

Wounds: *A. arborescens* (no detailed method of use); roasted *F. japonicum* leaves are applied; *I. balsamina* leaves; *P. foetida* leaves

3. Characteristics of medicinal plants in the Tokara Islands

In the Tokara Islands, 61 species belonging to 37 families of Spermatophyta and one species belonging to Rhodophyceae are used as medicinal plants (Appendices 1 and 2). Among 61 species of Spermatophyta, most of them are native to the Old World, except for e.g., potato (*S. tuberosum*) and corn (*Z. mays*), which are native to the New World. This suggests that people in the Tokara Islands tend to use plants native to the Old World as medicine, similar to populations on Tanega-shima and Yaku-shima islands in the Osumi Islands (YAMAMOTO 2017) and Tokuno-shima Island in the Amami Islands (YAMAMOTO 2016).

Among 62 species, seven species are recognized on more than five islands as a medical plant in the Tokara Islands: *Elaeagnus* spp. (seven islands); *C. asiaticum* (six islands); and *A. arborescens*, *Artemisia* spp., *C. revolute*, *F. japonicum*, and *P. asiatica* (five islands). Among them, *Elaeagnus* spp., *C. asiaticum*, *A. arborescens*, and *C. revolute* are used to treat two to four diseases/ailments, while *Artemisia* spp., *F. japonicum*, and *P. asiatica* are applied to 11, 6, and 7 diseases/ailments, respectively.

In addition to the above seven species, medicinal plants in the Tokara Islands, such as *Alocasia* spp., *A. tuberosum*, *C. asiatica*, *C. spinosum*, *D. simplex*, *H. sibthorpioides*, *M. azedarach*, *Musa* spp., *Paederia* spp., *Rumex* spp., *Smilax* spp., *Z. mays*, and *Z. officinale*, are also used as medicine in the Osumi Islands (YAMAMOTO 2017), Amami Islands (YAMAMOTO 2016), and Ryukyu Islands (MAEDA and NOSE 1989). This suggests that these 20 species are commonly used as medicine in the Nansei Islands. Moreover, some of them are well known as herbal medicines in Japanese herbalism developed during the Edo Period, which may influence the popularity of these remedies.

Conversely, *D. kaki*, *H. cordata*, and *Prunus* subg. *Cerasus* spp. are used as medicine in the Tokara and Osumi islands (northern part of the Nansei Islands), but not the Amami and Ryukyu islands (central and southern part of the Nansei Islands). *Diospyros kaki* and *Prunus* subg. *Cerasus* spp. are popular medicinal plants on the main islands of Japan, but they are better suited to temperate zones; thus, the people on the Amami and Ryukyu islands do not use them as medicine. *Houttuynia cordata* is also used as medicine in Southeast Asia (e.g., in Cambodia; KHAM [2004]), so it is unclear why it is not used as medicine in the Amami and Ryukyu islands.

To categorize or classify an island (or islands) in the Nansei Islands based on medicinal plants and traditional remedies related to plants, a field survey of medicinal plants in the Tokara Islands will be necessary because of the limited related literature.

References

HIGASHI, S., ABE, M., OGATA, S., TOBITA, H. and YOKOTA, K. 1975. Traditional Medicinal and Poisonous Plants in the Satsunan Islands Part I. Tanegashima, Yakushima, Kuchierabujima and Tokara Islands. Reports of the Faculty of Science, Kagoshima University: Earth Sciences and Biology, 8: 93–113. (in Japanese with English summary)

KHAM, L. 2004. Medicinal Plants of Cambodia: Habitat, Chemical Constituents and Ethnobotanical Uses. 631 pp., Bendigo Scientific Press, Australia.

MAEDA, M. and NOSE, H. (eds.) 1989. *Okinawa Minzoku Yakuyou Doushokubutsushi* (沖縄民俗薬用動植物誌, Medicinal Plants and Animals in Okinawa), 244 pp., Niraisha, Okinawa. (in Japanese)

SAITOU, S., TSUKADA, K. and YAMAUCHI, H. 1980. *Tokara Rettou Sono Shizen to Bunka* (トカラ列島−その自然と文化−, The Tokara Islands: Nature and Culture). 351 pp., Kokonshoin, Tokyo. (in Japanese)

SHIMONO, T. 1966. *Tokara Rettou Minzokushi Dai Ikkan Akusekijima Takarajima Hen* (吐咖喇列島民俗誌第1巻（悪石島・平島篇）, Ethnography of the Tokara Islands I: Akusekijima and Takarajima). 248 pp., Bunshousha, Tokyo. (in Japanese)

SHIMONO, T. 2009. *Tokara Rettou* (トカラ列島, The Tokara Islands). 352 pp., Nanpou Shinsha, Kagoshima. (in Japanese)

YAMAMOTO, S. 2016. Medicinal Plants on Tokuno-shima Island. In: The Amami Islands (eds. KAWAI, K., TERADA, R. and KUWAHARA, S.), pp. 22–29, Hokuto Shobo Publishing, Tokyo.

YAMAMOTO, S. 2017. Medicinal Plants of Tanega-shima and Yaku-shima Islands. In: The Osumi Islands: Culture, Society, Industry and Nature (eds. KAWAI, K., TERADA, R. and KUWAHARA, S.), pp. 50–68, Hokuto Shobo Publishing, Tokyo.

Appendix 1. Medicinal plants of the Tokara Islands.

Plant name	Kuchino-shima	Nakano-shima	Suwanose-jima	Taira-jima	Akuseki-jima	Kodakara-jima	Takara-jima
Ajuga decumbens	Ne	—	—	—	—	—	—
Allium bakeri	—	—	—	St	—	—	—
Allium sativum	—	—	—	Wo	—	—	—
Allium tuberosum	—	Dr	—	Ey	—	—	—
Alocasia odorum	—	—	So	—	Sk	—	—
Aloe arborescens	Bu, St	—	—	St, Wo	St	Wo	Bu, St, Wo
Ampelopsis glandulosa	—	Cm, Ey	Ey	Ey, Sk	—	—	Ey
Artemisia spp.	—	Li, Wo	—	An, Fa, Ha, Hy, St	Cm, Hs, St, To	Ar, St	An, Cm, St
Benincasa hispida	—	—	—	—	—	—	Ki
Camellia japonica	—	—	—	—	Wo	—	—
Centella asiatica	Hs	—	—	Hs	—	—	—
Cinnamomum camphora	—	—	—	—	Sk	—	Ne
Cirsium spinosum	—	—	—	—	—	Hy	—
Citrus aurantium	—	Cm	—	—	Lu	—	—
Clerodendrum trichotomum	—	—	—	—	St	—	—
Coix lacryma-jobi	—	—	—	Sk	—	—	—
Crepidiastrum lanceolatum	—	Ic, Sk, St	—	Sk, St	St	St	—
Crinum asiaticum	—	Sk	Sk	Sk	Se	Sk	Sk
Cucumis sativus	—	Bu	—	—	Bu	—	—
Cycas revoluta	Sk	Wo	Se, Wo	Wo	Ey	—	—
Digenea simplex	—	—	—	Ve	—	—	—
Diospyros kaki	—	—	—	—	—	—	Cm
Elaeagnus spp.	Se, Te	Se	Se	Se	Se, Wo	Te	Se, Te
Eriobotrya japonica	—	St	—	—	—	—	—
Farfugium japonicum	Se	Bu, Se, Sk, Wo	—	—	Sk, Wo	Sk	Cu, Te, Wo
Ficus superba	—	—	—	—	Sp	—	—
Gardenia jasminoides	—	Sp	—	Sp	—	—	—
Gynura bicolor	—	—	—	—	—	Wo	—
Houttuynia cordata	—	Sk	—	—	Al, Cn, Db, Se	—	—
Hydrocotyle sibthorpioides	—	Wo	—	—	Wo	—	—
Impatiens balsamina	Sk, Wo	Bu, Sk, Wo	—	—	Wo	—	Wo
Lagenaria siceraria	—	Ki	—	—	—	—	—
Luffa cylindrica	—	—	—	Ot	—	—	—
Lycoris radiata	Sk	—	—	—	—	—	—
Lygodium japonicum	—	—	—	Sk	—	—	—
Lythrum anceps	Ey	—	—	—	—	—	—
Melia azedarach	—	—	—	—	—	—	Ve
Mentha canadensis	—	—	—	—	Ey	—	—
Miscanthus sinensis	—	—	Wo	Wo	—	—	—
Momordica charantia	—	—	—	St	—	—	—

Appendix 1. Continued.

Plant name	Kuchino-shima	Nakano-shima	Suwanose-jima	Taira-jima	Akuseki-jima	Kodakara-jima	Takara-jima
Morella rubra	—	Sp	—	—	—	—	—
Musa basjoo	—	—	—	An	—	—	An
Oenanthe javanica	—	—	—	Te	—	St	Se, St, Te
Oryza sativa	—	—	—	Li, Se	Sk	—	—
Osmanthus insularis	—	—	—	—	—	—	Te
Oxalis corniculata	—	Hs	—	—	—	—	—
Paederia foetida	—	Wo	Wo	—	—	—	Wo
Peucedanum japonicum	—	—	—	—	—	Lu, St	—
Pittosporum tobira	—	—	—	—	Se	Se, Te	Se, Te
Plantago asiatica	Se, Sk, St	Ki, Sk, Wo	—	Go, Se, Sk	Gy, St	Sk	—
Prunus subg. *Cerasus* spp.	—	—	—	—	Ab	—	—
Rumex acetosa	—	Sk	—	—	—	—	—
Sambucus chinensis	Cn	—	—	—	—	—	—
Saururus chinensis	Sk	—	—	Ha	—	—	—
Saxifraga stolonifera	Ot	Ot	—	—	Na, Ot	—	—
Smilax spp.	—	—	—	Al	Al	—	—
Solanum tuberosum	—	So	—	—	—	—	—
Swertia japonica	—	—	—	St	St	—	—
Triticum aestivum	—	—	—	—	Ab	—	—
Zea mays	—	Ki, St	—	—	—	—	—
Zingiber officinale	—	Cu	—	—	Cm, Lu	—	—

Appendix 2. Abbreviations in Appendix 1.

Disease name		Disease name	
Abbre-viation	Meaning	Abbre-viation	Meaning
Ab	Abarticulation	Ic	Ichthyism
Al	all complaints	Ki	Kidney disease
An	Antipyretic	Li	Liver disease
Ar	Arthritis	Lu	Lung disease
Bu	Burns	Na	Nasal congestion
Cm	Common cold	Ne	Neuralgia
Cn	Constipation	Ot	Otorrhea
Cu	Cough medicine	Sk	Skin diseases/ringworm, scabies, etc.
Db	Diabetes	Sp	Sprain/fracture/bruise
Dr	Diarrhea	St	Stomachache/gastrointestinal disorder
Ey	Eye injury/disease	Se	Swelling/boils
Fa	Fatigue recovery	So	Swollen tonsils
Go	Gonorrhea	Te	Tetanus
Gy	Gynecopathy	To	Tooth disease
Ha	Headaches	Ve	Vermifuge
Hs	Hemostasis	Wo	Wounds
Hy	Hypertension		

Chapter 10
Current Status and Future Prospects of Broadband Services on the Tokara Islands

Masato MASUYA

Ultra-high-speed broadband services are widely available in Japan. However, in the Tokara Islands, the deployment of broadband infrastructure has been delayed. Broadband services can usually be realized as soon as the optical fiber is laid to a house or office. The only and biggest difficulty is how to secure the initial installation and running costs. Even in the Tokara Islands, residents and Toshima Village local government have a strong desire for broadband deployment, and various efforts have been made to realize a broadband service. In this article, I outline the process of broadband deployment in the Tokara Islands, the status of utilization, and future prospects.

1. Introduction

The Tokara Islands consist of seven inhabited islands (from north to south: Kuchino-shima Island, Nakano-shima Island, Suwanose-jima Island, Taira-jima Island, Akuseki-jima Island, Kodakara-jima Island, and Takara-jima Island) and five uninhabited islands. They are located between Yaku-shima Island and Amami-Oshima Island. Table 1 shows the population and number of households in the Tokara Islands at the end of March 2018.

Table 1. Population and number of households in the Tokara Islands (as of the end of March 2018).

Island	Population	Households
Kuchino-shima Is.	129	75
Nakano-shima Is.	159	90
Taira-jima Is.	64	31
Suwanose-jima Is.	79	44
Akuseki-jima Is.	73	35
Kodakara-jima Is.	53	32
Takara-jima Is.	131	68
Total	688	375

The total population is 688 and the number of households is 375. Nakano-shima Island, which has the largest number of households, has 159 people and 86 households, and the smallest, Taira-jima Island, has 64 people and 31 households. The only public transportation between the mainland and each island is the ship "Ferry Toshima 2", which is operated 2–3 times a week by the local government of Toshima Village. It takes about 6–7 hours from Kagoshima Port to the first port, Nishinohama fishing port in Kuchino-shima Island, and about 12–13 hours to the last port, Maegomori fishing port in Takara-jima Island. The ferry is often canceled due to adverse weather conditions, such as typhoons or stormy northwest seasonal winds in the winter, and residents sometimes cannot receive goods from the mainland for a long period. The Tokara Islands are unique geographically being seven small islands with small populations scattered 15 to 50 km away from each other by sea. The Toshima Village government office is located in Kagoshima city outside the village. The archipelago suffers from extremely disadvantageous geographical conditions.

If a high-speed broadband service becomes available, the distribution of information would be comparable to that of the mainland. Broadband is essential for improving living standards, economic development, and administrative efficiency. With broadband internet connectivity, it would be possible to promote content industries that do not require logistical operations, offer tourist information, and sell special local products over the internet. The internet can narrow the cultural and educational gap by providing various educational opportunities through e-learning, and by acquiring news, weather reports, and

Table 2. History of information communication infrastructure in the Tokara Islands before broadband.

Year	Matter
1935	Nakano-shima Post Office was established.
1949	Kuchino-shima Telegraph Station was established and a wireless telegraph with Naze was started.
1949	The lights were turned on for the first time in the hands of the youths at Nakano-shima West Youth Club and Nishi Onsen.
1952	Wireless telephony between Kagoshima and Nakano-shima Island, Kuchino-shima Island and Takara-jima Island was started.
1952	Electricity business of 8-hour power transmission began in all households at Nakano-shima Island.
1960	Telephone service began on Nakano-shima Island.
1961	A submarine underwater cable was laid between Nakano-shima Island and Kuchino-shima Island, and telephone service began on Kuchino-shima Island. However, there was only one line at the post office.
1961	The submarine underwater cable between Nakano-shima Island and Suwanose-jima Island was laid.
1962	Electricity-use agricultural cooperatives were established in Kuchino-shima Island, Nakano-shima Island, Takara-jima Island, Taira-jima Island, and Akuseki-jima Island, and an electricity business was introduced.
1963	A submarine underwater cable was laid between Takara-jima Island and Kodakara-jima Island, and telephone service began on Takara-jima Island. However, there was only one line at the post office.
1964	Rural telephone services were set up except for Gaja-jima Island. There was only one line on each island except Nakano-shima Island.
1970	By this time, telephone services were made to the clinics on each island.
1970	NHK TV relay station was set up in Nakano-shima Island.
1972	A microwave communication type TV relay station between Kagoshima and Naha was completed at Akuseki-jima Island.
1972	A microwave communication telephone line relay station between Kagoshima and Naha was completed at Akuseki-jima Island.
1976	MBC and KTS commercial TV relay stations were set up on Nakano-shima Island.
1979	The telephone switching station was automated and general subscriber telephone service began on Nakano-shima Island.
1982	General subscriber telephone service began on Kuchino-shima Island.
1984	General subscriber telephone services began on Taira-jima Island, Suwanos-jima Island, Akuseki-jima Island, Kodakara-jima Island and Takara-jima Island.
1985	KKB commercial TV relay station was set up on Nakano-shima Island.
1989	Captain System (text/image information provision service via telephone line) was introduced.
1991	Remote medical diagnosis (still image transmission) system at clinics was introduced on each island.

entertainment, such as music and movies. However, due to the disadvantageous geographical conditions, broadband deployment has been delayed in the Tokara Islands. The most significant barrier to broadband deployment has been its cost. Technically, broadband deployment is not difficult even in disadvantaged areas.

2. Information and communication infrastructure before the broadband

Telephone and TV are now indispensable for everyday life as a means of obtaining information. The same goes for people in the Tokara Islands. However, the deployment of information infrastructure has not been easy. Table 2 presents major events related to information communication infrastructure excerpted from the Record of

Toshima Village (Editorial Committee of Record of Toshima Village 1995).

Prior to the information and communication infrastructure deployment, there was a keen desire for electricity on the Tokara Islands. According to the Record of Toshima Village, under US military administration in 1949, the power generators which were received from a doctor were repaired, and only two lights were turned on at Nakano-shima Island. Youths of Nakano-shima Island purchased a 15 kW power generator in 1951 to generate electricity, but parts and materials were difficult to obtain under US military occupation. They raised funds by selling cedar trees in the district, leading to the launch of the electricity business in 1952. Therefore, residents gained electricity on their own. In parallel, separate efforts were made to send electricity to schools, and power generation facilities were established in all schools from 1959 to 1961 prior to general households. In 1962, electricity-using agricultural cooperatives were established in Kuchino-shima Island, Nakano-shima Island, Takara-jima Island, Taira-jima Island, and Akuseki-jima Island, and electricity transmission to households began. On the other hand, in Kodakara-jima Island and Suwanose-jima Island, residents used a school generator to transmit power to homes. The electric power business on the island required a large number of subsidies from national and local governments until the electricity facilities on each island were transferred to Kyushu Electric Power between 1978 and 1979. Since 1979, Kyushu Electric Power has transmitted 24-hour electricity stably, and the electrification of households has progressed rapidly.

At the same time as stable power supplies arrived, telephone services on each island became automated. In 1979, the Nakano-shima telephone switching station was automated, and general subscriber telephone services were launched in 1984 on all inhabited Tokara Islands. At that time, the Nakano-shima telephone switching station was connected to Yaku-shima Island via a wireless communication line. Submarine underwater cables were laid in Nakano-shima Island – Kuchino-shima Island (2 lines), Nakano-shima Island – Suwanose-jima Island, Suwano-jima Island – Taira-jima Island, Takara-jima Island – Kodakara-jima Island (2 lines), and wireless communication lines were installed on Nakano-shima Island – Taira-jima Island, Nakano-shima Island – Akuseki-jima Island, Suwanose-jima Island – Akuseki-jima Island, Akuseki-jima Island – Takara-jima Island (2 lines). All routes from Nakano-shima Island were duplicated, so that even if a failure occurred, the telephone line was connected. Prior to automation, only one telephone line was used for each island, with residents having to wait in turn. Automation made it much easier to talk on the phone and contributed greatly to residents' quality of life and industrial development. The inter-island lines for telephone services were replaced by technologically advanced wireless communication

equipment. Submarine underwater cables are not currently used.

The communication line connecting the mainland of Kagoshima and Okinawa, which is now connected by submarine underwater cables, was based on microwave radio that was launched in 1972. There are two routes: Miyanouradake in Yaku-shima Island – Akuseki-jima Island – Asato Pass in Amami-Oshima Island and Furutake in Kuchinoerabu-jima Island - Kuchino-shima Island – Takara-jima Island – Matsunagayama in Amami-Oshima Island. However, these lines are not used to provide telephone service to the Tokara Islands. The Tokara Islands were only used as relay sites. Currently, these lines are not used except for a part of the route between Kuchino-shima Island – Takara-jima Island, with the relay station on the top of Mitake in Akuseki-jima Island is completely abandoned. TV relays between Kagoshima and Naha also used the Tokara Islands. The current TV relay is via the Nakano-shima relay station, and only Nakano-shima Island can receive TV radio waves directly from the relay station.

There is no record of when internet use began in the Tokara Islands. However, when PC communications and the internet began, dial-up connections using general subscriber telephone services were used mainly nationwide, so it seemed that there was not much difference between the islands and other regions. However, while the spread of broadband services progressed rapidly on the mainland, broadband infrastructure was not deployed in the Tokara Islands. As a result, until 2009, internet users in the Tokara Islands used a dial-up connection from a general subscriber telephone service. However, the quality of the telephone line was poor compared to the mainland; therefore the connection was only 14.4 kbps maximum (actual value measured in 2006 in a household on Taira-jima Island). Even if a resident connected to a website that provided weather information to determine whether to go fishing, it took a long time to display a single image of weather forecast. Since an always connected service was not provided, the charge depended on the connection time. Some homes where junior high school students were using the internet paid more than 50,000 yen per month. In an era of strong demand for electricity and telephone services, the keen desire for a broadband service has increased.

3. Information and communication infrastructure as of 2009

On the Tokara Islands, a wired subscriber telephone service has been provided by NTT West and was available to all households. It is a matter of course that the telecommunications business law stipulates that a wired subscriber telephone service is indispensable for people's lives and they are therefore provided throughout Japan.

On the other hand, the ISDN service, which is a digital communication service by NTT West, was not available to ordinary households on most islands. There was no subscriber telephone service provided by operators other than NTT West.

As for mobile phones, NTT DOCOMO's mova and FOMA (including high-speed service) were available on six inhabited islands except for Kodakara-jima Island. Even on Kodakara-jima Island, it was possible to communicate with Takara-jima wireless base station by moving to the coastal vicinity. From June 2009, Kodakara-jima Island also became a FOMA service area. There were no mobile phone services provided other than NTT DOCOMO.

As the internet required a dial-up connection using an analog telephone line, or a dial-up connection using ISDN which is a digital telephone line, data communication using a mobile phone and packet communication became available. Moreover, although it was only for corporations, a satellite internet connection service by SKY Perfect JSAT that could be used all over Japan also became available.

However, FLET'S ISDN, an always-on fixed monthly charge internet connection service, was not provided. This is because NTT West had not established a regional IP network on the Tokara Islands. Although NTT DoCoMo's FOMA high-speed flat-rate connection service was available, the downlink speed was about 1 Mbps, which was slower than in urban areas (actual measurement in April 2009). As of 2009, the Tokara Islands had no broadband service in all areas. It was a so-called "broadband zero area" where neither FTTH services that laid optical fiber in each household nor ADSL services that used existing analog telephone lines were provided.

In addition, on the three islands of Nakano-shima Island, Akuseki-jima Island, and Takara-jima Island where submarine underwater cables were landed to provide the subscriber telephone service, which is a universal service, there were cases where a leased-line service for corporations (Digital Access 1500) could be used. If this was used, communication outside of the island was possible at the speed of 1.5 Mbps. In 2009, Mega Data Net's by NTT West, a high-speed leased-line service, began on Nakano-shima Island, Akuseki-jima Island and Takara-jima Island. As a result, high-speed communication up to 10 Mbps was possible between the islands and Kagoshima city.

4. Disaster Prevention Administrative Radio and Television

Although not an information and communication infrastructure, a disaster prevention administrative radio system is in place in the Tokara Islands. During normal times, it is used for administrative communication, to notify each island of the ferry entry/exit status at any time. The master station is located in Nakano-shima Island and is remotely controlled from a government office in Kagoshima city. There are two relay stations, Kindake in Nakano-shima Island and Mitake in Akuseki-jima Island, while mini relay stations are installed in Kuchino-shima Island and Taira-jima Island, and loudspeaker stations are installed in 23 locations on all seven islands. Also, 530 individual receivers are installed in each household. Although it is currently an analog system, it is scheduled to be updated to a new digital system by 2021 due to the aging of equipment.

As for the most widely used TV (terrestrial wave) for obtaining information in the Tokara Islands, Nakano-shima Island is a very important relay point for broadcast waves relayed from Makurazaki to Naze via Tanega-shima Island and Nakano-shima Island. The section between Nakano-shima Island and Naze is the longest section in Japan for terrestrial digital TV broadcast wave relay, and it is one of the most difficult places for the digitalization of terrestrial TV broadcasts. Fortunately, it was successfully relayed, and it is already possible to watch digital terrestrial TV broadcasting on Nakano-shima Island. The other six islands in the Tokara Islands receive radio waves from the joint reception facility. Kuchino-shima Island receives radio waves from Makurazaki TV relay station, and the remaining five islands receive radio waves from Naze TV relay station.

5. Activities for the deployment of broadband infrastructure

In general, the most significant barrier to broadband deployment in less favored regions has been its very high cost. In small remote islands and mountainous areas where there are few households, it is impossible to hope for the provision of broadband services by private telecommunication carriers. It is also very difficult for the local government of remote islands or mountainous regions to implement broadband infrastructure in a financially difficult situation. There is a Japanese government and prefectural government subsidy framework, but subsidies are not necessarily acquired, and the full amount is not subsidized.

Some urban residents profess that it is useless to spend a large amount of money on remote islands or mountain residents who are seeking broadband deployment. Certainly, in remote islands and mountainous areas where there are few employment opportunities, there is a small population in their 20's to 40's that are at the center of broadband use, alongside the notion that it should not be deployed if it is not cost-effective. However, those who argue that broadband is not necessary should look at children.

Elementary and junior high school classes are now premised on the use of the internet, and "investigative learning" is not only conducted daily, but "informatics" is a core subject taught at high schools. Adults may be free not to use a broadband service, but it is wrong not to offer children a chance to make such a decision. Providing a broadband environment for children who will play

a role in the advanced information society in the future is not wasteful, but indispensable, and it is no exaggeration to say that it is an adult's duty.

Nonetheless, there has been a significant cost problem with broadband deployment in the Tokara Islands.

Concrete efforts to deploy broadband infrastructure in the Tokara Islands can be traced back to the "Broadband Experience Class in Tokara - Satsumasendai" held in May 2005. This was organized by the Kyushu Bureau of Telecommunications, Ministry of Internal Affairs and Communications, and was co-sponsored by Kagoshima Prefecture, Satsumasendai City, Toshima Village, Kagoshima University, NTT West, and others. In addition to distance learning between Nakano-shima Elementary and Junior High School and Sendai Elementary School in Satsumasendai City, a broadband internet experience class was held in Nakano-shima Island. The Computing and Communications Center of Kagoshima University played a major role in planning and implementation, referring to the "Broadband Experience Class in Io-jima" sponsored by themselves in the previous year.

The internet access line used at that time was NTT West's Digital Access 1500. This service had been provided for a long time and was widely used as a trunk line for an ISP (Internet Service Provider). The price-setting depended on the distance, so it was expensive compared to current leased-lines, and if Nakano-shima Island and Kagoshima city were connected, the monthly fee would be over 500,000 yen. At that time, 100 Mbps connection service by FTTH (Fiber to the Home) was already available in urban areas, and the monthly fee was around 5,000 yen. The speed rate was 1/100, 100 times the charge, and the disparity was 10,000 times. Even in the 2005 Tokara Islands, it was possible to use broadband-grade internet access lines, but it required 10,000 times the burden.

The "Broadband Experience Class in Tokara – Satsumasendai" increased residents' desire for broadband deployment. It was not just Nakano-shima Island where the event was held. Takara-jima Island, which had already been working on

ICT utilization, including a PC study youth group, was not silent. Mr. M who lived on Takara-jima Island said, is there anything that residents can do to deploy a broadband infrastructure? I was inspired by him to develop the "community broadband" (MASUYA 2007) and broadband deployment in the Tokara Islands was in sight.

6. Community Broadband Project

The concept of "community broadband" was close to the early days of the internet. It existed before the connection via ISP became common and the internet expanded explosively. At that time, you could join the internet by laying a line to a place that was already connected to the internet. In the same way, "community broadband" was a way to achieve broadband internet access by connecting one place in the area to broadband in some way and connecting each household in the area to the hub. High-cost issues could be solved by using the cheapest equipment possible and having every household user contribute to the cost.

The research group centered on the Computing and Communications Center of Kagoshima University which filed a grant application to the Ministry of Internal Affairs and Communications, and was selected as a SCOPE (Strategic Information and Communications R&D Promotion Programme) in 2006 to conduct research and development over three years. The field of research and development included the Tokara Islands, and the group was named the "community broadband project" and research and development began.

Nevertheless, the biggest challenge was "connecting one place in the area." If it could be done easily, it was not a broadband zero area in the first place. Anyway, any communication line was enough. If you can see the sky, you can connect to the internet using a satellite internet connection service. NTT West's Digital Access 1500 was used in Nakano-shima Island, Akuseki-jima Island and Takara-jima Island. The former was 100,000 yen per month, and the latter was more than 500,000 yen per month, which was too expensive. However, if it was divided by 10 households, it would be 10,000 to 50,000 yen, and 100 households would pay 1,000 to 5,000 yen per month, which was

Fig. 1. Parabolic antenna for satellite internet service installed on the campus of Kodakara-jima Elementary and Junior High School. The antenna diameter is 1.2 m. The stand was embedded in concrete so that it would not be blown away even by strong winds caused by a typhoon.

reasonable. Therefore, the "community broadband project" began an experiment using satellite internet on Kodakara-jima Island (Fig. 1) and Digital Access 1500 on Takara-jima Island.

"Community broadband" expenses were borne by the community, as the participation of many households enables the use of broadband-grade internet access lines at a monthly rate equal to or less than that of urban areas. The ability to achieve "community broadband" in the Tokara Islands depended on how many households were allowed to participate.

7. How to connect between islands using Community Broadband

The Tokara Islands had attracted attention in the "Broadband Experience Class in Tokara - Satsumasendai", and became a research site for the study of broadband deployment in broadband zero areas, conducted by the Ministry of Internal Affairs and Communications in 2006. This was entitled the "Research and Study for Promoting Broadband Deployment in Toshima Village." In addition to surveying residents' needs by questionnaire, some wireless communication devices between Nakano-shima Island and Kuchino-shima Island were demonstrated across the 15.44 km section to construct a practical broadband deployment model.

As a result, it became clear that communication between islands could be realized stably using 18 GHz to 5 GHz band wireless devices.

If sufficient participating households could not be recruited on one island, the line could be shared across multiple islands. However, both 18 GHz and 5 GHz band wireless devices are expensive and require a radio station license. They are useful for local governments and telecommunication carriers but not suitable for residents' "community broadband." Thus, we considered whether wireless LAN equipment using the 2.4 GHz band, which does not require a radio station license and is relatively inexpensive, could be used for the "community broadband project." Although the equipment that could be obtained for less than 1 million yen was guaranteed for about 10 km only, it connected easily when we tried between Akuseki-jima Island and Suwanose-jima Island across a section of 18.7 km. In May 2007, wireless LAN equipment using 2.4 GHz band was installed in Akuseki-jima Island and Suwanose-jima Island and were connected by wireless LAN.

As a result, the broadband internet access in Kagoshima city via leased-lines such as Digital Access 1500 and Mega Data Net's were used on Akuseki-jima Island and Suwanose-jima Island. In addition, the 17.4 km section of Suwanose-

jima Island and Taira-jima Island were connected by wireless LAN which could also be used from Taira-jima Island. Three islands were therefore connected to broadband access lines (Fig. 2).

8. How to connect households to Community Broadband

It was not possible to use broadband internet access by connecting the islands only. "Community broadband" could be established only after each household was connected. Therefore, the "community broadband project" constructed a wireless LAN network that covered the entire area of Taira-jima Island. This model was resident maintained, so was completed as cheaply as possible. Usually, wireless LAN devices for outdoor use with waterproofing measures are expensive. Thus, we installed indoor wireless LAN equipment in a rainproof box. As a result, the cost per site was reduced to about 30,000 to 50,000

Fig. 3. Wireless LAN equipment installed on Taira-jima Island by "community broadband project." We chose 12 outdoor locations and connected them with wireless LAN to create a wireless LAN network that covered the entire island.

Fig. 2. Parabolic antennas for wireless LAN installed on the roof of the Suwanose-jima Elementary and Junior High School assembly hall by the "community broadband project." The upper antenna communicates with Akuseki-jima Island and the lower antenna communicates with Taira-jima Island.

yen (Fig. 3).

We decided to install wireless LAN devices in public facilities as much as possible, but there were cases where installation in ordinary households was unavoidable. Even in such cases, we were able to obtain active cooperation from everyone in Taira-jima Island. It was thought that it was natural that there was a voice that I did not cooperate because I did not use it, but there is no. The unique "Yui no Kokoro" (heart to help each other) of the Tokara Islands where residents help each other daily could be seen in the way people worked on "community broadband", which was an effective way to deploy broadband due to this characteristic of the region.

Research and development by the Ministry of Internal Affairs and Communications to subsidize the "community broadband project" was completed in 2008. However, the demonstration experiment of the broadband service for residents conducted on Kodakara-jima Island, Takara-jima Island, Taira-jima Island, and Suwanose-jima Island was continued until the broadband service was launched. In July 2009, when the broadband infrastructure was being deployed by Toshima Village, the Tokara Islands attracted attention from all over the country as a place where a total solar eclipse could be observed. Complimentary use of Kagoshima University's equipment and the communication lines for the "community broadband project" facilitated a broadband connection on all seven inhabited Tokara Islands, and a "Live Streaming of the Total Solar Eclipse in Tokara Seven Islands Project" was held (MASUYA *et al.* 2010).

Fig. 4. FWA antenna installed in Nakano-shima Island.

Kodakara-jima Island and Toshima Village government office (in the mainland) were networked so that a remote health consultation system, a distance learning system, a disaster prevention information provision system, were operated to improve residents' services.

9.2. Grants for Regional Intranet Infrastructure Deployment in 2009 (expenses 498,260 thousand yen)

Following the deployment of Nakano-shima Island, Akuseki-jima Island, Takara-jima Island, and Kodakara-jima Island in 2008, various facilities were connected to facilities at the Toshima Village office on the mainland of Kagoshima via Kuchino-shima Island, Suwanose-jima Island, and Taira-jima Island. The public facilities were networked with optical fiber, and the public service was improved by using the village assembly streaming system, the port monitoring system, and the weather information system.

9. Broadband deployment by Toshima Village government

The broadband infrastructure was deployed in the Tokara Islands by Toshima Village using three Japanese government subsidies in 2008 and 2009.

9.1. Grants for Regional Intranet Infrastructure Deployment in 2008 (expenses 497,490 thousand yen)

Various public facilities in Nakano-shima Island, Akuseki-jima Island, Takara-jima Island, and

9.3. Grants for the Promotion of Regional Information and Communication Infrastructure Deployment in 2009 (expenses 182,787 thousand yen)

It was possible to provide high-speed internet access service by establishing Fixed Wireless Access (FWA) with a public intranet infrastructure such as a trunk line, thereby correcting the information and communication gap between the village areas and revitalizing the region.

The total grants for the three projects were 1,178,537 thousand yen. The report on the "Research and Study for Promoting Broadband Deployment in Toshima Village" by the Kyushu Bureau of Telecommunications, Ministry of Internal Affairs and Communications was incorporated in the deployment method.

The island mainline connected three submarine underwater cable landing islands (Nakano-shima Island, Akuseki-jima Island, and Takara-jima Island) and the Toshima Village office located in Kagoshima city with NTT West's leased-line service, Mega Data Nets, and the other four islands connected with the three landing islands with 18 GHz band radio equipment and a 5 GHz band wireless device. The radio sections were Nakano-shima Island – Kuchino-shima Island, Akuseki-jima Island – Suwanose-jima Island, Akuseki-jima Island – Taira-jima Island, and Takara-jima Island – Kodakara-jima Island.

The report concluded that the overhead method for installing optical fiber on the utility pole was optimal in terms of cost, but due to the location being vulnerable to typhoons overhead wire breakage was assumed and maintenance costs would be high. Also, if the communication line was not available during a disaster, there was a risk that it would hinder information gathering by the local government. For this reason, a simplified underground wiring method was adopted for the intranet network connection with branch offices, schools, and clinics. Port surveillance cameras were connected by a 25 GHz band wireless access device that did not require a radio station license. On the other hand, the broadband service for residents adopted the FWA (Fixed Wireless Access), which did not require laying cable (Fig. 4).

The broadband infrastructure deployed by Toshima Village consisted of two parts: a part used for public services and a broadband service for residents. Various systems such as a remote health consultation system, a distance learning system, a disaster prevention information provisioning system, a village assembly streaming system, and a port monitoring system were introduced and used for public services. In many cases, other local governments could see examples of utilization, but the port monitoring system used to track the operation of the village ferry was unique to the local governments of the offshore islands, and very important. In addition to informing government office ferry operation decisions, it was also used by local residents to evaluate sea conditions. Near real-time images were published on the Toshima Village website, allowing residents of the island to check the state of the harbor while staying at home.

Meanwhile, the residents' broadband service was of high interest to residents due to various public awareness activities prior to broadband deployment, and about 60% of households subscribed. This was the highest municipality participation rate in Kagoshima Prefecture.

10. Broadband issues in the Tokara Islands

The broadband service was operated by the government. The operation, maintenance and management of facilities and services were all conducted by Toshima Village. The initial cost was subsidized by the Japanese government, except the running costs. For this reason, running costs put pressure on village finances. In particular, the cost of leased-line services contracted on three landing islands was expensive. Although a monthly fee of 4,000 yen was collected from broadband service subscribers, the annual running cost was more than 30 million yen, so not profitable. If the monthly fee was set at 10,000 yen or more, it would barely profit, but it was not realistic to ask for a user burden twice as large as an urban area. Renewal costs for aging equipment were increasingly difficult to secure.

Another issue was the lack of line capacity. Initially, the leased-line service used on the three islands was 10 Mbps maximum, and the total capacity of the seven islands was only 30 Mbps. Since this was shared by all participating households and local governments, there was a chronic shortage of bandwidth. In particular, there was a big problem with low image quality when conducting video conferences at eight locations, including the village office in Kagoshima city. In Toshima Village, additional line equipment was introduced to increase the bandwidth by using

Table 3. The broadband history of the Tokara Islands.

Year	Matter
2005	Broadband Experience Class in Tokara - Satsumasendai
2006	Community Broadband Project (−2009)
2007	Research and Study for Promoting Broadband Deployment in Toshima Village
2008	Grants for Regional Intranet Infrastructure Deployment (−2009)
2009	Internet live streaming of total solar eclipse from all seven islands
2009	Grants for the Promotion of Regional Information and Communication Infrastructure Deployment
2010	Toshima Village broadband service began (wireless system).
2019	Started laying submarine underwater optical cable between islands
202X	Toshima Village ultra-high-speed broadband service is scheduled to begin (optical fiber system).

services through a wavelength lending service. This increased the line capacity between the three islands where the submarine underwater cables were landed, and made a slight improvement.

However, there has been no change in the wireless connection between the four islands without submarine underwater cable, and there is no change in residents' FWA for broadband services. The radio link between islands is only about 20 Mbps, and the FWA section has only about 5 Mbps, so the lack of bandwidth in these sections has not been resolved, and residents' complaints about slow internet are increasing year by year. Also, the potential for equipment failure has increased due to aging equipment, and it has become difficult to repair malfunctioning parts.

11. Ultra-high-speed broadband in the Tokara Islands

By Toshima Village, the old equipment update will begin to replace all the wireless sections causing the speed reduction with optical fiber.

In order to improve the communication speed between islands, submarine underwater cables will be laid on Nakano-shima Island – Kuchino-shima Island, Nakano-shima Island – Suwanose-jima Island, Suwano-jima Island – Taira-jima Island, and Takara-jima Island - Kodakara-jima Island instead of the radio equipment connecting the islands. This will connect four islands that are not connected to the mainland, Kuchino-shima Island, Suwanose-jima Island, Taira-jima Island, and Kodakara-jima Island. As a result, all inhabited Tokara Islands will be connected to the mainland by submarine underwater cables, and

the communication environment will be similar to that on the mainland. Although laying submarine underwater cables is enormously costly, the village is considering deployment with subsidies from the Japanese government. After deployment, the submarine underwater cable will be loaned to the telecommunications carrier by an IRU contract, and the running cost reduced to zero by offsetting the rental and maintenance fees. Submarine underwater cables can be used for a long period of time, so renewal costs will not need to be studied for the time being, and running costs reduced to zero will result in a significant reduction in costs. Currently, maintenance of wireless devices are required, and wireless equipment must be renewed every 5 to 6 years.

Also, in order to realize the same internet connection environment as the mainland, the FTTH method will be introduced instead of FWA for lines on the islands. This is a publicly-owned private system where maintenance management is entrusted to a private telecommunications carrier, and a loan obtained through an IRU contract for maintenance costs. The burden of the direct broadband service on the village will be reduced. When the optical cable is routed to the island, a simplified underground wiring method will be used to reduce the risk of cable breakage due to typhoons.

As a result, an internet access environment equivalent to the mainland can be realized at a low cost.

12. Conclusion

It took many people a lot of time and effort to deploy

an information and communication infrastructure, especially broadband, in the Tokara Islands (MASUYA 2009). Table 3 shows the broadband history of the Tokara Islands. In contrast to urban areas where broadband deployment is performed by telecommunications carriers, residents and local governments have never worked on deployment or improvement. Nevertheless, this is the reason a high penetration rate has been achieved in the Tokara Islands. Toshima Village is a municipality with the highest population growth rate in the whole country, but the existence of the broadband infrastructure seems to contribute indirectly to this. Moreover, due to residents' high expectations, dissatisfaction with the speed increased, and an ultra-high-speed broadband service equivalent to the mainland was expected. Running costs were expected to decrease, and current information and communication infrastructure problems solved. Information and communications disparities will soon be completely eliminated from the Tokara

Islands which are no longer "remote" in these terms.

It is hoped that the deployment of the ultra-high-speed broadband infrastructure in the Tokara Islands will provide a model for broadband deployment in similar unfavorable geographical conditions, such as other remote islands and mountainous areas throughout the country.

References

Editorial Committee of Record of Toshima Village 1995. Record of Toshima Village 1758 pp. (in Japanese)

MASUYA, M. 2007. Development of Community Broadband Infrastructure on Remote Areas, IEICE technical report, CS107(18): 31–36. (in Japanese)

MASUYA, M. 2009. Chapter 5 – *Joho no Michi* (Road to Information Infrastructure). In: *Nihon-ichi Nagai Mura Tokara* (Tokara – The Longest Village in Japan) (eds. NAGASHIMA, S., FUKUZUMI, T., KINOSHITA, K, and MASUYA, M.), Azusa-Shoin, Tokyo. (in Japanese)

MASUYA, M., AIBA, S. and SHIMOZONO, K. 2010. Internet Streaming of Total Solar Exlipse in 2009 at Tokara Islands. Academic information processing environment research, 13: 73–84. (in Japanese)

Nature

Nakano-shima Island. Photo: Ryuta TERADA

Otsuka, Y., Terada, R. and Nishimura, S. (eds.), *The Tokara Islands*
Kagoshima University International Center for Island Studies; Hokuto Shobo Publishing, Tokyo. 10 March 2020.

Chapter 11
Tephrochronology in the Tokara Islands

Hiroshi MORIWAKI

1. Introduction

Tephras, meaning ash in Greek, refer to fragmental products, which originally eject as solid by explosive eruptions in contrast to the other volcanic products, i.e. lava as liquid and volcanic gas. Because tephras broadly disperse in a short time period and deposit on the surfaces with various environments, they are used as isochrones connecting the palaeoenvironmental and cultural records between distant places, and once their ages are determined by various methods, tephras can be used as age indices.

The term, 'tephrochronology' was originally defined by S. Thorarinsson in 1940's, who used it as the studies on stratigraphy, dating and distribution of tephras, and their application to the chronology of palaeoenvironmental and archaeological records in Iceland (Thorarinsson 1981). In recent

years, the term has been used more broadly to describe all aspect of tephra studies including those chronological aspects as a stratigraphic linking, dating and synchronizing tool (Lowe 2008). In Japan, in which numerous Quaternary tephras broadly occur, tephras have been used as quite useful tools for linking, correlating and synchronizing palaeoenvironmental and cultural records as well as explosive volcanic eruption histories (Machida and Arai 2003).

In this paper, the studies of tephrochronology of the Tokara Islands are reviewed in the light of stratigraphy of tephras.

In the context of arc-trench system, Tokara Islands are situated in inner volcanic arc of the Ryukyu Island arc. (Fig. 1). Outer arc without volcanic islands such as Tanega-shima, Amami-Oshima, and Yoron-jima is arranged to the east of

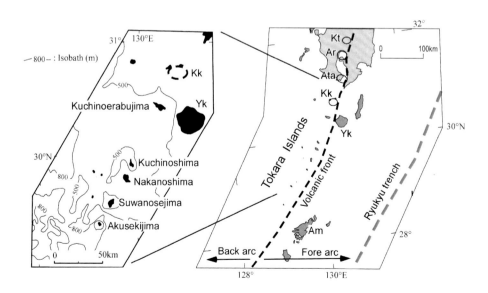

Fig. 1. Physiography of the Tokara Islands and their surrounding region. Kt: Kakuto caldera, Ar: Aira caldera, Ata: Ata cladera, Kk: Kikai caldera, Am: Amami-Oshima Island Yk: Yaku-shima Island.

Fig. 2. Recent eruption of Suwanose-jima Island (October 8th in 2005).

this arc in the direction of northeast to southwest. The inner arc of the Ryukyu Island arc is featured by Quaternary volcanoes, various types of which volcanoes occur from Kakuto volcanic field in the north to Io-Tori-shima in the south in southern Kyushu and northern half of the Ryukyu (Nansei) Islands of this arc. The volcanoes in the northern half of the arc are characterized by gigantic calderas, in which many volcanoes are concentrated in and around those calderas. Each caldera together with their associated volcanoes constitutes a caldera volcanic field. The southernmost one is the Kikai caldera volcanic field (Fig. 1).

On the other hand, no such gigantic caldera occurs in southern half of the arc, i.e. Tokara Islands. Several types of volcanoes including small calderas occur in these islands. Thus, Tokara Islands refer to the volcanic islands from Kuchinoerabu-jima in the north to Io-Tori-shima in the south in this paper. The tephras produced by those volcanoes of southern Kyushu from Kakuto caldera volcanic field to the Tokara Islands amount to around 100 layers in tha past c. 100,000 yeras (MORIWAKI 2010).

Tokara Islands are volcanologically divided into two zones, i.e. dormant volcanic island zone such as Kuro-shima and Gaja-jima in the west side, and active volcanic island zone such as Kuchinoerabu-jima in the northernmost and Io-Tori-shima in the southernmost (MACHIDA *et al.* 2001). Some volcanoes are presently very active

and eruptions sometimes occur (Fig. 2). The volcanoes of those islands have repeatedly caused explosive eruptions in the Quaternary, which have produced fall out tephras and pyroclastic flows (Fig. 3). In the following, tephrochronology of the Tokara Islands in the Holocene and late Pleistocene in the past around 50,000 years are examined.

2. Tephrochronology of the islands

Erecting robust framework of tephrochronology, i.e. stratigraphy and age of tephras in each island is essential for linking and dating the records of palaeoenvironments, explosive volcanic eruptions and archaeological remains etc. It is critical to give the stratigraphic positions of foreign widespread tephras in the local tephra stratigraphy, because foreign widespread tephras link the tephras of the Tokara Islands as tiepoints to the other local tephras in far distant areas as well as those between the Tokara Islands, and thus more reliable tephrochronology of each island can be erected.

Of the several widespread tephras of the late Pleistocene and Holocene in southern Kyushu, Aira-Tn tephra (AT) and Kikai-Akahoya tephra (K-Ah) are most useful for erecting the framework of tephrochronology of the Tokara islands, because the two tephras are extensively identified in the tephra sequences of Japan (MACHIDA and ARAI 2003). AT is derived from a gigantic ignimbrite (pyroclastic flow) erupted from Aira caldera in the head of the Kagoshima Bay, 30,000 years ago, and

K-Ah, 7,300 years in age, from Kikai caldera close to the Tokara Islands, which lies in Osumi Strait between Satsuma Peninsula and Yaku-shima Island (Fig. 1). Those two tephras are distinctively vitric in distal area and their petrological and chemical properties are well known, and thus we can rather easily identify those by using their identification indices.

In the following, stratigraphy and chronology of the tephras of the Tokara Islands are described in the light of AT and K-Ah stratigraphic positions in the tephra sequences of the islands on the basis of MORIWAKI *et al.* (2009), and in addition, some issues for the chronology of the explosive eruption histories in and around Tokara Islands are examined.

2.1. Kuchinoerabu-jima Island

Kuchinoerabu-jima Island to the west of Yaku-shima Island has Shindake and Furudake volcanoes in the central part. Shindake volcano, younger than Furudake is very active. Of more than four tephras from those volcanoes, Noike-Yumugi tephra (N-Ym) (GESHI and KOBAYASHI 2006) is most voluminous (Fig. 4). According to MORIWAKI *et al.* (2009), the features and chronology of the tephras in this island are summarized as follows. N-Ym attains more than 4.6 m thick on the eastern flank of the Noike vent and its isopachs indicate that the distribution axis lie from the vent to the east within this island.

On the other hand, identification of N-Ym at the marine core (MD982195) in the East China Sea, 220 km northwest of the island, and Tanega-shima 80km east of the island indicates that this tephra is widely distributed to the northwest as well as east (Moriwaki *et al.* 2011). This tephra occurs at the stratigraphic position below Sakurajima-Satsuma tephra (Sz-S, c. 13,000 cal BP) at those sites. Fingerprints of every fall unit suggest that upper fall unit flew to Tanega-shima, and lower one to northwest. Two radiocarbon ages obtained for this

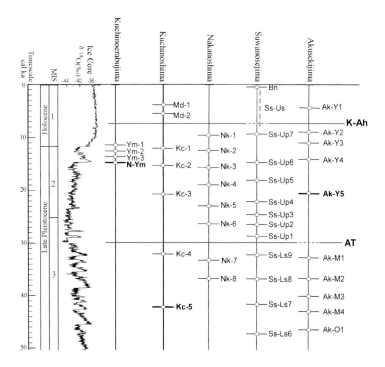

Fig. 3. Tephrochronology of the Tokara Islands. MIS: Marine oxegine isotope stage. Full tephra names are shown in the text. Based on MORIWAKI *et al.* (1996, 2009, 2010). Based on LOW, J. J. *et al.* (2008), INTIMATE Group (2008), and STUIVER and GROOTES (2000) for the ice core δ18O records.

Fig. 4. Noike-Yumugi tephra in the northern part of Kuchinoerubu-jima Island.

Fig. 5. Tephra sequence on the northern rim of older caldera in Kuchino-shima Island.

tephra (GESHI and KOBAYASHI 2006, MORIWAKI *et al.* 2009) present that this tephra is at 14,500–14,900 cal BP. On the other hand, stratigraphic position in marine oxygen isotope records obtained from the marine core (MD982195) suggests that the age is 13,000–13,200 cal BP (MORIWAKI *et al.* 2011).

Although three tephras above N-Ym consisting of scoria (Ym1 and Ym3) and pumices (Ym2) are not so voluminous, the stratigraphic positions are around at Younger Dryas cooling stage, and hence those tephras are useful for correlating the palaeoenvironments in such stage. No distinctive tephra occurs above K-Ah.

2.2. Kuchino-shima Island

Two calderas, younger one called Ogochi caldera and older, Yokodake collapsed caldera (GESHI and NAKANO 2007) , form entire frame of this island. Three intra-caldera cones occur within the Yokodake collapsed caldera. Tephrostratigraphy and depositional features of the tephras well correspond to the eruptions of those volcanoes. In the volcanological point of view, volcanic eruptions of this island are reported by GESHI and NAKANO (2007). According to MORIWAKI *et al.* (2009) based on the tephrochronological point of view, more than seven tephras mainly derived from the calderas and intra-caldera cones occur in this island (Figs. 3, 5). Of those tephras, uppermost Md-1 and Md-2 tephras possibly derived from Yokodake collapsed caldera or younger cones are thin even on the rim of the cone, suggesting small

eruptions.

Lowest one, Kc-5 is the most voluminous. It is called Ogachi pyroclastic flow (GESHI and NAKANO 2007). Its pumice deposit is around 5 m thick on the caldera (Fig. 5). In addition to such thick pumice deposits, this tephra overlies on older somma of the northwestern part of the island, but not within older and younger calderas, possibly suggesting that it ejected in the time of Ogochi caldera eruption. Kc-5 tephra is c. 42,000 cal BP (MORIWAKI *et al.* 2009). Kikai-Tozurahara tephra (K-Tz: 95,000 yr BP, MACHIDA and ARAI 2003) from Kikai caldera occur in the soil below Kc-5 (GESHI and NAKANO 2007). It is hard to observe this tephra on the area to the southeast of Ogochi caldera, because this area is occupied by Yokodake collapsed caldera and older somma with steep slope. A thick pumiceous bed, c. 2m thick is recognized on the northern tip of the island.

The Kc-1 consisting of a pumice bed and lower a lithic fragment bed occurs in younger somma, Yokodake and within older caldera (Ogochi caldera) as well as older somma, suggesting that Kc-1 is derived from Yokodake collapsed caldera-forming eruption. Kc-2 consists of pumice and ash fall deposits with many thin layers, suggesting a phreatomagmatic eruption likely under the environment of sea or lake within the younger caldera. Kc-3 and Kc-4 are scoria tephras, likely corresponding to the eruptions of the younger somma, Yokodake.

AT is recognized in the soil between Kc-3 and

Kc-4. K-Ah lying at near land surface underlies scoriaceous tephras, Md-1 and Md-2.

2.3. Nakano-shima Island

Nakano-shima has a rather high stratovolcano, Otake volcano (979 m high) on its northwestern part. A depression landform similar to caldera with a steep slope occurs in the central part of the island, but it is not caldera, because there are not voluminous volcanic products suggesting caldera forming eruptions such as Kc-5 of Kuchino-shima. Tephrostratigraphy of this island is established on the eastern part of the island, on which a suite of tephras is recognized. According to MORIWAKI *et al.* (2009), around eight tephra beds named Nakano-shima-1 (Nk-1) ~ Nakano-shima-8 (Nk-8) from younger to older are recognized in this island (Fig. 3). As a whole, scoriaceous tephras dominate in this island. Of these tephras, uppermost two tephras, Nk-1 and Nk-2 are most thick with a thickness of around 1 m in the central part of this island. Nk-1 consists of a distinctive pumice unit overlying a scoria unit, and Nk-2, scoria beds.

AT is detected in the light brown soil between Nk-6 scoria bed and Nk-7 pumice bed, although it is very thin. K- Ah lies in the near-surface soil. Distinctive tephras are not observed above K-Ah.

2.4. Suwanose-jima Island

Suwanose-jima Island consists of several volcanoes, of which Otake volcano is very active and has occasionally caused vulcanian eruptions (Fig. 2). Volcanological studies for the historical tephras are well conducted (IMURA 1991, SHIMANO and KOYAGUCI 2001). According to MORIWAKI *et al.* (1996), a continuous sequence of Holocene and late Pleistocene tephras was found on the flank of older volcano, Negamidake in the southern part of the island (Fig. 6). The sequence of the tephra beds is divided into five groups: Suwanose south lower tephra group (Ss-L), Suwanose south lower scoria fall group (Ss-Ls), Suwanose south upper pumice fall group (Ss-Up), Suwanose south upper scoria group (Ss-Us), Bunka, post-Bunka scoria group (Bn-PBs). Stratigraphy of the upper half of these tephras is shown in Fig. 3. Ss-L consists of a lowest pyroclastic flow deposit overlying a pre-plinian pumice fall. Ss-Ls consists of nine scoria beds, of which the lowest one with a thickness of c. 2.5 m is the thickest of this group. Ss-Up consists of seven pumiceous beds. Ss-Us is an aggregate consisting of numerous vulcanian scoriaceous ashes occasionally intercalating with humic soils. Thus it is hard to recognize each bed corresponding to one cycle of eruption, although some thin coarse scoria beds are contained. Ss-Us is overlain by a thick scoria bed, called Bunka scoria, which erupted in 1813 AD.

AT lies in between Ss-Ls9 and Ss-Ls10, of which the stratigraphic position well constrains the age of Ss-Ls and Ss-Up. K-Ah has not yet been reported in this sequence, but stratigraphic position of AT and Ss-Us deposits with a thickness of more than 10 m suggest K-Ah likely lies at lower to middle part of Ss-Us.

Fig. 6. Tephra sequence in the southern part of Suwanose-jima Island.

Fig. 7. Ak-Y5 tephra in the southern part of Akuseki-jima Island.

2.5. Akuseki-jima Island

Landforms of this island are dominated by younger and older calderas, younger and older sommas, and a intra-caldera cone, Mitake, 584 m high. Younger somma is a part of the intra-caldera cone of the older caldera, of which its western part was disappeared in the time of the younger caldera eruption. Mitake is a intra-caldera cone of the younger caldera.

Tephras from those volcanoes are divided into three groups: Akuseki Older (Ak-O), Akuseki Middle (Ak-M) and Akuseki Younger (Ak-Y) (Moriwaki *et al.* 2009). Stratigraphy and lithofacies of those tephra deposits well reflect eruption styles of those calderas and intra-caldera cones. Ak-O consisting of only one tephra is a pyroclastic flow and only occurs on the older somma in the southeastern tip of the island, suggesting a product of the time of older caldera-forming eruption. Ak-M consists of four tephras, Ak-M1~M4. Those tephras are scoria and occur not on the areas of the younger caldera and Mitake volcano, but on older and younger sommas, suggesting that Ak-M1~M4 are the products of the eruptions of the younger somma. Ak-Y1~Y5 consisting of pumice and scoria deposits are the products of younger caldera and Mitake. In particular, Ak-Y5, oldest one of the younger tephras is most voluminous, widely overlies younger and older sommas, undoubtedly suggesting it was produced by the younger caldera forming eruption (Fig. 7). Ak-Y2 consists of thin ash layers containing many charcoals and scattered coarse pumices. Those features present base surge deposits, suggesting an eruption in a water environment such as caldera lake.

Although stratigraphic position of AT in the sequence of Akuseki-jima tephras is unclear, Ak-Y tephras seem to be younger than AT, judging from soil developments. K-Ah clearly lies above the Ak-Y2. Although stratigraphic relation of it to AK-Y1 is unclear, Ak-Y1is very thin scoriaceous ash, and its distribution is limited, showing no distinct explosive eruption has not occurred since K-Ah.

2.6. Chemical compositions of major tephras in the Tokara Islands

Voluminous tephras, N-Ym tephra of Kuchinoerabu-

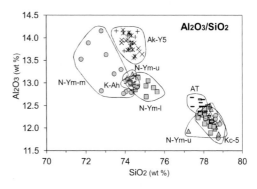

Fig. 8. Oxide variation diagrams of glass composition (wt %) showing properties of N-Ym, Kc-5, Ak-Y5 tephras. N-Ym-u, -m, -l indicate upper, middle, lower units of N-Ym respectively. Based on Moriwaki *et al.* (2009).

jima Island, Kc-5 tephra of Kuchino-shima and Ak-Y5 tephra of Akuseki-jima make us to anticipate widespread distributions, which means that those tephras are useful for the widespread correlations of palaeoenvironmental and cultural records. In order to identify those tephras in distant areas, it is necessary to fingerprint those tephras. Major element compositions of individual volcanic glass shards forming the tephras are most useful for fingerprinting and identifying such tephras (Lowe 2011). Therefore, it is critical for reliable identification of those tephras in other islands and marine cores to obtain major element compositions of glasses. Major element compositions are commonly detected using electron probe-micro analyzer (EPMA).

The distinctions of the properties of major element compositions for N-Ym, Kc-5, and Ak-Y5 can be well understood by oxide variation diagrams of glass composition. Major elements of several glass shards measured for each tephra occupy a characteristic position distinguished each other in the diagram. For example, Al_2O_3/SiO_2 diagram indicates the following characteristics as shown in Fig. 8. For N-Ym, there are not only differences between its units, but it bears a wide variety of composition. For exenple, a part of the upper unit of N-Ym (N-Ym-u) is close to K-Ah, but others, to AT. SiO_2 of N-Ym-m is low in content, which is clearly different from that of N-Ym-l.

Those differences between units of N-Ym enable to identify each unit in distal area. Thus units of N-Ym were identified in the marine core of the East China Sea and Tanega-shima (MORIWAKI *et al.* 2011). Kc-5 is close to, but significantly different from AT. It is high SiO_2 in content, but low AL_2O_3. Conversely, Ak-Y5 bears high Al_2O_3 content. Those properties of the chemical compositions of those tephras are useful for identifying them in other distant places

3. Summary

Following two are pointed out for the tephrochronology of the Tokara Islands. First, in the context of explosive volcanic history, no distinct explosive eruption has occurred to the present since K-Ah, i.e. in the past 7,300 years, besides Bunka eruption of Suwanose-jima, which is scoria eruption, but not pumice eruption. This may likely be due to the change in outer environment, i.e. sea-level change and thus it matches to postglacial high sea-level stand as well as underground volcanological context.

Second, in the context of the application of tephras of the Tokara Islands to the chronology of palaeoenvironmental and cultural records, N-Ym is identified in the places far distant from the island, and used as an important time marker of the Late Glacial records. Kc-5 and Ak-Y5, which are not yet recognized in around marine cores and on other islands, will be possibly identified in those areas, and in addition , the other tephras of the Tokara Islands may be likely fined out around those islands and be used as time markers in the future.

References

GESHI, N. and KOBAYASHI, Y. 2006. Volcanic Activities of Kuchinoerabujima Volcano within the Last 30,000 years. Bulletin of the Volcanological Society of Japan, 51: 1–20. (in Japanese with English Abstract)

GESHI, N. and NAKANO, S. 2007. Volcanic Activity of Kuchinoshima Volcano, Tokara Islands, Kagoshima Prefecture. Bulletin of the Geological Survey of Japan, 58: 105–116. (in Japanese with English abstract)

IMURA, R. 1991. Pyroclastic deposits of Suwanosejima Volcano for the last 200 year—A Reconstruction of Volcanic Activity Using the Volcanic sand Formation. The Journal of the Geological Society of Japan, 97: 865–868. (in Japanese)

LOWE, D. J. 2008. Globalization of Tephrochronology: New Views from Australia. Progress in Physical Geography, 32: 11–335.

LOWE, D. J. 2011. Tephrochronology and its Application: A Review. Quaternary Geochronology, 6: 107–153.

LOWE, J. J., RASMUSSEN, S. O., BJORCK, S., HOEK, W. Z., STEFFENSEN, J. P., WALKER, M. J. C., YU, Z. C. and the INTIMATE Group 2008. Synchronization of Palaeoenvironmental Events in the North Atlantic Rregion during the Last Termination: A Revised Protocol Recommended by the Intimate Group. Quaternary Science Reviews, 27: 6–17.

MACHIDA, H. and ARAI, F. 2003. Atlas of Tephra in and around Japan (revised edition). 336 pp., University of Tokyo Press, Tokyo. (in Japanese)

MACHIDA, H., OTA, Y., KAWANA, T., MORIWAKI, H. and NAGAOKA, S. 2001. Regional Geomorphology of the Japanese Islands, vol. 7, Geomorphology of Kyushu and the Ryukyus. 355 pp., University of Yokyo Press, Tokyo. (in Japanease)

MORIWAKI, H. 2010. Late Pleistocene and Holocene Tephras in Southern Kyushu. In: Intra-conference Field Trip Guides. INTAV International Field Conference and Workshop on Tephrochronology, Volcanism, and Human Activity, (eds. MORIWAKI, H. and LOWE, D. J.), pp. 44–53, Kirishima City, Kyushu, Japan, 9–17, May, 2010.

MORIWAKI, H., NAGASAKO, T. and ARAI, F. 2009. Late Pleistocene and Holocene Tephras in the Tokara Islands, Southern Japan. The Quaternary Research, Japan (*Daiyonki-Kenkyu*), 48: 271–287. (in Japanese with English abstract)

MORIWAKI, H., SUZUKI, T., MURATA, M., IKEHARA, M., MACHIDA, H. and LOWE, D. J. 2011. Sakurajima-Satsuma (Sz-S) and Noike-Yumugi (N-Ym) tephras: New Tephrochronological Marker Beds for the Last Deglaciation, Southern Kyushu, Japan. Quaternary International, 246: 203–212.

MORIWAKI, H., WESTGATE, J. and ARAI, F. 1996. Quaternary Tephra Layers of Suwanose Island, in the Tokara Islands, South Japan. Geographical Reports of Tokyo Metropolitan University, 31: 1–10.

SHIMANO, T. and KOYAGUCHI, T. 2001. Eruption Styls and Degassing Process of Ascending Magma of 1813 Eruption of Suwanose-jima Volcano, Southwest Japan. Bulletin of the Volcanological Society of Japan, 46: 53–70. (in Japanese with English abstract)

STUIVER, M. and GROOTES, P. M. 2000. GISP2 oxygen isotope ratios. Quaternary Research, 53: 277–284.

THORARINSSON, S. 1981. Tephra Studies and Tephrochronology: a Historical Review with Special Reference to Iceland. In: Tephra Studies (eds. SELF, S. and SPARKS, R.), pp. 1–12, D. Reidel Publishing Company, Dordrecht.

Chapter 12
Endemism and Diversity of Plant Communities in the Tokara Islands

Motohiro KAWANISHI, Jinshi TERADA and Akio TACHIKUI

1. Introduction

The Tokara Islands is an archipelago consisting of twelve small islands located between the Osumi Islands (which include Yaku-shima Island and Tanega-shima Island) and the Amami Islands. The geology of the Tokara Islands is volcanic, which has a major impact on the island environment. In particular, the ground disturbances caused by eruptions and steep volcanic landforms created by lava and pyroclastic flows have a significant impact on the vegetation of these islands. The Tokara Islands are an important biogeographical area because the fauna differs significantly between the north and south side of the Tokara Channel. This boundary line is called Watase Line and it has been established as the boundary between the Oriental and the Palaearctic region.

The Tokara Islands have a long history of human settlement, except for the Suwanose-jima Island, where human residence was restricted because of active volcanic activity. Therefore, a great part of the vegetation on the islands was formed under the influence of traditional human lifestyles (Sᴀɪᴛᴏ *et al.* 1980). The plants of these islands are important food resources for humans and livestock as well as for traditional human usages, such as sacred events. Wild plants, such as bamboo (*Pleioblastus linearis* (Hack.) Nakai), Chinese fan palm (*Livistona chinensis* (Jacq.) R.Br. ex Mart.), and Japanese Bay tree (*Machilus thunbergii* Siebold et Zucc.) are used in making the costume of the famous masked god named "Boze" in the traditional festival on Akuseki-jima Island (Kᴜʙᴏ 2018). Although the island industry changed from year to year, people of all generations have utilized the land in different ways, which had a strong impact on the vegetation and landscape of these islands.

On the other hand, in the mountains, relatively old forests with large trees are protected from human influence. Steep landforms created by volcanic activity and sea erosion prevent human invasion, and here, magnificent coastal vegetation is developed. The vegetation structure created under the influence of these environmental factors is not simple. As a consequence of geological history, geography, different habitats, and plant use by humans, the Tokara Islands are a very interesting area from the aspects of vegetation structure, plant uniqueness, diversity, and interactions with human beings. In this chapter, we will give an overview of the Tokara Islands vegetation and describe its structure and diversity, focusing on natural forests and coastal vegetation.

2. Environmental conditions of the Tokara Islands

There are big differences in the land square areas among the Tokara Islands. Among the islands inhabited by humans, the land area of the largest Nakano-shima Island is 34 km^2, and the land are of the smallest Kodakara-jima Island is 0.98 km^2 (Table 1, Editorial Committee of Toshima Village Magazine supplementation 2019). Uninhabited islands, such as the islands of Kogaja-jima and Ko-shima, have even smaller square areas, even though some currently uninhabited islands, such as the Gaja-jima Island which was once inhabited by humans, are relatively large.

The highest elevation of all the islands is Mt. Otake on Nakano-shima at 979 m a.s.l. Although it has a lower elevation than that of the highest peak of the Yaku-shima Island in Kyushu, it has a higher elevation than that of the larger islands of the Amami Islands, such as the Amami-Oshima and Tokuno-shima Islands. The highest peak altitudeof the island is higher as the area of island is larger in the Nansei Islands. The Tokara Islands have smaller square areas than those of the other islands of the Nansei Islands (SHIUCHI and HOTTA 2015). This is because of the fact that the Tokara Islands were mainly formed by volcanoes, and their topography is steep, the coastline consists of many cliffs formed by strong sea erosion, and there are few low plains, such as the uplifted coral reefs. On the Tokara Islands, most of the relatively larger low-altitude plains of elevated coral reefs are located on the Takara-jima and Kodakara-jima Islands. Some villages are located on the small flatland, and the population of each island is less than 200, with a small number of households (Table 1). One of the Tokara Islands, the Takara-jima Island, has a relatively large population because of the presence of relatively large flatlands. On the other hand, human population and number of households are few in the Suwanose-jima Island because of limited settling areas because volcanic areas occupy most of the island.

In the hythergraph shown in Fig. 1, the monthly mean temperatures and precipitation of Nakano-shima (belongs to the Tokara Islands; location of the Japan Meteorological Agency observation station), Nase (Amami-Oshima Island), and Kagoshima (Kyushu district) are indicated. The

Meteorological Station of the Nakano-shima Island is located 220 m a.s.l., and thus, the information on the average temperature of this area can be obtained using the temperature lapse rate of -0.6 °C/100 m. This would indicate that the monthly average temperature of the lowlands on the Nakano-shima Island is 12 °C or higher during the cold season from January to March. The lowest daily temperature in the period from 2003 to 2018 was 0.0 °C in February 2003. On Kagoshima, 13 years with daily minimum temperatures falling below freezing point were recorded since 1999. The lowest temperature was -5.3 °C in 2016. The mean annual precipitation in the period from 1999 to 2018 was 2412.3 mm in Kagoshima, 2915.1 mm in Naze, and 3586.0 mm in Nakano-shima. This shows that the Tokara Islands have milder winters and more precipitation than those of the Kagoshima prefecture located on the mainland of the Japan archipelago.

The Warmth Index (WI), which is used when describing the relationship between the vegetation zone and the climate, can be obtained by subtracting 5 °C from the mean temperature of month in > 5 °C, and sum up their value (KIRA 1949). Based on the observation data from 1999 to 2018, the mean annual temperature and WI are 18.9 °C and 166.1, respectively, for the Kagoshima Island, and 21.8

Table 1. Geographical characteristics and number of plant species of each island of the Tokara Islands.

	Island area*	Peak altitude*	Population†	Number of plant species §		
	(km^2)	(m)	(households)	native	alien	total
Kuchino-shima Is.	13.33	628.3	129 (75)	602	29	631
Nakano-shima Is.	34.42	979.0	159 (90)	771	34	805
Kogaja-jima Is.	0.37	301.0	–	–	–	–
Gaja-jima Is.	4.05	497.2	–	331	9	340
Taira-jima Is.	2.08	242.9	64 (31)	338	20	408
Suwanose-jima Is.	27.61	799.0	79 (44)	406	25	431
Akuseki-jima Is.	7.49	584.0	73 (35)	520	24	544
Ko-shima Is.	0.31	56.0	–	–	–	–
Kodakara-jima Is.	0.98	102.7	53 (32)	297	14	311
Takara-jima Is.	7.07	291.9	131 (68)	648	42	690
Kaminone-jima Is.	0.45	280.0	–	–	–	–
Yokoate-jima Is.	2.75	409.8	–	92.0	1.0	93.0

*Data in Editorial Committee of Toshima Village Magazine supplementation (2019). † Data in March 31, 2018. Web site of Toshima Village (accessed in 2019 Oct.). § Data in SUZUKI and MIYAMOTO (2018).

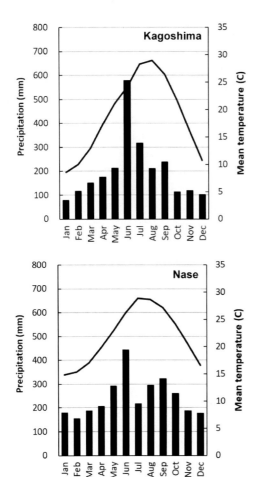

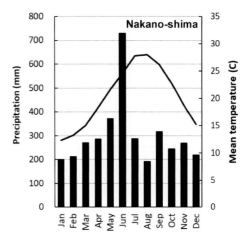

Fig. 1. Hythergraph of Kagoshima (Kyusyu district), Nakano-shima (Tokara Islands), and Nase (Amami-Oshima Island of the Amami Islands) based on the observation results from the Japan Meteorological Agency. The data for Kagoshima and Nase shows the average values of observation sites from January 1999 to December 2018. Values for Nakano-shima were obtained from the observation data of the weather station (altitude 220 m) by converting data to obtain data for the altitude of 0 m with a lapse rate of 0.6 °C/100 m, and the average values from December 2002 to December 2018 are shown.

°C and 201.8, respectively, for Nase, Amami-Oshima. On the Nakano-shima Island, these values are 20.3 °C and 183.5, respectively (data obtained from December 2002 to December 2018). The observation data was converted based on the lapse rate of -0.6 °C/100 m).

According to KIRA (1976), the border line of vegetation zone between the warm temperate vegetation zone and the subtropical vegetation zone is the line at the WI of 180, and therefore, the Nakano-shima Island is right on the boundary of both zones. OONO (2005) indicated that the WI value in this boundary area is because of the fact that the boundary of the vegetation zone was set to the south of Yaku-shima Island. However, if the based on view that Yaku-shima lowland also belongs to the subtropical zone, WI of boundary will be lower. In this regard, as indicated by AIBA

(2018), it is difficult to exclude biogeographical factors because the area that is the basis of this WI180 almost matches the position of the Watase Line. So, the boundary of the vegetation zone determined by temperature factors may be better applied to WI = 144 (SU 1984), the border between warm temperate and subtropical forests in Taiwan (AIBA 2017). According to this theory, the Tokara Islands, including not only the lowlands but also relatively high mountain areas, belong to the subtropical zone.

2. 1. Biogeography of the Tokara Islands

The Tokara Islands have always attracted attention because they are located at the border of two large biogeographical regions, the Palearctic region and the Oriental region (MAEKAWA 1977). In particular, it is famous for its fauna which changes greatly between the north and the south on the Tokara Channel located between the Akuseki-jima Island and the Kodakara-jima Island (Tokara Gap). This boundary is called the "Watase Line". This area is also the boundary between the Holarctic region and Continental South East Asian region belonging the Palaeotropical region, in the plant biogeographical system. KOIZUMI (1933) noted that the Tokara Channel corresponds to this boundary. However, there are several views on floral changes in the north and south area of Watase Line as below.

NAKAMURA *et al.* (2009) stated that the flora change greatly along the Tokara tectonic strait. SHIUCHI and HOTTA (2015) showed that some plant species show irregular distribution patterns along the Tokara tectonic channel. They indicated that besides geological factors, it is necessary to consider the patterns caused by various physiological and ecological characteristics as well as by the movement of plants with humans. SUZUKI and MIYAMOTO (2018) compared the flora of each Nansei Island using 3110 sheets of native species specimen information. As a result, the south part of the Watase Line, from Yonaguni-jima Island (part of the Yaeyama Islands) to the Kodakara-jima Island (part of the Tokara Islands), along with the islands on the north side of the Watase Line formed another cluster. These results are same to conclusion of NAKAMURA *et al.* (2009). Therefore, SUZUKI and MIYAMOTO (2018) also supported the view that the Watase Line is an important boundary for flora.

If we examine the distribution pattern of plants considering the difference in habitat variables, for example in altitude, the connection between the north and south regions will be different. Evergreen broad-leaved forest which mainly consists of *Castanopsis sieboldii* (Makino) Hatus. ex T.Yamaz. et Mashiba, *Machilus thunbergii*, *Distylium racemosum* Siebold et Zucc., and *Ardisia sieboldii* Miq. is established in the mountainous area of the Ryukyu Islands over 300 m a.s.l. This species composition at a high altitude indicates that the southern Ryukyu Islands are essentially related to the Sino-Japanese region, though there are some different because some species had endemic evolution in the islands. On

the other hand, in the lower areas lower than 300 m a.s.l., tropical plants characteristic for the Oriental region are widely distributed (YASUMA 2001). The development of an evergreen broad-leaved forest in this high altitude region is unusual because the region is an active volcano. This may be one of the factors that obscure the north-south connection pattern of vegetation elements of the evergreen broad-leaved forest.

2.2. Flora of the Tokara Islands
Plants in the Tokara Islands have been thoroughly investigated and a large number of specimen sampling records is available for many islands, including the Kuchino-shima Island (WAKI 1990, MORITA 2004, OOYA 2011b), Nakano-shima Island (MORITA 2002, OOYA 2011a), Suwanose-jima Island (TACHIKUI 1992, MORITA 2001), Taira-jima Island (TACHIKUI 1991, MORITA 2005), Akuseki-jima Island (TACHIKUI 1993, MORITA and MARUNO 2003), and Kodakara-jima Island (MORITA 2006). The flora of Tokara Islands was summarized in SHIUCHI and HOTTA (2015). SUZUKI and MIYAMOTO (2018) compiled specimen information and the number of plant species on each island of the Nansei Islands. The number of species of the Tokara Islands is shown in Table 1. They clarified the relationship between the island area and number of species in major islands of the Nansei Islands and found a positive correlation. In addition, they pointed out that the currently active volcanic islands, such as the Suwanose-jima Island and uninhabited small islands like the Yokoate-jima Island, have lower number of species despite of their large land area. In the following section, we will introduce some of the notable species from SHIUCHI and HOTTA (2015) that inhabit the Tokara Islands.

2.2.1. Endemic species
ARISTOLOCHIACEAE
Asarum tokarense Hatus
The species is endemic to three islands, Kuro-shima, Kuchino-shima, and Nakano-shima Island. It is considered to be closely related to *Asarum kumageanum* Masam., which inhabits the Yaku-shima Island, *Asarum kumageanum* Masam. var. *satakeanum* (F.Maek.) Hatus., which inhabits the

Tanega-shima Island, and *Asarum lutchuense* (Honda) Koidz., which inhabits the Amami-Oshima Island (SHIUCHI and HOTTA 2015).

LILIACEAE
Lilium nobilissimum (Makino) Makino

The species is an endemic lily which grows only on the cliff facing the coast of the Kuchino-shima Island. Species related to this lily include *Lilium speciosum* Thunb. and *Lilium japonicum* Houtt., both inhabiting Japan, as well as *Lilium rosthornii* Diels inhabiting southern China. *Lilium longiflorum* Thunb., a lily species native to Nansei Island, and *Lilium formosanum* Wallace, a species native to Taiwan and invasive in Japan, have low affinity to *L. nobilissimum* (HAYASHI and KAWANO 2000). In recent years, the concerns of the Wild Extinction of *L. nobilissimum* have been increasing because of the excessive collection and goat feeding damage (SHIUCHI and HOTTA 2015), but Hayashi (2014) confirmed the presence of a small wild population. *L. nobilissimum* was classified as Critically Endangered (CR) in the Red List of the Japanese Ministry of the Environment, and it was classified as Data Deficient (DD) in the Red List of the Kagoshima prefecture (Kagoshima Prefecture Environment and Forestry Affairs Department Nature Conservation Division 2016).

ASPARAGACEAE
Aspidistra elatior Blume

Aspidistra elatior is native to three islands, Uji-Mukai-jima, Kuro-shima, and Suwanose-jima (TAMURA 2015). The populations in Uji-Mukai-jima (Uji Islands) and Kuro-shima Island (Osumi Islands) are large enough to cover the forest floor. On the other hand, the population in Suwanose-jima Islands is restricted to the area around Mt. Nabedao (SHIUCHI and HOTTA 2015), and the number of individuals is low. Although this species is considered to originate in southern China, it has not been confirmed as native in China. The results of the phylogenetic analysis showed that *A. elatior* is closely related to *Aspidistra attenuata* Hayata and *Aspidistra daibuensis* Hayata, which are endemic to Taiwan (YAMASHITA and TAMURA 2004).

CYPERACEAE
Carex conica Boott var. *scabrocaudata* (T.Koyama) Hatus.

This sedge species is endemic to Kuro-shima Island (Osumi Islands) and Tokara Island (Kuchino-shima, Nakano-shima, Gaja-jima, Suwanose-jima, Akuseki-jima, and Takara-jima) (SHIUCHI and HOTTA 2015). It was indicated that it is cytologically related to *Carex conica* Boott distributed from Hokkaido to Kyushu and Jeju Island, or *Carex oshimensis* Nakai distributed on the Izu Islands (YANO *et al.* 2010).

Carex tokarensis T.Koyama

This endemic sedge species inhabits the islands of Kuro-shima and Nakano-shima. According to YANO *et al.* (2010), just as *Carex reinii* Franch. Et Sav.. *C. reinii* is distributed on Honshu, Shikoku, and Kyushu, but was not recorded on the islands of Tanega-shima and Yaku-shima (SHIUCHI and HOTTA 2015).

HYDRANGEACEAE
Hydrangea involucrata Siebold var. *tokarensis* M.Hotta et T.Shiuchi

The species only grows on the islands of Kuro-shima, Kuchino-shima, and Suwanose-jima (OHBA 2017). It was indicated that the mother species of *H. involucrata* var. *tokarensis* is *Hydrangea involucrata* Siebold which is native to Honshu and has a hybrid origin (SHIUCHI and HOTTA 2015).

STYRACACEAE
Styrax japonicus Siebold et Zucc. var. *tomentosa* Hatus.

This taxon is considered to be unique for Kuchino-shima, Nakano-shima, Suwanose-jima, Gaja-jima, and Akuseki-jima. It is a variety of *Styrax japonicus* Siebold et Zucc. with dense hairs on the sepals (SHIUCHI and HOTTA 2015). Still, the opinions on its taxonomic status differ. For example, YONEKURA (2012) describes this taxon as one form, *Styrax japonicus* Siebold et Zucc. var. *kotoensis* (Hayata) Masam. et T. Suzuki f. *tomentosus* (Hatus.) T. Yamaz. On the other hand, OHASHI (2017) describes this species as an intraspecific variation of *Styrax japonicus*.

OLEACEAE

Ligustrum japonicum Thunb. var. *spathulatum* Mansfeld

This taxon has thick leaves and is unique to the Ryukyu limestone area in the Kodakara-jima and Takara-jima Island. This taxon was observed in the wild on the Amami-Oshima Island (NOSHIRO 2017), but it is considered to be cultivated there (SHIUCHI and HOTTA 2015).

Osmanthus rigidus Nakai

The species is an endemic tree which inhabits the islands of Kuro-shima. Kuchino-shima, Nakano-shima, Suwanose-jima, and Uji (SHIUCHI and HOTTA 2015, NOSHIRO 2017).

COMPOSITAE

Chrysanthemum ornatum Hemsl. var. *tokarense* (M.Hotta et Y.Hirai) H.Ohashi et Yonek.

This *Chrysanthemum* species is endemic to the Tokara Islands (Kuchino-shima, Nakano-shima, Gaja-jima, Taira-jima, Akuseki-jima, Kodakara-jima, and Takara-jima) and to the islands of Kuchinoerabu-jima and Yaku-shima (SHIUCHI and HOTTA 2015). The species *Chrysanthemum ornatum* Hemsl. is an octaploid (2n = 72) distributed from the southern part of the Satsuma Peninsula to the Uji Islands (SHIUCHI and HOTTA 2015, KADOTA *et al.* 2017). As a related species, the hexaploid *Chrysanthemum japonense* (Makino) Nakai. (2n = 54) is distributed in the eastern areas of the Osumi and Noma Peninsulas. *Chrysanthemum crassum* (Kitam.) Kitam. (decaploid, 2n = 90) is distributed on the Amami-Oshima Island. According to this taxonomy, the *Chrysanthemum* plants determined as *Chrysanthemum ornatum* and *Chrysanthemum crassum* in the vegetation survey report of the coastal vegetation of the Tokara Islands, which will be described later, are classified as the taxon *Chrysanthemum ornatum* var. *tokarense*.

2.2.2. Remarkable plants of the Tokara Islands

SHIUCHI and HOTTA (2015) cite the following taxonomic groups as quasi-endemic species with a center of distribution in the Tokara region. Most of them show distribution patterns that replace closely-related species in around the Tokara region.

In addition, because of their small morphological differences from closely-related species the authors indicated that these species recently started to differentiate due to.

Cinnamomum daphnoides Siebold et Zucc.

This species is the most common shrub in coastal windswept shrub forests on the Tokara Islands. It is distributed from the Danjo Islands (Nagasaki prefecture) and Oshima (Fukuoka prefecture) in the north, via the southern part of Kyushu (Osumi and Satsuma Peninsulas) to the islands of Amami-Oshima and Iwo-Tori-shima (Okinawa prefecture). However, its population size is small outside the Tokara region (SHIUCHI and HOTTA 2015, YONEKURA 2015). *Cinnamomum doederleinii* Engl, a related species, is distributed on the Nansei Islands south of the Amami-Oshima Island (YONEKURA 2015).

Rhododendron eriocarpum (Hayata) Nakai

This azalea species is distributed from the southern part of Kyushu mainland and Yaku-shima to the Takara-jima Island (Tokara Islands). The greatest share of its populations is distributed in the Tokara Islands (SHIUCHI and HOTTA 2015). On volcanic soils such as those on the Nakano-shima, Suwanose-jima, and the top of Satsuma-Iwo-jima Island, the branches of this plant spread like a mat and bear very small leaves, whereas individuals growing in shrub forests on the coast and planted in villages are about 3 m tall and have relatively broad leaves. The shape of the shrub changes greatly depending on the environmental conditions.

Rhododendron tashiroi Maxim. var. *lasiophyllum* Hatus.

This azalea species is distributed in areas that have experienced volcanic explosions over the past tens of thousands of years, which can be found in the Tokara region and the Satsuma Peninsula. The closely related species *Rhododendron tashiroi* Maxim spread from Tanega-shima to the area of Tokara and is also distributed on the Amami-Oshima Island (SHIUCHI and HOTTA 2015).

Peucedanum japonicum Thunb. var. *latifolium* M.Hotta et Shiuchi

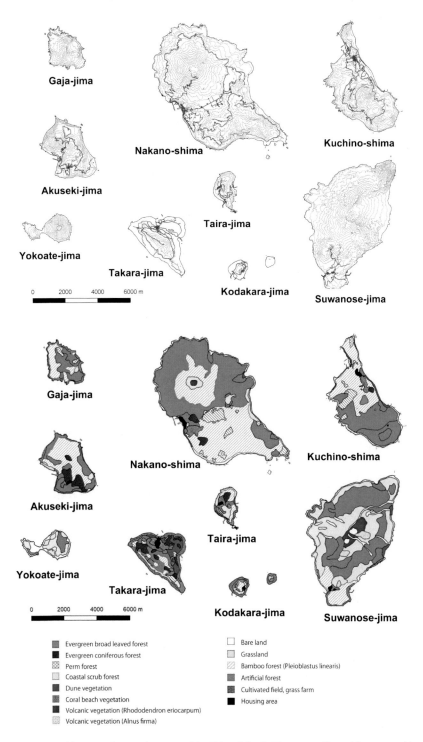

Fig. 2. Topographic map and vegetation maps of the Tokara Islands. The contour lines of the topographic map are 50 m apart. Red dots and brown lines indicate houses and roads, respectively. The vegetation map is based on the data from the 1/50,000 vegetation map obtained from the Ministry of the Environment made until 1998 (base map is the topographical map of the Geographical Survey Institute).

This species is a variety of *Peucedanum japonicum* Thunb. which is a taxon present only in the Tokara and the neighboring region. (HOTTA and SHIUCHI (1996). A related taxon, *Peucedanum japonicum* Thunb. var. *australe* M. Hotta et A. Seo, inhabits the Takara-jima Island (SEO and HOTTA 2000, SHIUCHI and HOTTA 2015).

Hydrangea kawagoeana Koidz. var. *kawagoeana*
This is a plant endemic to the Tokara Islands, Amami-Oshima Island, and Tokuno-shima Island. However, it is possible that the population in Amami-Oshima has gone extinct (SHIUCHI and HOTTA 2015). It was indicated that the different forms present on each island are grouped morphologically and that it is necessary to reexamine this taxon (SHIUCHI and HOTTA 2015).

Buddleja curviflora Hook. et Arn. f. *venenifera* (Makino) T.Yamaz.
This species is distributed from southern Shikoku and southern Kyushu to Amami-Oshima. There is considerable variation in leaf size and leaf back hair density between individuals of these species (SHIUCHI and HOTTA 2015).

Disporum sessile D.Don ex Schult. et Schult.f. var. *micranthum* Hatus. ex M.N.Tamura et M.Hotta
This species is distributed from the Tokara Islands to Tokuno-shima. The closely related species *Disporum sessile* D.Don ex Schult. et Schult.f. var. *sessile* is distributed from the south Kyusyu to the Honshu. Both species are replaced each other in the Tokara area (SHIUCHI and HOTTA 2015).

3. Vegetation of the Tokara Islands

According to the 1/50,000 vegetation map obtained from the Ministry of the Environment made up to 1998 (base map is the topographical map of the Geographical Survey Institute), the vegetation in the Tokara Islands consists of natural vegetation (such as evergreen broad-leaved forest, coastal vegetation, and volcanic vegetation) and secondary vegetation (such as grasslands and bamboo forests under human influence). There is a difference in the composition of the vegetation elements in each island, and this is visible as a difference in the landscape of each island.

The evergreen broad-leaved forests occupy the largest area (4,134.1 ha) among all the vegetation elements of the Tokara Islands, followed by bamboo forests (*Pleioblastus linearis* community) which occupy 2,585.5 ha. The evergreen coniferous forests (including planted pine forests of *Pinus luchuensis* Mayr on the Takara-jima Island and of *Pinus thunbergii* Parl. on the other islands) occupy 225.1 ha. There are also planted forests with Japanese cedar (*Cryptomeria japonica*

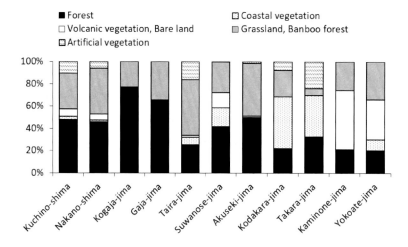

Fig. 3. The composition ratio of vegetation elements on each of the Tokara Islands. The original data used to calculate the vegetation area are shown in Fig. 2 and Table 2.

(L.f.) D.Don), Japanese cypress (*Chamaecyparis obtusa* (Siebold et Zucc.) Endl.), and beefwood (*Casuarina equisetifolia* L.). Volcanic vegetation covers an area of 140.5 ha and is mostly developed on the islands of Nakano-shima and Suwanose-jima. Coastal vegetation is the second largest vegetation element after the bamboo community. The area of the coastal vegetation, as shown in the vegetation map, is mostly distributed on the Suwanose-jima Island, even though coastal vegetation is established on every island. Uplifted coral vegetation is mainly established on the Takara and Kodakara-jima Island. Natural bare land includes volcanic and coastal bare land. The largest part of the bare areas is the natural bare land located in the volcanic area of the islands of Nakano-shima and Suwanose-jima. The islands of Kuchino-shima, Nakano-shima, and Takara-jima, which are relatively flat and have large human populations, have a lot of cultivated land and pasture areas.

In the original data from the vegetation map shown in Fig. 2, there are lots of community types in the forests, and a relatively complicated community arrangement is shown. However, the purpose of this chapter was to grasp the pattern of global vegetation elements, which is why the individual community types shown in the original data of the vegetation map were not taken into account. The Japanese Ministry of the Environment is currently in the process of creating a new vegetation map with more detailed community types (topographic vegetation map on 1/25,000 scale) than those in the vegetation map shown in this paper.

Vegetation surveys were conducted on the following islands of the Tokara Islands: Kuchino-shima (TERADA 1999b), Nakano-shima (TERADA 1997), Taira-jima (TERADA and TACHIKUI 2017), Akuseki-jima (TERADA and OHYA 2008), Kodakara-jima, Ko-jima (TERADA 1995), Takara-jima (TERADA 2000), etc.

4. Forests of the Tokara Islands

As mentioned above, forests, grasslands, and bamboo forests occupy large areas on the main islands of the Tokara Islands (Table 2, Fig. 3). Forests are representative of the mountainous natural vegetation, and most of the forests of the Tokara Islands are evergreen broad-leaved forests which are established in large areas of the islands of Nakano-shima and Suwanose-jima.

Fig. 4. Mt. Megamiyama on Takara-jima Island. The pale green community at the foothills of the mountain is the *Livistona* community, and the dark green community at the top of the mountain is the *Quercus phillyreoides* community.

Fig. 5. Forest of *Quercus phillyreoides* f. *wrightii* in Megamiyama with many epiphytic orchids (*Luisia teres*) growing on the tree trunks.

Although these islands continue to experience active volcanic activity, these islands are relatively large in island area, and evergreen broad-leaved forests are mainly established in the areas that have not been affected by volcanoes and that are not close to human settlements. Evergreen broad-leaved forests can be found on other islands covering smaller areas, and these forests include many forests stands that are attracting research interest because of their constituent species and distribution characteristics.

The evergreen broad-leaved forests of the Tokara Islands mainly consist of forests dominated by evergreen Fagaceae plants, such as *Castanopsis sieboldii*, *Quercus phillyreoides* A.Gray (*Quercus phillyreoides* A.Gray f. *wrightii* (Nakai) Makino), *Lithocarpus edulis* (Makino) Nakai, and Lauraceae tree *Machilus thunbergii*. Table 3 shows the species richness and community structure of the main evergreen broad-leaved forest elements (*Castanopsis sieboldii* forest, *Machilus thunbergii* forest, *Ficus microcarpa* L.f. forest, *Livistona chinensis* forest) on each of the Tokara Islands. Here, species richness was shown by index D derived from GLEASON (1922) as follows,

$$D = S / \log_{10}A$$

then, S is the number of species, and A is plot size. Species richness and community structure differ between the same community types on different islands. Details will be discussed later.

The *Castanopsis sieboldii* forest has developed stands on the islands of Nakano-shima and Kuchino-shima. *Machilus thunbergii* forests are widely distributed on the Takara-jima Island, Akuseki-jima Island, Suwanose-jima Island, Gaja-jima Island, and Kuchino-shima Island, as well as on some other islands, and they have a strong secondary forest character. In slightly drier habitats, *Lithocarpus edulis* forests are developed, and on the Akuseki-jima Island, *Beilschmiedia erythrophloia* Hayata community is present (OHNO 1989, 1991). The relatively natural evergreen broad-leaved forests of the Tokara Islands are established on low altitude hills or mountains, excluding currently active volcanoes. TERADA and OHYA (2008) cited the human worshiping of the several mountains in the Tokara region as the reason why the natural forest were preserved in this hilly terrain, and they indicated that the mountain with a moderate height close to the village has been a ritual place since ancient times.

For example, Mt. Megamiyama on the Takara-jima Island was a sacred place where people

Table 2. Area (ha) of vegetation elements on each island derived from the 1/50,000 vegetation map obtained from the Ministry of the Environment made until 1998 (base map is the topographical map of the Geographical Survey Institute).

	Kuchino-shima Is.	Nakano-shima Is.	Kogaja-jima Is.	Gaja-jima Is.	Taira-jima Is.	Suwanose-jima Is.	Akuseki-jima Is.	Kodakara-jima Is.	Takara-jima Is.	Kaminone-jima Is.	Yokoate-jima Is.	Total
Forest												
Evergreen broad leaved fores	621.1	1537.1	22.8	249.2	36.6	1143.6	280.0	19.0	159.2	9.7	55.8	4134.1
Evergreen coniferous forest	8.3	39.9	6.3	–	16.6	–	92.2	–	61.7	–	–	225.1
Perm forest	12.1	10.7	–	18.6	–	–	–	9.0	10.8	–	–	61.2
Coastal vegetation												
Coastal scrub forest	–	35.7	–	–	–	445.0	8.3	–	29.2	–	26.6	544.9
Dune vegetation	34.3	10.1	–	–	11.5	21.3	–	–	103.7	–	–	180.9
Coral beach vegetation	–	–	–	–	3.9	–	–	59.2	129.1	–	–	192.1
Volcanic vegetation, Bare land												
Volcanic vegetation	–	10.9	–	–	-	129.6	–	–	–	–	–	140.5
Natural bare land	88.9	180.1	–	–	3.6	248.0	–	–	–	24.5	99.7	644.7
Grassland, Bamboo forest												
Grassland	–	62.9	–	6.9	52.4	556.0	26.1	12.0	–	12.0	93.9	822.2
Bamboo forest	429.8	1368.6	8.8	135.2	53.7	199.2	326.4	18.7	45.1	–	–	2585.5
Artificial vegetation												
Artificial forest	18.4	–	–	–	–	–	–	–	23.8	–	–	42.2
Cultivated field, grass farm,	115.5	197.3	–	–	30.3	9.2	7.9	6.4	131.9	–	–	498.7
Housing area	10.7	14.6	–	–	4.5	7.1	4.5	3.6	15.4	–	–	60.3

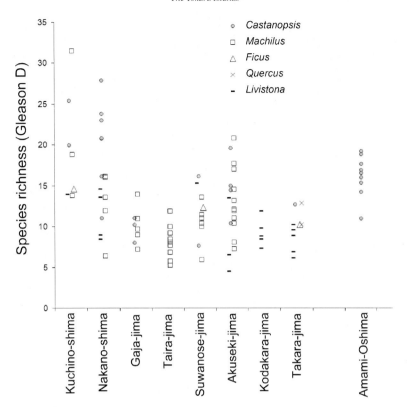

Fig. 6. The comparison of species richness index (Gleason's D) of forest communities that compose the evergreen broad-leaved forests of the Tokara Islands. The abbreviations for the forest types and the data set are the same as in Table 3.

practiced rituals. For this reason, natural forests were preserved in this area (TERADA and OOYA 2012) (Fig. 4). The *Livistona chinensis* community developed in the foothills of Mt. Megamiyama. In this palm forest, the species *Livistona chinensis* dominates in the canopy layer along with other species, such as *Ardisia sieboldii*, *Machilus thunbergii*, *Schefflera heptaphylla* (L.) Frodin, and *Turpinia ternate* Nakai (TERADA 2000). This species composition is close to that of the *Ardisia sieboldii–Machilus thunbergii* community, but the forest floor plants are hardly present and the herbaceous layer is not as developed as in the *Livistona* community. This tendency is also common in the *Livistona* forests of Akuseki-jima (TERADA and OHYA 2008). The top of Mt. Megamiyama is the habitat of the pure forest of *Quercus phillyreoides* f. *wrightii* with trees shorter than 5 m (TERADA 2000, TERADA and OOYA 2012).

This community has unique species composition and structure. For instance, it is densely populated with epiphytic orchids growing on tree trunks and on the rocks on the forest floor, and the species *Carex conica* var. *scabrocaudata* and *Trachelospermum gracilipes* Hook.f. var. *liukiuense* (Hatus.) Kitam. are growing on the forest floor (Fig. 5).

The distribution of *Quercus phillyreoides* in the Nansei Islands is unique. It has a scattered distribution on the islands of Kuro-shima, Tanega-shima, Yaku-shima (Osumi Islands), Takara-jima (Tokara Islands), Okinawa-jima, Izena-jima, and Iheya-jima (Okinawa Islands). Among the Tokara Islands, it is distributed only on Takara-jima, and it is not present on the Amami Islands (SHUICHI and HOTTA 2015).

A long time has passed since HONDA (1912) discussed the vegetation of the Nansei Islands, and this area has been investigated from various perspectives since then. The history of vegetation research in this area was explained in detail by MIYAWAKI (1989). The vegetation of the Nansei Islands was systematized by SUZUKI (1979) and the results of vegetation surveys in this area obtained by other researchers were compiled by MIYAWAKI (1989). According to MIYAWAKI (1989), the evergreen broad-leaved forests on the Nansei Islands belong to the class Camellietea japonicae Miyawaki et Ohba 1963, The evergreen broad-leaved forests, which are distributed from the northern part of Honshu to relatively high altitudes of the Yaku-shima Island belong to the order Illicio-Quercetalia acutae Fujiwara 1981 (scientific name of phytosociological unit is referred from Miyawaki & Okuda 1994. The same hereinafter). The order Myrsino-Castanopsietalia sieboldii Fujiwara 1981 is distributed in relatively low-latitude and low-elevation areas, such as the non-limestone area from central Honshu to the Nansei Islands. In addition, the Ryukyu limestone upland and uplifted coral reefs in the Nansei Islands are considered to belong to the order Diospyro maritimae-Mallotetalia philippensis Fujiwara 1981 (FUJIWARA 1981).

As mentioned above, the changing pattern of the flora of the Nansei Islands is one of the important and interesting topics in vegetation research in Japan. For example, MIYAWAKI *et al.* (1971) concluded that the boundary between the class Quercion acuto-myrsinaefoliae Fujiwara 1981 (order Illicio-Quercetalia acutae) and the alliance Psychotrio-Castanopsion sieboldii Miyawaki *et al.* 1971 (order Myrsino-Castanopsietalia sieboldii) is between the Yaku-shima Island and the Osumi Peninsula based on the difference in the amount of winter frost. SUZUKI (1979) described the alliance Psychotrio-Castanopsion sieboldii as an evergreen broad-leaved forest in the non-limestone area of the Ryukyu Islands. And, SUZUKI (1979) suggested that the *Castanopsis sieboldii* forest in the south of the Amami Islands belongs to the alliance Psychotrio-Castanopsion sieboldii. FUJIWARA (1981) recognized the boundary between the islands of Yaku-shima, Tanega-shima, and Ryukyu, and described that the alliance Maeso japonicae-Castanopsion sieboldii Fujiwara 1981 (order Myrsino-Castanopsietalia

sieboldii) is distributed in the region east of Yaku-shima and Tanega-shima. She also indicated that Yaku-shima is the northern limit of the distribution of the alliance Psychotrio-Castanopsion sieboldii. Following this research, MIYAWAKI (1989) described the alliance Psychotrio-Castanopsion sieboldii as an evergreen broad-leaved forest with the dominant species being *Castanopsis sieboldii*, and he stated that this alliance is distributed south of the Yaku-shima lowlands. Furthermore, MIYAWAKI (1989) described that this alliance is subdivided into three groups: the ones distributed on the Amami Islands, the ones centered on the Okinawa Islands, and the ones centered on the Sakishima Islands. However, the forests of the Tokara Islands were excluded from these three groups and their phytosociological affiliation was hardly mentioned.

The *Castanopsis* forest distributed on the Tokara Islands belongs to the phytosociological association Tarenno–Castanopsietum sieboldii Miyawaki *et al.* 1974 that is a vegetation unit of substitutional vegetation. Natural *Castanopsis* forests are not present on the Tokara Islands. This is the one of the reasons why it is difficult to compare the vegetation of Amami and Tokara Islands. As the boundary of the flora is located on the Tokara Islands, some viewpoints indicated that it would be best to set the boundary of the phytosociological alliances (between Psychotrio-Castanopsion sieboldii and Myrsino-Castanopsietalia) here as well (AIBA 2018, YONEDA 2018). More detailed research of ecological character of species in the future is necessary to recognize the mechanism of plant distribution pattern.

4.1. *Castanopsis* forest

This evergreen broad-leaved forest is developed in the foothills of Mt. Otake (below 450 m a.s.l.) and Mt. Jin-nyom-dake on the Nakano-shima Island, the largest of the Tokara Islands (Table 2). The remains of the primeval forest (mainly *Castanopsis* forest) are visible in this forest (OHNO 1989, 1991). The average number of species recorded in the vegetation survey data is 51.3 ± 14.1 and Gleason's D is 20.5 ± 5.5 (Table 3), meaning that the species richness of *Castanopsis* forest on Nakano-shima Island is greater than that in the

Table 3. Community structure and species richness of the forest communities that compose the evergreen broad-leaved forests in the Tokara Islands.

Forest type *		Number of stands	Gleason D †	Number of species §	Canopy height (m)	Coverage of herb layer (%)
Kuchino-shima Is.						
	Castanopsis	2	22.7±3.9	57.5±7.8	18.5±2.1	50±14.1
	Machilus	3	21.4±9.1	54.3±21.5	16.7±3.5	60±26.5
	Ficus	1	14.6	38	22	60
	Livistona	1	13.9	29	15	70
Nakano-shima Is.						
	Castanopsis	7	20.5±5.5	51.3±14.1	14.4±3.2	42.1±21.2
	Machilus	5	12.8±4	30.6±8.2	15±6	54±11.4
	Livistona	5	11.9±2.9	28.4±8.2	11±3.8	31±15.2
Gaja-jima Is.						
	Castanopsis	3	9.8±1.6	23.3±3.1	16±1	16.7±20.2
	Machilus	5	10.2±2.5	22±4.8	11.2±3.3	11±8.2
Taira-jima Is.						
	Machilus	10	7.9±2.1	20.1±5	17.1±3.6	31±17.9
Suwanose-jima Is.						
	Castanopsis	2	11.9±6	30±17	13.5±2.1	10±0
	Machilus	6	10.4±2.5	23.2±5.4	10.7±1.8	36.7±18.6
	Ficus	1	12.3	32	14	90
	Livistona	1	15.3	36	14	60
Akuseki-jima Is.						
	Castanopsis	4	14.9±3.8	37.8±10.1	16±4.6	36.3±28.1
	Machilus	12	13.1±3.9	30.7±8.1	14.9±4.2	27.1±18.1
	Livistona	3	8.2±4.7	17.7±9	10±2.6	23.7±20.3
Kodakara-jima Is.						
	Livistona	5	9.3±1.7	22.2±4.3	11.4±7.1	42.2±24.5
Takara-jima Is.						
	Castanopsis	1	12.7	33	15	50
	Ficus	1	10.2	24	12	30
	Livistona	5	8.4±1.7	21±3.9	12.4±1.7	20±10
	Quercus	2	11.5±1.9	26±2.8	6.5±0.7	45±7.1
Amami Oshima Is.						
	Castanopsis	9	16.2±2.5	40.3±8.9	20.1±1.2	31.1±20.3

*Forest types are indicated as follow: Castanopsis: Castanopsis sieboldii community, Machilus: Machilus thunbergii community, Ficus: Ficus microcarpa community, Livistona: Livistona chinensis community, Quercus: Quercus phillyreoides community. † Gleason Index was derived from the formula: D=S/log10A which tightly corresponded with the species-area curve (GLEASON 1922). § "Number of species" shows the mean number of species that is actual number occurred in investigation plot area including different area (64–400 m2). Fundamental data was obtained from previous reports as follows: Kuchino-shima Island (TERADA 1999b), Nakano-shima Island (TERADA 1997), Gaja-jima Island (TERADA 1999a), Taira-jima Island (TERADA and TACHIKUI 2017), Suwanose-jima Island (TERADA *et al.* in press), Akuseki-jima Island (TERADA and OOYA 2008), Kodakara-jima Island (TERADA 1995), Takara-jima Island (TERADA 2000, TERADA and OOYA 2012), Amami Oshima Island (KAWANISHI, unpublished data).

other Tokara Islands. In addition, *Castanopsis* forest on Nakano-shima Islandis greater than that in the *Castanopsis* natural forest developed on the Amami-Oshima Island (Fig. 6). On Nakano-shima, the average community height is 15 m to 20 m, which is a little lower than that of the natural *Castanopsis* forest on Amami-Oshima (Table 3). The vegetation coverage of the herbaceous layer varies greatly from island to island and is relatively large in the *Castanopsis* forests on Kuchino-shima,

Nakano-shima, and Akuseki-jima, whereas it is below 20 % on Gaja-jima and Suwanose-jima Islands.

The *Castanopsis* community in Nakano-shima is composed of *Ardisia sieboldii*, *Myrsine seguinii* H.Lev., *Livistona chinensis*, *Lithocarpus edulis*, and *Osmanthus rigidus*. In addition, the herbaceous layer is developed with many ferns, such as *Bolbitis subcordata* (Copel.) Ching and *Angiopteris lygodiifolia* Rosenst., and notable herbaceous plants, such as *Calanthe triplicata* (Willem.) Ames, *Calanthe* x *dominyi* Lindl., *Ainsliaea macroclinidioides* Hayata var. *okinawensis* (Hayata) Kitam., and *Asarum tokarense* (TERADA 1997).

The *Castanopsis* forests established on heights of over 300 m a.s.l. in Kuchino-shima include notable species such as *Asarum tokarense*, *Empusa formosana* (Rchb.f.) T.C.Hsu, and *Pilea aquarum* Dunn subsp. *brevicornuta* (Hayata) C.J.Chen. The common species of the *Machilus* forest include *Ardisia sieboldii*, *Machilus thunbergii*, *Schefflera heptaphylla*, etc. (TERADA 1999b). If these secondary forest elements are included, the above mentioned *Castanopsis* forest is considered to correspond to the phytosociological association

Fig. 7. *Machilus* forest on Taira-jima Island.

Tarenno-Castanopsietum sieboldii Miyawaki *et al.* 1974, which is a secondary forest of the *Castanopsis* forest on the Ryukyu Islands (TERADA 1997, 1999b). The average number of species of association Tarenno-Castanopsietum sieboldii in Kuchino-shima obtained from the vegetation survey data is 57.8 ± 7.8, and D is 22.7 ± 3.9, which is the largest value of D on the Tokara Islands (Table 3, Fig. 6). This can be attributed to the mix of secondary forest elements.

On Akuseki-jima Island, secondary *Castanopsis* forest belonging to the association Tarenno-Castanopsietum sieboldii is developed on the cliffs and on Mt. Megamiyama, which is a sacred area (TERADA and OHYA 2008). The dominant species of this forest stand in the tree and sub-tree layer are *Castanopsis sieboldii*, *Ardisia sieboldii*, *Machilus thunbergii*, and *Schefflera heptaphylla*, and the dominant species in the shrub layer are *Hydrangea kawagoeana* var. *kawagoeana*, *Tarenna kotoensis* (Hayata) Kaneh. et Sasaki var. *gyokushinkwa* (Ohwi) Masam., *Gardenia jasminoides* Ellis, *Camellia japonica* L., *Maesa perlaria* (Lour.) Merr. var. *formosana* (Mez) Yuen P.Yang, etc.. In the herbaceous layer, species such as *Arachniodes sporadosora* (Kunze) Nakaike, *Ctenitis subglandulosa* (Hance) Ching, *Damnacanthus indicus* Gaertn. f. var. *intermedius* Matsum., and *Alpinia intermedia* Gagnep. are present (TERADA and OHYA 2008). The plant coverage varies widely in Akuseki-jima, but on average it is slightly higher on Akuseki-jima (36.3 ± 28.1%) than on Amami-Oshima Island (Table 3).

4.2. Machilus forest

Many secondary forests are established on the Tokara Islands as a consequence of human influence. In some islands, large areas of *Castanopsis* forests are developed, but *Machilus* forests are more common evergreen broad-leaved forests on the Tokara Islands (Fig. 7). The average community height of *Machilus* forestsis lower than that of the *Castanopsis* forests and the species richness (Gleason D) tends to be smaller as well, except on Nakano-shima (Table 3). On Kuchino-shima Island, evergreen broad-leaved forests are developed in the southern part of Mt. Maedake and on the southern half of the island from Mt. Yokodake. These forests are considered to belong to the association Arisaemato ringentis–Perseetum thunbergii Miyawaki *et al.* 1971 (TERADA 1999b), and are composed of woody plants, including *Cinnamomum yabunikkei* H.Ohba, *Morus australis* Poir., and *Litsea japonica* (Thunb.) Juss., and herbaceous plants, including *Ctenitis subglandulosa*, *Ophiopogon jaburan* (Siebold) G.Lodd., *Microlepia strigosa* (Thunb.) C.Presl, *Piper kadsura* (Choisy) Ohwi, *Leptochilus neopothifolius* Nakaike, and *Arisaema ringens* (Thunb.) Schott.

In Nakano-shima, along the valley below 100 m a.s.l., a small area of Machilus forest is developed, creating a community that includes many tree species, such as *Ardisia sieboldii, Ficus microcarpa, Ficus virgata* Reinw. ex Blume, and *Ficus superba* (Miq.) Miq. var. *japonica* Miq. (OHNO 1989, 1991). These species are found in secondary forests in proximity to villages. We often can see large trees such as *Ficus microcarpa* and *Ficus superba* var. *japonica* in such forests. The large *Ficus microcarpa* trees create a unique landscape which can be observed in the *Machilus* forest on the Taira-jima Island (association Arisaemato ringentis–Perseetum thunbergii, which is a secondary forest) (TERADA and TACHIKUI 2017) (Fig. 8). The forest which can be seen on Kotakara-jima probably belongs to the association Arisaemato ringentis–Perseetum. In this forest, *Ficus microcarpa* trees predominate, along with *Machilus thunbergii, Ficus virgata*, and *Ardisia sieboldii*. On Kuchino-shima Island, the *Ficus superba* var. *japonica–Ficus microcarpa* community was also confirmed, and this community corresponds to the association Arisaemato ringentis–Perseetum thunbergii (TERADA 1999b).

The low-lying forest vegetation of Akuseki-jima Island corresponds to the *Ficus superba* var. *japonica–Machilus thunbergii* community, including the species *Crateva formosensis* (Jacobs) B.S.Sun, *Morus australis, Leptochilus neopothifolius, Oplismenus compositus* (L.) P.Beauv., *Polystichum lepidocaulon* (Hook.) J.Sm., *Cyrtomium falcatum* (L.f.) C.Presl, etc., and characteristic species *Pisonia umbellifera* (J.R. et

Fig. 8. A large stand of *Ficus microcarpa* in an evergreen broad-leaved forest on Taira-jima Island.

G.Forst.) Seem., *Beilschmiedia erythrophloia*, etc. (TERADA and OHYA 2008).

On Mt. Imakiradake (291.9 m a.s.l.), the highest peak on Takara-jima Island, the community *Pleioblastus linearis* is developed at the mountain tops and ridges that stretch from the southeastern to the northwestern part of the island, and *Machilus thunbergii–Ardisia sieboldii* community is established at the foothills of the mountain (TERADA 2000). A small area where *Castanopsis sieboldii* predominates belongs to the community *Machilus thunbergii* in terms of species composition.

According to OHNO (1989), the forests of the Gaja-jima Island which is currently uninhabited, include *Machilus thunbergii* forests, *Castanopsis sieboldii* forests, and *Livistona chinensis* communities. Some ferns, such as *Angiopteris lygodiifolia.*, *Cyathea spinulosa* Wall. ex Hook., and *Ctenitis subglandulosa* can be found in the wetlands along the small valley. Near the summit of Mt. Mitake on Gaja-jima Island, the species *Quercus glauca* Thunb., *Ligustrum japonicum* Thunb., *Eurya japonica* Thunb. var. *japonica*, *Hydrangea chinensis* Maxim., *Arachniodes exilis* (Hance) Ching, *Conandron ramondioides* Siebold et Zucc., *Lemmaphyllum microphyllum* C.Presl, and *Selaginella involvens* (Sw.) Spring can be found growing on rocky habitats. Kogaja-jima Island is an even smaller uninhabited island with steep cliffs dominated by forest communities including *Machilus thunbergii* and *Ardisia sieboldii*, coastal windswept shrub forests mainly consisting of *Cinnamomum daphnoides*, *Rhaphiolepis indica* (L.) Lindl. var. *umbellata* (Thunb.) H.Ohashi, and *Euryaemarginata* (Thunb.) Makino, and a *Livistona chinensis* community. On Yokoate-jima Island, forests vegetation includes the *Ficus microcarpa* community, *Machilus thunbergii* community, *Ardisia sieboldii* community, *Livistona chinensis* community, and *Pinus luchuensis* community with a lower tree form (OHNO 1989, 1991).

4.3. Deciduous broad-leaved forests

The deciduous broad-leaved forests distributed on the Tokara Islands are mostly pioneer communities which consists of tree of sun plant. In Nakano-shima, several broad-leaved communities are present: *Ardisia sieboldii–Styrax japonicus*, *Idesia polycarpa* Maxim., *Alnus firma* Siebold et Zucc., *Litseacubeba–Mallotusjaponicus* (L.f.) Müll. Arg., and *Hydrangea kawagoeana* var. *kawagoeana*. Along with these communities, deciduous pioneer trees, such as *Zanthoxylum ailanthoides* Siebold et Zucc., *Trema orientalis* (L.) Blume, *Aralia elata* (Miq.) Seem., *Rhus javanica* L. var. *chinensis*

Fig. 9. Large *Cerasus jamasakura* var. *chikusiensis* tree on Suwanose-jima.

(Mill.) T.Yamaz., *Callicarpa japonica* Thunb. var. *luxurians* Rehder, and *Clerodendrum trichotomum* Thunb. var. *fargesii* (Dode) Rehder were recorded on the Tokara Islands (Terada 1997). Suwanose-jima Island is the southern border of the community of *Alnus firma* and the *Rhododendron eriocarpum* community are developed around a high-altitude volcano. The natural habitat of *Cerasus jamasakura* (Siebold ex Koidz.) H.Ohba var. *chikusiensis* (Koidz.) H.Ohba is near Nabetao Hill (Fig. 9). *Rhododendron eriocarpum* and *Alnus firma* communities on Suwanose-jima and Nakano-shima are the dominant communities of volcanic habitats, which will be described later.

On Akuseki-jima Island, the community *Clerodendrum trichotomum* var. *fargesii–Trema orientalis* was reported. Its main constituent species are pioneer deciduous trees (*Mallotus japonicus*, *Zanthoxylum ailanthoides*, *Morus australis*, *Litsea cubeba* (Lour.) Pers., *Rhus javanica* var. *chinensis*, *Callicarpa japonica* var. *luxurians*, *Clerodendrum trichotomum* var. *fargesii*, etc.), *Rubus* species (*Rubus okinawensis* Koidz., *Rubus grayanus* Maxim., *Rubus sieboldii* Blume, *Rubus ribisoideus* Matsum.), *Thelypteris acuminata* (Houtt.) C.V.Morton, and *Miscanthus condensatus* Hack. On Suwanose-jima Island, pioneer communities with *Clerodendrum trichotomum* Thunb. var. *esculentum* Makino can often be found near villages.

4.4. Coniferous forests

The dominant tree species of the coniferous forests on the Tokara Islands are *Pinus luchuensis* and *Pinus thunbergii*. The northern limits of natural distribution of *Pinus luchuensis* are considered to be the islands of Takara-jima and Kodakara-jima. *Pinus luchuensis* was confirmed on Nakano-shima (KAWAGOE 1916) and Akuseki-jima (TERADA and OHYA 2008), but according to SHIUCHI and HOTTA (2015), these records are plantations or individuals that have escaped from plantations. The southern limit of natural distribution of *Pinus thunbergii* is the Akuseki-jima Island, and the populations of *P. thunbergii* in the islands of Taira-jima, Gaja-jima, Suwanose-jima, Kodakara-jima, and Takara-jima are considered to be as a

Fig. 10 *Livistona chinensis* communities on Takara-jima Island.

Fig. 11. Volcanic vegetation on Suwanose-jima Island.

unnatural population formed by invaded trees that consequence of afforestation (Ohno 1989, 1991, SHIUCHI and HOTTA 2015). Plantation trees except pine are cedar (*Cryptomeria japonica*) and cypress (*Chamaecyparis obtusa*). these are all brought in from outside the island and have no natural distribution in Tokara Islands.

4.5. Palm communities

The dominant species of palm communities on the Tokara Islands is *Livistona chinensis*, and developed this palm communities can be found on the islands of Takara-jima, Akuseki-jima, and Nakano-shima (Fig. 10). The *Livistona chinensis* communities on Kuchino-shima are scattered all over Mt. Seiriidake and other areas, whereas the *Livistona chinensis* communities on Gaja-jima Island are established on steep slopes. From the viewpoint of species composition of this community, these stands are not different from evergreen broad-leaved forests mainly composed of *Machilus thunbergii* (OHNO 1989, 1991).

According to vegetation survey reports on Kuchino-shima and Nakano-shima (TERADA 1997, 1999b), the *Livistona* forest has many species that are common to *Ardisia sieboldii–Machilus thunbergii* community or to the *Arisaemato ringentis–Perseetum thunbergii* association. It is considered that this community is a one type of this association with a high degree of dominance of the *Livistona*. The number of species that appear in this *Livistona* forest is less than 30, except for one

stand on Suwanose-jima Island, and Gleason's D is often around 10. The structure of this community tends to be simple (Table 3, Fig. 6).

5. Volcanic vegetation

The highest peak of the Tokara Islands, i.e., Mt. Otake (979 m) on Nakano-shima, and Mt. Otake (796 m) on Suwanose-jima are active volcanoes with spectacular volcanic vegetation inhabiting their slopes (Fig. 11). The main element of the volcanic vegetation on the Tokara Islands is the Rhododendron eriocarpum community which is established from the middle to the upper slope of the volcano Suwanose-jima and Nakano-shima Islands (Fig. 12).

On Suwanose-jima Island, around 350 m a.s.l., the *Alnus firma* community is developed with trees about 6 m tall (Fig. 2). This is a shrub community whose tree height decreases as the altitude increases to about 400 m (OHNO 1989). The *Rhododendron eriocarpum* forest is developed from 450 to 650 m a.s.l., and it is accompanied by a population of *Miscanthus condensatus* and *Fallopia japonica* (Houtt.) Ronse Decr. var. *japonica*. Around the crater, *Rhododendron eriocarpum* disappears, and the community shifts to a community consisting only of *Miscanthus condensatus* and *Fallopia japonica* var. *japonica*. The crater wall at the top of the mountain is bare land as a consequence of the eruption of smoke. As lava accumulates on both east and west side of the volcano, plants do not inhabit this habitat and it is also bare land.

109

On Nakano-shima, the *Rhododendron eriocarpum* community is established above 800 m a.s.l., whereas on the steep slopes where the gravel flows, low-density *Rhododendron eriocarpum* grows (Fig. 2). Accompanying species include *Rhododendron tashiroi* var. *lasiophyllum*, *Miscanthus condensatus*, *Lycopodiella cernua* (L.) Pic.Serm., *Drosera spatulata* Labill., *Odontosoria biflora* (Kaulf.) C.Chr., etc. (TERADA 1997). The inside of the crater is natural bare land. Although this is not shown in the vegetation map in Fig. 2, a small *Rhododendron eriocarpum* community is also developed on the cliffs at 100 m a.s.l. on Akuseki-jima Island.

6. Bamboo forest (*Pleioblastus linearis* community)

As can be seen from the vegetation map (Fig. 2), large areas of bamboo forests are developed on all islands except Kaminone-jima and Yokoate-jima (Table 2). *Pleioblastus linearis* community occupies the northern half of Kuchino-shima (Fig. 13), southern half of Nakano-shima, middle part of Mt. Mitake, most of the Akuseki-jima Islands

except for the mountain regions, and most part of the middle slope on the southwest side and around the settlement on Gaja-jima Island (Fig. 2). This indicated that the *Pleioblastus linearis* community is distributed in wide range habitat, from the plains to the cliffs, from the coastal to the mountainous areas, and this community is an important factor in the vegetation landscape of the Tokara Islands.

Natural habitats of *Pleioblastus linearis* are coastal windswept steep slopes. However, most Pleioblastus communities in the Nansei Islands, including the Tokara region, are established as secondary vegetation affected by human use. The development of the *Pleioblastus* community in Tokara is thought to be a consequence of extreme forest interference by humans, i.e., the former slash-and-burn agricultural practices in this area (OHNO 1989, 1991, TERADA and OHYA 2008).

7. Coastal vegetation
7.1. Coastal shrub forests

Unlike the Amami Islands, the Tokara Islands are characterized by volcanic topography. Along the coastline, the volcanic rocks and sediment often form cliffs eroded by the sea waves. For this reason, there is not a lot of sand dune vegetation and uplifted reef vegetation, and the shrub forests established on the steep coastal slopes or cliffs is representative of the coastal windswept vegetation on the Tokara Islands. Relatively large area coastal shrubs can be found on the islands of Suwanose-jima and Takara-jima (Fig. 2). As the areas where

Fig. 12. *Rhododendron eriocarpum* forming the volcanic vegetation of the Tokara Islands.

Fig. 13. *Pleioblastus linearis* community on the northern part of Kuchino-shima.

Fig. 14. A windswept shrub forest dominated by *Cinnamomum daphnoides* on Takara-jima Island.

people can enter Suwanose-jima are limited, there is currently not much available information on the vegetation of this area. However, according to reports on the vegetation of this area by OHNO (1991, 1989), a shrub forest with tree height of about 2-3 m is developed on the upper edges of the coastal cliffs of Suwanose-jima Island, predominantly consisting of *Cinnamomum daphnoides* mixed with *Eurya emarginata*, *Pittosporum tobira* (Thunb.) W.T.Aiton, *Litsea japonica* (Thunb.) Juss., *Daphniphyllum teijsmannii* Zoll. ex Kurz, and other species.

On the islands of Takara-jima, Akuseki-jima, and Nakano-shima, shrub communities consisting of tree species *Cinnamomum daphnoides*, *Litsea japonica*, *Rhaphiolepis indica* var. *umbellata*, *Pittosporum tobira*, *Eurya emarginata*, *Elaeagnus macrophylla* Thunb., etc., and herbaceous species *Crepidiastrum lanceolatum* (Houtt.) Nakai, *Farfugium japonicum* (L.) Kitam., *Carex wahuensis* C.A.Mey. var. *bongardii* (Boott) Franch. et Sav., *Cyrtomium falcatum* etc. are established (Fig. 14). These communities are equivalent to the associations Cyrtomio-Litseetum japonicae Sumata, Mashiba et Suz.-Tok. 1969 and Crepidiastro-Cinnamometum daphnoidis H. Nakanishi et H. Suz (TERADA 1997, TERADA and OHYA 2008, TARADA and OOYA 2012). In the windswept coastal shrub forests in Nakano-shima, the parasitic plant species *Balanophora tobiracola* Makino is present and an endemic species *Ligustrum japonicum*

var. *spathulatum* is present in this community on the Takara-jima Island (TARADA and OOYA 2012). A similar community is developed on wind-exposed cliffs, such as coastal cliffs and steep slopes on Taira-jima, but on small areas. On the Kodakara Island, the *Ficus pumila* L. community, Volkameria inermis L. community, *Cycas revoluta* Thunb. community, *Chrysanthemum ornatum* var. *tokarense–Crepidiastrum lanceolatum* community, and *Ischaemum aureum* (Hook. et Arn.) Hack. community were reported as windswept vegetation types.

Ton the windswept steep slopes on the coast of the Kuchino-shima Island, similar shrub forests are developed. An endemic lily species, *Lilium nobilissimum*, inhabits these slopes and it is restricted to the island of Kuchino-shima. *Lilium nobilissimum* is classified as Data Deficient (DD) in the Kago-shima Prefecture (Kagoshima Prefecture Environment and Forestry Affairs Department Nature Conservation Division 2016), and as Threatened IA (Critically Endangered; CR) in the Japanese Red List of 2019 (Japanese Ministry of the Environment; https://ikilog.biodic. go.jp/Rdb/booklist, accessed October 2019). In the Edo period, feudal lord of the Satsuma Domain dedicated *Lilium nobilissimum* as an item presented to the generals of Japan "Shogun" (HAYASHI 2014). The natural habitat of this lily was protected because it was kept secret under the policy of the Satsuma Domain in the Edo period. Under the occupation after WW2, the number of bulbs of this lily was drastically reduced as a consequence of smuggling to the Western countries. Although this species has not been confirmed in the wild for the past ten years, HAYASHI (2014) confirmed its presence in the wild.

7.2. Rock wall vegetation

Adjacent to the windswept shrub communities, perennial herb communities are developed on the seaside rocky terrain. As there are many steep shores and cliffs on the Tokara Islands, rocky vegetation can also be considered to be very important in the vegetation landscape of the Tokara Islands.

In the Japanese archipelago, one of the

main taxa that grow in the rocky coasts is a species of *Chrysanthemum*. In the report on the vegetation of the Tokara Islands, it was reported that *Chrysanthemum crassumgrows* in these coasts, but Sʜɪᴜcʜɪ and Hᴏᴛᴛᴀ (2015) reported the species *Chrysanthemum ornatum* var. *tokarense* to be growing on the Tokara Islands. In addition, the dominant species that grow naturally in the coastal rock walls are *Peucedanum japonicum* Thunb. (now classified as *Peucedanum japonicum* var. *latifolium*, Hotta and Shiuchi 1996), *Crepidiastrum lanceolatum*, *Zoysia pacifica* (Goudswaard) M.Hotta et Kuroki, *Carex wahuensis* var. *bongardii*, *Lysimachia mauritiana* Lam., *Lreptopetalum strigulosum* (DC.) Neupane et N.Wikstr. var. *parvifolium* (Hook. et Arn.) T.C.Hsu, *Limonium wrightii* (Hance) Kuntze var. *arbusculum* (Maxim.) H.Hara, *Euphorbia jolkinii* Boiss., etc. (Oʜɴᴏ 1989).

7.3. Sand dune vegetation and uplifted coral reef vegetation

As described above, there is not a lot of vegetation of the sand dunes and uplifted coral reefs on the Tokara Islands, and the range of this vegetation is smaller than that in the islands of Kikai-jima and Okinoerabu-jima (Amami Islands) . However, the islands of Kuchino-shima and Nakano-shima are the northern limits of the distribution of *Pandanus* communities (Oʜɴᴏ 1989, Tᴇʀᴀᴅᴀ 1999b), and different types of communities are reported from the small areas of coastal sand dunes.

Relatively large sandy beach vegetation is developed on the islands of Kuchino-shima, Kodakara-jima and Takara-jima (Figs. 2 and 15). On Kuchino-shima, the association of *Vigna marina* (Burm.) Merr. and *Ipomoea pes-caprae* (L.) Sweet (belonging to the association Vigno-Ipomoeetum pedis-caprae Miyawaki et K. Suzuki 1976, which consist almost only of *Ipomoea pes-caprae*) and the communities *Euphorbia jolkinii* and *Pandanus odoratissimus* L.f. are reported (Terada 1999b). On Kodakara-jima, the community *Pandanus odoratissimus* and the association of *Heliotropium arboreum* (Blanco) Mabb. and *Scaevola taccada* (Gaertn.) Roxb. (belonging to the association Messerschmidio-Scaevoletum taccadae Miyawaki *et* K. Suzuki 1976) were reported in the coastal forests, and *Vitex rotundifolia* L.f., *Cassytha filiformis* L. and *Indigofera trifoliata* L. communities were reported in the sand dune vegetation (Terada 1995). Additionally, *Wedelia biflora* (L.) DC community and *Wollastonia dentata* (H.Lév. et Vaniot) Orchard–*Panicum repens* L. community were reported in Nakano-shima (Tᴇʀᴀᴅᴀ 1997).

Regarding the uplifted coral reef vegetation, the association of *Lreptopetalum strigulosum* var. *parvifolium* and *Zoysia pacifica* (association Hedyotido-Zoysietum tenuifoliae Miyawaki 1967), association of *Artemisia chinensis* L. and *Limonium wrightii* var. *arbusculum* (association Limonio wrightii-Crossostephietum Miyawaki *et* K. Suzuki 1976), and association of *Blutaparon*

Fig. 15. Coastal vegetation of Takara-jima Island.

Fig. 16. The uplifted coral reef vegetation on Takara-jima Island.

wrightii (Hook.f. ex Maxim.) Mears (association Philoxeretum wrightii Miyawaki *et* K. Suzuki 1976) are developed on the Kodakara Island (TERADA 1995). On inland habitats, a community of uplifted coral reef which includes species such as *Juniperus taxifolia* Hook. et Arn. var. *lutchuensis* (Koidz.) Satake, *Osteomeles anthyllidifolia* (Sm.) Lindl., *Lotus taitungensis* S.S.Ying and *Peucedanum japonicum* var. *latifolium* is developed (OHNO 1989).

Takara-jima Island has a flat coastal terrace topography which develops around the mountains, and a wide sand dune is developed in the northeastern part of the island. The island is surrounded by uplifted coral reefs (Fig. 16). On this island, reef and dune vegetation is developed on the largest scale of all the Tokara Islands. Various coastal herbaceous and shrub communities are established here, and some notable communities, such as the uplifted reef vegetation consisting of *Osteomeles anthyllidifolia* and *Limonium wrightii* var. *arbusculum*, as well as communities such as *Spinifex littoreus* (Burm.f.) Merr. and *Dodonaea viscosa* Jacq. are developed (OHNO 1989). In the hinterland of the sand dune vegetation, the communities of *Pandanus odoratissimus* and *Hibiscus tiliaceus* L. are developed.

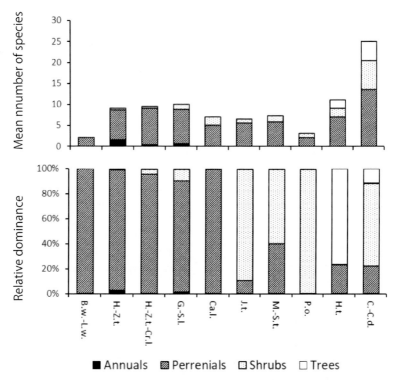

Fig. 17. Life form spectra of the coastal vegetation on the Takara-jima Island. Data sets were based on vegetation survey data by TERADA and OOYA (2012). Relative dominance values were calculated as the sum of relative coverage of each species in each community. Abbreviations of community types are as follows; B.w.-L.w: *Blutaparon wrightii*–*Limonium wrightii* var. *arbusculum* community, H.-Z.t.: A typical sub-association of Hedyotido-Zoysietum tenuifoliae (an association of *Lreptopetalum strigulosum* var. *parvifolium* and *Zoysia pacifica*), H.-Z.t.-Cr.l.: *Crepidiastrum lanceolatum* sub-association of Hedyotido–Zoysietum tenuifoliae (an association of *Lreptopetalum strigulosum* var. *parvifolium* and *Zoysia pacifica*), G.-S.l.: Glehnio–Spinificetum littorei Ohba, Miyawaki et Tx. 1973 (grassland community of *Glehnia littoralis* F.Schmidt ex Miq. and *Spinifex littoreus*), Ca.l.: *Canavalia lineata* community, J.t.: *Juniperus taxifolia* var. *lutchuensis* community, M.-S.t.: Messerschmidio–Scaevoletum taccadae (association of *Heliotropium arboreum* and *Scaevola taccada*), P.o.: *Pandanus odoratissimus* community, H.t.: *Hibiscus tiliaceus* community, C.-C.d.: Crepidiastro–Cinnamometum daphnoidis.

7.4. Ecological character of coastal vegetation

In Figs. 17 and 18, the plant communities that make up the coastal vegetation of Takara-jima Island from the coast side to the inland side are compared in terms of life forms and growth forms (data are based on vegetation survey data by TERADA and OOYA 2012). In Figs. 17 and 18, mean number of species and relative dominance of coastal plant communities are shown. The two sub-association (A typical sub-association (H.-Z.t.) and a *Crepidiastrum lanceolatum* sub-association (H.-Z.t.-Cr.l.)) of Hedyotido–Zoysietum tenuifoliae (an association of *Lreptopetalum strigulosum* var. *parvifolium* and *Zoysia pacifica*) are developed on the uplifted coral reefs, and Glehnio-Spinificetum littorei Ohba, Miyawaki et Tx. 1973 (G.-S.l.: grassland community of *Glehnia littoralis* F.Schmidt ex Miq. and *Spinifex littoreus*), *Canavalia lineata* community (Ca.l.), and *Juniperus taxifolia* var. *lutchuensis* community (J.t.) are developed on the sand dunes composed of coral sand behind the uplifted coral reefs. In addition,

in the habitats on the inland side, a tropical coastal forest Messerschmidio-Scaevoletum taccadae (M.-S.t.: association of *Heliotropium arboreum* and *Scaevola taccada*), *Pandanus odoratissimus* community (P.o.), and *Hibiscus tiliaceus* community (H.t.) are developed, and the Crepidiastro-Cinnamometum daphnoidis (C.-C.d.) which is a windswept shrub forest developed on the coastal slopes. Although coastal vegetation on the Takara-jima Island forms a complex mosaic pattern of the above mentioned communities distributed in patches, from a broader perspective, the community is changed from the coastline to the inland side as above mentioned, and form a band structure.

There are only two species in the *Blutaparon wrightii* and *Limonium wrightii* var. *arbusculum* communities of the uplifted reef vegetation. The other communities comprise about five to ten species, and the association Crepidiastro–Cinnamometum daphnoidis in the coastal

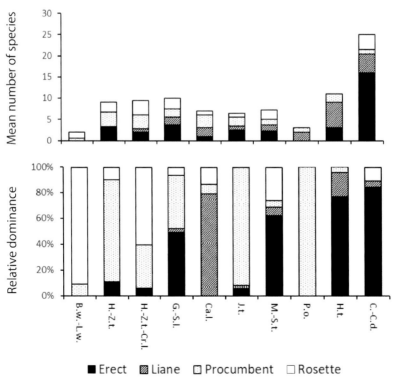

Fig. 18. Growth form spectra of the coast vegetation on the Takara-jima Island. See Fig. 17 for explanation of this analysis and abbreviations of community type.

windswept forests has the largest number of species (Figs. 17 and 18). Uplifted reef vegetation and dune vegetation mostly comprise perennial herbs, and annual plants are only rarely found in the Hedyotido-Zoysietum tenuifoliae and the Glehnio-Spinificetum littorei associations. There are many species of rosette growth form in the *Blutaparon wrightii* and *Limonium wrightii* var. *arbusculum* community located near the sea (Fig. 18). Although the communities A typical sub-association (H.-Zt) and *Crepidiastrum lanceolatum* sub-association (H.-Zt-Cr.l) of Hedyotido-Zoysietum tenuifoliae comprise plants of all growth forms, their relative dominances differ greatly among different community types. The plants of the A typical sub-association (H.-Zt) community are predominantly lianas and the plants of the *Crepidiastrum lanceolatum* sub-association (H.-Zt-Cr.l) community are predominantly rosette plants. The community dominated by lianas is the *Canavalia lineata* community (Ca.l.).

On the other hand, only one or two shrub species appear from the sand dune communities to tropical shrub forests. In terms of proportion of number of species, perennials are larger than shrubs, but the relative dominance of shrubs showed large value remarkably in communities located on the inlandside of the sand dunes. In particular, in the *Juniperus taxifolia* var. *lutchuensis* community (J.t.) and the *Hibiscus tiliaceus* community (H.t.), procumbent shrubs are greatly dominant, but with only one or two species. The high relative dominance of shrubs is also characteristic for the association Crepidiastro–Cinnamometum daphnoidis (C.-C.d.) in the windswept shrub forests. However, this association differs greatly from the dune shrub communities by the number of its constituent species. The dense windswept shrub forests, are comprised of multiple species, whereas the coastal dune forest are comprised only one or two shrub species (e.g. M.-S.t. and P.o.).

8. Marsh vegetation

There are no large freshwater lakes on the Tokara Islands, and wetland environments are scarce because large rivers are not developed on the islands (OHNO 1989). Wetland vegetation is developed only in small swamps and paddy fields on the islands of Nakano-shima and Akuseki-jima. A relatively large amount of marsh vegetation can be seen in the Sokonashi-ike pond in the northeastern part of the central plateau on the Nakano-shima Island. In this area, TERADA (1997) reported the presence of the *Trapa japonica* Flerow community, *Schoenoplectiella triangulata* (Roxb.) J.D.Jung et H.K.Choi community, *Cyperus malaccensis* Lam. subsp. *monophyllus* (Vahl) T.Koyama community, *Persicaria muricata* (Meisn.) Nemoto–*Philydrum lanuginosum* Banks et Sol. ex Gaertn. community, *Ischaemum aristatum* L. var. *aristatum* community, *Isachne globosa* (Thunb.) Kuntze community, *Phragmites karka* (Retz.) Trin. ex Steud. community, *Scirpus ternatanus* Reinw. ex Miq. community, *Lobelia chinensis* Lour. community, and *Fimbristylis subbispicata* Nees et Meyen community. According to OHNO (1989), communities with dominant species such as *Potamogeton distinctus* A.Benn. and *Cladium jamaicense* Crantz are also developed here. In addition, the wetland forests along the Sokonashi-ike pond are composed of *Glochidion zeylanicum* var *zeylanicum, Rhaphiolepis indica* var. *umbellata, Pittosporum tobira, Carex alopecuroides* D.Don ex Tilloch et Taylor var. *chlorostachya* C.B.Clarke, *Thelypteris interrupta* (Willd.) K.Iwats., *Persicaria sagittata* (L.) H.Gross var. *sibirica* (Meisn.) Miyabe, and other species. This area is also the northern limit of ash forests (*Fraxinus insularis* Hemsl.) which are indigenous to this area (OHNO 1989, TERADA 1997).

On the Akuseki-jima Island, wetland communities with species such as *Cyperus malaccensis* subsp. *monophyllus, Eleocharis dulcis* (Burm.f.) Trin. ex Hensch., *Schoenoplectus tabernaemontani* (C.C.Gmel.) Palla, and *Cladium jamaicense* are established in coastal wetlands and inland ponds (TERADA and OHYA 2008). There are almost no swamp communities on the other islands, but the community *Isachne globosa–Panicum repens* is developed on abandoned paddy fields on the Kodakara-jima Island. In addition, the presence of wetland plants such as *Ludwigia octovalvis* (Jacq.) P.H.Raven, *Commelina diffusa* Burm.f., *Alternanthera sessilis* (L.) R.Br. ex

115

DC., *Schoenoplectiella juncoides* (Roxb.) Lye, *Phragmites karka*, and *Typha domingensis* Pers. was confirmed (TERADA 1995). On Kuchino-shima, communities with species such as *Thelypteris interrupta*, *Isachne globosa*, *Ischaemum aristatum* var. *aristatum*, *Sphagneticola calendulacea* (L.) Pruski, and *Scirpus ternatanus* are established on abandoned paddy fields.

9. Riparian vegetation

Large rivers are not present on the Tokara Islands, but small riparian environments are present on some islands. In Nakano-shima, which is a relatively large island, vegetation is not very developed around the Okawa River on the east side and Miyagawa River on the west side of the island (OHNO 1989). On the Akuseki-jima Island, *Pilea aquarum* subsp. *brevicornuta* community was confirmed in a small stream near the water source west of Mitake. On the Suwanose-jima Island, a riparian vegetation along mountain stream did not develop. Nevertheless, endangered species, including *Hydrangea involucrata* var. *tokarensis* and *Blechnum hancockii* Hance are distributed along a narrow valley at the mountain slope in Suwanose-jima. Such small streams are important habitats for the growth of plants which inhabit humid habitats and which could not inhabit dry environments, such as on the slopes of volcano in Suwanose-jima.

10. Grasslands

On the Tokara Islands, we can find different types of grasslands, including those related to volcanoes, such as the *Miscanthus condensatus* community and the *Fallopia japonica* var. *japonica* community, windswept meadows, pastures, and secondary grasslands around villages. These grasslands are interesting because of their diverse origins and species composition, including the invasion of many exotic plants.

11. Characteristics of the vegetation of the Tokara Islands and the effects of alien species on natural flora

Because of the diversity of habitats, the flora of the Tokara Islands changes greatly, and an interesting distribution pattern of plants can be seen in these islands. Although their areas are small, each island has a unique vegetation landscape with many endemic species. The vegetation closely related to the volcanic habitats is represented by the *Rhododendron eriocarpum* community, windswept shrub forests, and uplifted reef vegetation formed along the coast.

In addition, on these islands we can find forests with many endemic species and epiphytic orchids, as well as with biogeographically interesting communities, such as *Quercus phillyreoides* forests, even though the forest vegetation includes many secondary forests. The Tokara Islands are inhabited by native endemic plants and many species whose northern and southern limits are on these islands, meaning these among the Nansei Islands, these islands are extremely important in maintaining high species diversity of plants.

In recent years, concerns have grown over the damage of feral goats to the vegetation of the Tokara Islands. Feral goats are listed as one of the 100 of the World's Worst Invasive Alien Species (IUCN 2000, LOWE *et al.* 2000) and one of the 100 of the Japan's Worst Invasive Alien Species (The Ecological Society of Japan 2002). In Japan, the number of feral goats increased drastically in recent years, which could be problematic because of their impact on the vegetation of the islets such as the islands of Ogasawara (SHIMIZU 1993, TOMIYAMA 1998), Senkaku (YOKOHATA and YOKOTA 2000), and Amami-Oshima (NAKANISHI 2017). In the islands of Akuseki-jima and Gaja-jima on Tokara, the influence of feral goats is increasing while the vegetation is declining.

In addition, Table 1 shows the number of alien plants species on the Tokara Islands, but a greater number of alien plants was confirmed by results of a survey of flora. For example, 30 naturalized plants and 57 cultivated plants were confirmed on Taira-jima (TERADA and TACHIKUI 2017). It is expected that the number of alien species is actually larger than the number of alien species recorded from specimen materials. In the future, it will be important to investigate the flora of this area and collect specimens in order to investigate the share of alien and native species. Although many problems concerning alien species were not mentioned here, these plants are the main obstacles in conserving the natural world of the Tokara Islands.

References

AIBA, S. 2017. Vegetation Zones and Biogeography of Conifer Dominance in the Humid Regions of the Western Pacific. Japanese Journal of Ecology, 67: 313–321. (in Japanese and English abstract)

AIBA, S. 2018. *Amami-Oshima to Tokuno-shima no Santi Shouyou Jyurin* (Mountain Lucidophyllous Forest in Amami-Oshima Island and Tokunoshima Island). In: Kagoshima University Biodiversity Research Group (eds.), Wild Plants and Cultivate plants in Amami Islands, pp. 35–59, Nanpo-shinsha, Kagoshima. (in Japanese)

The Ecological Society of Japan (ed) 2002. Handbook of Alien Species in Japan. 390 pp., Chijin-shokan, Tokyo. (in Japanese)

Editorial Committee of Toshima Village Magazine Supplement 2019. *Toshima Sonshi Tsuiroku ban* (Toshima Village Magazine Supplement). 1059pp., Toshima Village, Kagoshima. (in Japanese)

FUJIWARA, K. 1981. Phytosociological Investigation of the Evergreen Broad-leaved Forests of Japan–I. Bulletin of the Institute of Environmental Science and Technology, Yokohama National University, 7: 67–133. (in Japanese with English synopsis)

GLEASON, H. A. 1922. On the Relation between Species and Area. Ecology, 3: 158–162.

HAYASHI, K. 2014. The Current Status of the Endangered Noble Lily *Lilium nobilissimum* Who is Also the Mating Parent of *Lilium* "Casa Blanca". Abstract of the 14th Annual Meeting of the Japanese Society for Plant Systematics. (in Japanese)

HAYASHI, K. and KAWANO, S. 2000. Molecular Systematics of *Lilium* and Allied Genera (Liliaceae): Phylogenetic Relationships among *Lilium* and Related Genera Based on the *rbcL* and *matK* Gene Sequence Data. Plant Species Biology, 15: 73–93.

HONDA, S. 1912. *Nihon Shinrin Shokubutsutai Ron* (Forest Plants Zones of Japan). 440 pp., Chikuma Shobo, Tokyo. (in Japanese)

HOTTA, M. and Shiuchi, T. 1996. Notes on the Flora of the Ryukyu Islands 1. Two New Varieties from the Tokara Islands, *Peucedanum japonicum* Thunb. var. *latifolium* (Umbelliferae) and *Hydrangea involucrata* Sieb. var. *tokarensis* (Hydrangeaceae). The Journal of Japanese Botany, 71: 183–187.

IUCN 2000. IUCN Guidelines for the Prevention of Biodiversity Loss due to Biological Invasion.

KADOTA, Y., SETOGUCHI, H., SOEJIMA, K., TOUMA, T., CHUGOKU, M., MORITA, T. and YONEKURA, K. 2017. Asteraceae (Compositae). In: OHASHI H., KADOTA Y., MURATA J. YONEKURA K. and KIHARA H. (eds), Wild Flowers of Japan (revised edition). vol. 5 Convolvulaceae–Caprifoliacea. pp. 198–369, Heibonsya, Tokyo. (in Japanese)

Kagoshima Prefecture Environment and Forestry Affairs Department Nature Conservation Division 2016. *Kaitei Kagoshima Ken no Zetsumetsu no osore no aru Yasei Dousyokubutsu. –Shokubutu hen–* (Red Data Book 2016 –Threatened Wildlife of Kagoshima Prefecture. Plants (revised edition)–). 499 pp., Kagoshima Prefecture. (in Japanese)

KAWAGOE, S. 1916. *Tokara Rettou Tokuni Nakano-shima oyobi Takara-jima no Shokubutsu nit suite* (Plants in the Tokara Islands, Especially Nakanoshima Island and Takarajima Island). *Kagoshima Koutou Nourin Gakkou Gakujutsu Houkoku* (Academic Reports of Kagoshima Higher School of Agriculture and Forestry), 1: 93–203. (In Japanese)

KIRA, T. 1949. *Nippon no Shinrintai* (Forest zones of Japan). 41 pp., Ringyô Gizyutu Kyôkai, Tokyo. (In Japanese)

KIRA, T. 1976. *Rikujou Seitaikei –Gairon–* (Terrestrial Ecosystems–An Introduction) (Handbook of Ecology, Vol. 2). 166 pp., Kyôritsu Shuppan, Tokyo. (in Japanese)

KOIZUMI, G. 1933. *Hutatabi Shokubutsu Kukei no Kyoukai Tokara Suidou ni tsuite* (Phytogeographical Region of Tokara Channel). Acta Phytotaxonomica et Geobotanica, 2(3): 206. (In Japanese)

KUBO, K. 2018. Plants Used for the Akusekijima Island's Masked God Boze. Research reports of Kagoshima Prefectural Museum Kagoshima, 37: 67–69. (In Japanese).

LOWE, S., BROWNE, M., BOUDJELAS, S. and DE POORTER, M. 2000. 100 of the World's Worst Invasive Alien Species–A selection from the Global Invasive Species Database–. 12 pp., The Invasive Species Specialist Group (ISSG) a specialist group of the Species Survival Commission (SSC) of the World Conservation Union (IUCN).

MAEKAWA, F. 1977. *Nippon no Shokubutsu Kukei* (Phytogeographical region of Japan). 178 pp., Tamagawa University Press. (in Japanese)

MIYAWAKI, A. (ed) 1989. Vegetation of Japan vol.10, Okinawa & Ogasawara. Shibundo co. ltd. publishers, Tokyo. (in Japanese)

MIYAWAKI, A., FUJIWARA, K., HARADA, H., KUSUNOKI, T. and OKUDA, S. 1971. Vegetationskundliche Untersuchungen in der Stadt Zushi bei Yokohama– Besondere Betrachtung mit Camellietea japonicae Wald (immergruner Laubwald) Japans. 151 pp., Zushi Educational Community, Kanagawa. (in Japanese)

MORITA, Y. 2001. The Report of the Plant Collection on Suwanosejima in the Tokara Islands, Kagoshima Prefecture. Research reports of Kagoshima Prefectural Museum Kagoshima, 20: 25–38. (in Japanese)

MORITA, Y. 2002. The Report of the Plant Collection on Nakanoshima in the Tokara Islands, Kagoshima Prefecture. Research Reports of Kagoshima Prefectural Museum Kagoshima, 21: 71–80. (in Japanese)

MORITA, Y. 2004. The Report of the Plant Collection on Kuchino-shima in the Tokara Islands, Kagoshima Prefecture. Research Reports of Kagoshima Prefectural Museum Kagoshima, 23: 55–60. (in Japanese)

MORITA, Y. 2005. The Report of the Plant Collection on

Taira-jima in Tokara Islands, Kagoshima Prefecture. Research Reports of Kagoshima Prefectural Museum Kagoshima, 24: 20–27. (in Japanese)

MORITA, Y. 2006. The Report of the Plant Collection on Kodakara-jima in the Tokara Islands, Kagoshima Prefecture. Research reports of Kagoshima Prefectural Museum Kagoshima, 25: 30–37. (in Japanese)

MORITA, Y. and MARUNO, K. 2003. The Report of the Plant Collection on Akuseki-jima in the Tokara Islands, Kagoshima Prefecture. Research reports of Kagoshima Prefectural Museum Kagoshima, 22: 88–99. (in Japanese)

NAKAMURA, K., SUWA, R., DENDA, T. and YOKOTA, M. 2009. Geohistorical and Current Environmental Influences on Floristic Differentiation in the Ryukyu Archipelago, Japan. Journal of Biogeography, 36: 919–928.

NAKANISHI, Y. 2017. *Satsunan-Shotou no Noyagi Mondai to Taisaku ni tsuite* (Problems and Countermeasure of Feral Goats in Satsunan Islands). In: Kagoshima University Biodiversity Research Group (ed), Alien species in Amami Islands, pp. 206–214, Nanpo-shinsha, Kagoshima. (in Japanese)

NOSHIRO, S. 2017. Oleaceae. In: OHASHI H., KADOTA Y., MURATA J., YONEKURA K. and KIHARA H. (eds), Wild Flowers of Japan (revised edition). vol. 5 Convolvulaceae–Caprifoliacea, pp. 59–66, Heibonsya, Tokyo. (in Japanese)

OHBA, H. 2017. Hydrangeacea. In: OHASHI H., KADOTA Y., MURATA J., YONEKURA K. and KIHARA H. (eds.), Wild Flowers of Japan (revised edition). vol. 4 Malvaceae –Apocynaceae, pp. 157–172, Heibonsya, Tokyo. (in Japanese)

OHASHI, H. 2017. Styracaceae. In: OHASHI H., KADOTA Y., MURATA J., YONEKURA K. and KIHARA H. (eds.), Wild Flowers of Japan (revised edition). vol. 4 Malvaceae –Apocynaceae, pp. 216–218, Heibonsya, Tokyo. (in Japanese)

OHNO, T. 1989. Vegetation of Tokara Islands. In: MIYAWAKI, A. (ed.), Vegetation of Japan vol.10 Okinawa & Ogasawara, pp. 507–512, Shibundo Co. Ltd. Publishers, Tokyo. (in Japanese)

OHNO, T. 1991. Vegetation of Tokara Islands. In: Kagoshima prefecture (ed.), Research Reports of Tokara Islands, 197pp., Kagoshima prefecture, Kagoshima. (in Japanese)

OONO, K. 2005. Sub-tropical Laurel Forest. In: HUKUSHIMA T. and IWASE T. (eds.), Vegetation of Japan, pp. 20–21, Asakura-Shoten, Tokyo. (In Japanese)

OOYA, S. 2011a. Record of the Plant Collection on Nakanoshima Island, Kagoshima Prefecture. Research reports of Kagoshima Prefectural Museum Kagoshima, 30: 29–32. (in Japanese)

OOYA, S. 2011b. Record of the Plant Collection on Kuchinoshima Island, Kagoshima Prefecture. Research reports of Kagoshima Prefectural Museum Kagoshima, 30: 33–36. (in Japanese)

SAITO, T., TSUKADA, K. and YAMANOUCHI, H. 1980. *Tokara Rettou –Sono Shizen to Bunka–* (Tokara Islands – the Nature and culture–). Kokon-shoin, Tokyo. (in Japanese)

SEO, A. and HOTTA, M. 2000. Taxonomical Notes on Plants of Southern Japan V. Infraspecific Variation of *Peucedanum japonicum* Thunb. (Umbelliferae) in Kyushu and Ryukyu Islands. Acta Phytotaxonomica et Geobotanica, 51(1): 99–116. (in Japanese and English abstract)

SHIMIZU, Y. 1993. Vegetation of Mukojima Island Group in the Bonin (Ogasawara) Islands with Reference to the Ecology of *Ardisia* Dominant Forest and the Influence of Feral Goats. Komazawa Geogr, 29: 9–58. (In Japanese)

SHIUCHI, T. and HOTTA, M. 2015. Flora of Tokara Islands. 367 pp., The Kagoshima University Museum. (In Japanese)

SU, H. J. 1984. Studies on the Climate and Vegetation Types of the Natural Forests in Taiwan (II) Altitudinal Vegetation Zones in Relation to Temperature Gradient. Quarterly Journal of Chinese Forestry, 17: 57–73.

SUZUKI, E. and MIYAMOTO, J. 2018. *Nansei Shotou ni okeru Toushokan no Shokubutsu Sou Hikaku* (Comparison of flora among islets in Nansei Island). In: Kagoshima University Biodiversity Research Group (ed), Wild plants and cultivate plants in Amami Islands, pp. 26–34, Nanpo-shinsha, Kagoshima. (in Japanese)

SUZUKI, K. 1979. Vegetation der Ryukyu-Inseln, Japan: Pflanzensoziologische Studien der Ryukyu-Inseln VI. Bulletin of the Institute of Environmental Science and Technology, Yokohama National University, 5: 87–159. (in Japanese)

TAMURA, M. 2015. Asparagaceae. In: OHASHI, H., KADOTA, Y., MURATA, J., YONEKURA, K. and KIHARA, H. (eds.), Wild Flowers of Japan (revised edition). vol. 1 Cycadaceae–, Cyperaceae), pp. 246–260, Heibonsya, Tokyo. (in Japanese)

TACHIKUI, A. 1991. Flora of Taira-jima, Toshima-mura, Kagoshima Prefecture. Research reports of Kagoshima Prefectural Museum Kagoshima, 10: 11–20. (in Japanese)

TACHIKUI, A. 1992. Flora of Suwanose-jima, Toshima-mura, Kagoshima Prefecture. Research Reports of Kagoshima Prefectural Museum Kagoshima, 11: 17–27. (in Japanese)

TACHIKUI, A. 1993. Flora of Akuseki-jima, Toshima-mura, Kagoshima Prefecture. Research Reports of Kagoshima Prefectural Museum Kagoshima, 12: 1–14. (in Japanese)

TERADA, J. 1995. Vegetation of Kodakara-jima and Ko-jima. Research Reports of Kagoshima Prefectural Museum Kagoshima, 14: 1–32. (in Japanese)

TERADA, J. 1997. Vegetation of Nakanoshima, Tokara Islands. Research Reports of Kagoshima Prefectural Museum Kagoshima, 16: 1–48. (in Japanese)

TERADA, J. 1999a. Effect of Alien Animal to Natural Vegetation of an Uninhabited Island. –Flora and Actual Vegetation in Gajajima Island–. Minami Nihon Bunka, 33: 59–108. (in Japanese)

TERADA, J. 1999b. Vegetation of Kuchinoshima, Kagoshima Prefecture. Research Reports of Kagoshima Prefectural Museum Kagoshima, 18: 43–78. (in Japanese)

TERADA, J. 2000. Vegetation of Takarajima in the Tokara Islands, Kagoshima Prefecture. Research Reports of Kagoshima Prefectural Museum Kagoshima, 19: 1–44. (in Japanese)

TERADA, J. and OHYA S. 2008. Akusekijima Island's Slash-and-Burn Agriculture and the Megamiyama Protected Areas: The Effects on Vegetation. Research Reports of Kagoshima Prefectural Museum Kagoshima, 27: 1–32. (in Japanese)

TERADA, J. and OOYA, S. 2012. The Forest Vegetation of Megamiyama and the Vegetation of the Upheaved coral Reefs around the East Cast of Takara-jima, Kagoshima Prefecture. Research Reports of Kagoshima Prefectural Museum Kagoshima, 31: 31–57. (in Japanese)

TERADA, J. and TACHIKUI, A. 2017. The Vegetation of Tairajima Island, Part of the Tokara Islands in Kagoshima Prefecture, Which Has the Giant Machilus thunbergi Forest in the Sacred Mountain. Research Reports of Kagoshima Prefectural Museum Kagoshima, 36: 39–71. (in Japanese)

TERADA, J., TACHIKUI, A., KAWANISHI, M. and HASEGAWA, Y. (in press) The Vegetation of Active Volcano Suwanosejima Island, Located on the Tokara Islands, in Kagoshima Prefecture. Kagoshima Prefectural Museum Kagoshima, 39. (in Japanese)

TOMIYAMA, K. 1998. Disturbance of Island Ecosystem by Introduced Species in Ogasawara Islands. Japanese Journal of Ecology, 48: 63–72. (in Japanese and English abstract)

WAKI, T. 1990. Flora of Kuchinoshima Island, Kagoshima. Research Reports of Kagoshima Prefectural Museum Kagoshima, 9: 23–29. (in Japanese)

YAMASHITA, J. and TAMURA, M. 2004. Phylogenetic Analyses and Chromosome Evolution in Convallarieae (Ruscaceae sensu lato), with some Taxonomic Treatments. Journal of Plant Research, 117: 363–370.

YANO, O., MASAKI, T., KATSUYAMA, T. and HOSHINO, T. 2010. Carex (Cyperaceae) of the Kuroshima Island in the Osumi Islands, Kagoshima Prefecture. The Journal of Japanese Cyperology, 15: 11–18. (in Japanese)

YASUMA, S. 2001. Ryukyu Islands: Species Diversity and History of Archipelago. 195 pp., Tokai University Press, Tokyo.

YOKOHATA, Y. and YOKOTA, M. 2000. The Problem of Introduced Goats on Uotsuri-Jima in the Senkaku Islands. Wildlife Conservation Japan, 5(1–2): 1–12. (in Japanese and English abstract)

YONEDA, T. 2018. *Nansei Shotou no Shinrin to Hozen* (Conservation of Forest in Nansei Island). Shinrin Kagaku, 84: 3–7. (in Japanese)

YONEKURA, K. 2012. An Enumeration of the Vascular Plants of Japan. 379 pp., Hokuryukan Co., Ltd., Tokyo. (in Japanese)

YONEKURA, K. 2015. Lauraceae. In: OHASHI, H., KADOTA , Y., MURATA , J., YONEKURA, K. and KIHARA, H. (eds.), Wild Flowers of Japan (revised edition). vol. 1 Cycadaceae –Cyperaceae, pp. 78–88, Heibonsya, Tokyo. (in Japanese)

Chapter 13
The Butterflies in the Tokara Islands

Kenichi KANAI and Taiji MORIYAMA

1. Introduction

The Tokara Islands lie between Yaku-shima Is. and Amami-Oshima Is., consisting of 7 populated islands (Kuchino-shima, Nakano-shima, Taira-jima, Suwanose-jima, Akuseki-jima, Kodakara-jima, and Takara-jima) and 5 unpopulated islands (Gajya-jima, Kogajya-jima, Ko-jima, Kaminone-jima, and Yokoate-jima). The area is administered by Toshimamura Village.

Between the Akuseki-jima and Kodakara-jima islands, the border between the Palearctic and Oriental regions, i.e. Watase line (Tokara gap), has been proposed (e.g. ANMA 2001). However, when OKADA (1927) proposed the concept of gap, he drew no clear line between the islands. Therefore, the gap would be better regarded as a transitional zone between Palearctic and Oriental subregions (NAGASHIMA 2019).

The insect fauna of this area has attracted much attention with regard to the commonality with and differences from Kagoshima Prefecture mainland and the Amami Islands. The oldest literature in record is OKAJIMA's (1928) survey. As a historical review of such studies, FUKUDA (1995) presented a comprehensive synopsis in Tokara Village Records (Toshimamura Village 1995). Thereafter, studies have been continued, and we wrote a review with some new findings in Bulletin of the Kagoshima Prefectural Museum (KANAI and MORIYAMA 2018). Here in this article, we supplement KANAI and MORIYAMA (2018) with additional new findings to present an updated and comprehensive list of butterflies found in the Tokara Islands. As to the scientific names of butterflies, we followed the Current Checklist of Japanese Butterflies (INOMATA *et al.* 2010–2013). As to the botanical taxonomy, we followed SHIUCHI and HOTTA (2015), and as to the botanical names YList (YONEKURA and KAJITA 2013–).

2. The butterflies found in the Tokara Islands

Table 1 lists the 69 butterflies recorded in the Tokara Islands. Those which are regarded resident in respective areas are marked with ○. Those difficult to determine resident or non-resident or which show great fluctuations in number by years are marked with ◎. Non-resident or temporary visitor species are marked with ●. Dubious records are marked with ? . Those only recorded in the past but not seen at present are marked with ○×.

Among these species, we comment on: (1) those of which residency (resident or temporary visitor) needs to be confirmed, (2) those showing changes in distribution or with unstable distribution, and (3) those of which taxonomical treatment could be changed in future. Note that the numbers tagged before the species names are the same as in Table 1. For any comment on species not listed in the table, * is tagged before the species name.

2.1. Species of which residency needs to be confirmed
Hesperiidae

3) *Potanthus flavus* (Murray, 1875) (Japanese Dart)

In the Tokara Islands, the first record was from Nakano-shima in 1953 (MIYAMOTO *et al.* 1954). Thereafter, 7 reports have been added, including 11 records, though no record for a while after a single case in 1989 (TANAKA 1991).

However, Moriyama confirmed its presence on Nakano-shima in August and September in 2013 (MORIYAMA and KANAI 2014), and on Kuchino-shima in August 2014, as evidence of continued residence in the area. From now on, particular topics necessary to probe into are whether the Tokara population of this species has any notable

Table 1. Distribution of the butterflies recorded in Tokara.

	Tanega-shima Is	Yaku-shima Is	Kushinoerabu-jima Is	Kuchino-shima Is	Gaiya-jima Is	Kogaya-jima Is	Nakano-shima Is	Tara-jima Is	Suwanose-jima Is	Akuseki-jima Is	Kodakara-jima Is	Takara-jima Is	Kaminone-jima Is	Yokoate-jima Is	Amami-Oshima Is
Hasora chromus 1 Common Banded Awl												●			○
Badamia exclamationis 2 Brown Awl		●?									●				●
Potanthus flavus 3 Japanese Dart	○	○	○	○			○								
Pelopidas mathias 4 Small branded Swift	○	○	○	○			○	○	○	○	○	○		○	○
Parnara guttata 5 Straight Swift	○	○	○	○			○	○	○	○	○	○			○
Notocrypta curvifascia 6 Restricted Demon	○	○	○	○			○								○
Atrophaneura alcinous 7 Chinese Windmill	○	○									●				○
Graphium sarpedon 8 Common Bluebottle	○	○	○	○			○	○	○	○	○	○		○	○
Papilio machaon 9 Common Yellow Swallowtail	○	○										?			
Papilio xuthus 10 Asian Swallowtail	○	○	○	○			○	○	○	○	○	○			○
Papilio polytes 11 Common Mormon	●	●	●	◎			◎	◎	◎	◎	◎	◎			○
Papilio protenor 12 Spangle	○	○	○	◎			◎				◎	◎			○
Papilio memnon 13 Great Mormon	○	○	○	○			○	○	○	○	○	○			○
Papilio helenus 14 Red Helen	○	○	○	○			○	○	○	○	○	○			○
Papilio dehaanii 15 Chinese Peacock	?	●	?	○			○		○		●	●			
Papilio ryukyuensis 16 Okinawa Peacock											●	●			○

Those which are regarded resident in respective areas are marked with ○ . Those diffifult to determine resident or non-resident or which show great fluctuations in number by years are marked with ◎ . Non-resident or temporary visitor species are marked with ● . Dubious records are marked with ? . Those only recorded in the past but not seen at present are marked with ○× .

features distinguishable from those in mainland Kyushu, Yaku-shima and Tanega-shima islands.

4) *Pelopidas mathias* (Fabricius, 1798) (Small Branded Swift)

This species is very commonly seen, and regarded as resident ○. However, it is still needed to confirm its habitation on each island of Tokara all the year round by checking presence of adults and larvae in various seasons.

5) *Parnara guttata* (Bremer et Grey, 1852) (Straight Swift) (Fig. 1)

As *Pelopidas mathias* (Small Branded Swift), its status of being resident needs to be confirmed. In Kagoshima prefecture on mainland Kyushu, in particular, the brood following the overwintering one (to emerge as adults from April to May) of this species is expected to be dependent on the cultivated rice (*Oryza sativa* L.) (FUKUDA 2012b). Therefore, in Tokara where rice is now not cultivated, whether this species is resident there or not, and, if so, what is used as the larval food plant in May would be important questions to solve in future.

6) *Notocrypta curvifascia* (C. Felder et R. Felder,

Table 1. Continued.

	Tanega-shima Is	Yaku-shima Is	Kushinoerabu-jima Is	Kuchino-shima Is	Gaja-jima Is	Kogaja-jima Is	Nakano-shima Is	Tara-jima Is	Suwanose-jima Is	Akuseki-jima Is	Kodakara-jima Is	Takara-jima Is	Kaminone-jima Is	Yokoate-jima Is	Amami-Oshima Is
Colias erate 17 Eastern Pale Clouded Yellow	○	○		○	○				○	○	○	○			○
Catopsilia pyranthe 18 Mottled Emigrant	●	●					●					●			●
Catopsilia pomona 19 Lemon Emigrant	●	●	●						●	●	●	●		●	○
Eurema mandarina 20 Mandarin Grass Yellow	○	○	○	◎			○			◎	◎	◎			◎
Eurema hecabe 21 Common Grass Yellow									●			◎			○
Eurema laeta 22 Angulated Grass Yellow	○	○	◎	●				●		●	●				●
Appias paulina 23 Ceylon Lesser Albatross	●	●		●						◎	◎	◎			●
Appias albina 24 White Albatross		●										●			●
Pieris rapae 25 Cabbage White	○	○	○	○	○		○	○	○	○		○			○
Pieris canidia 26 Indian Cabbage White		●		●								●			
Pieris melete 27 Gray-veined White	○	○					●		●						●
Hebomoia glaucippe 28 Great Orange Tip	○	○	○	◎			○		○	○	◎	○			○
Arhopala japonica 29 Japanese Oakblue	○	○					○								○
Arhopala bazalus 30 Powdered Oakblue	○	○		◎	●		○	◎	◎	●	●	●			◎
Lampides boeticus 31 Long-tailed Blue	○	○	○	○			○	○	○	○		○			○
Nacaduba kurava 32 Transparent Six-line Blue	◎	○	◎	○			○	○	○	○	◎	○		○	○
Jamides bochus 33 Dark Cerulean	●	●	●	●					●			●			●
Euchrysops cnejus 34 Gram Blue		●						●			◎	◎			○
Zizeeria maha 35 Pale Grass Blue	○	○	○	○	○		○	○	○	○		○			○
Zizina otis 36 Oriental Lesser Grass Blue		●		◎				○				○			○
Celastrina argiolus 37 Holly Blue	○	○	○						○	○		◎			○
Megisba malaya 38 Malayan		●		●			●			●					○
Everes argiades 39 Short-tailed Blue	○	○		◎				●							◎
Everes lacturnus 40 Indian Cupid	○	○	○				○	○×							○×
Chilades pandava 41 Plains Cupid	●	●	●	●			●	●	●	●	●	●			●
Curetis acuta 42 Angled Sunbeam	○	○	○				◎					◎			○

Table 1. Continued.

	Tanega-shima Is.	Yaku-shima Is.	Kushinoerabu-jima Is.	Kuchino-shima Is.	Gaja-jima Is.	Kogaja-jima Is.	Nakano-shima Is.	Taira-jima Is.	Suwanose-jima Is.	Akuseki-jima Is.	Kodakara-jima Is.	Takara-jima Is.	Kaminone-jima Is.	Yokoate-jima Is.	Amami-Oshima Is.
Libythea lepita 43 Snout Butterfly	○	○					○			◎	◎	○×			○
Parantica sita 44 Chestnut Tiger	○	○	○	○			○	○	○	○	○	○			○
Ideopsis similis 45 Ceylon Blue Glassy Tiger	●	●	●	◎			◎		◎	◎	◎	◎			○
Tirumala septentrionis 46 Dark Blue Tiger	●	●					●					●			●
Tirumala hamata 47 Blue Tiger		●										●			●
Tirumala limniace 48 Oriental Blue Tiger	●	●					●				●	●			●
Danaus genutia 49 Orange Tiger	●	●	●	●					●	●	●	●			●
Danaus chrysippus 50 Plain Tiger	◎	◎	◎	◎			◎	◎	◎	◎	◎	◎			○
Idea leuconoe 51 Rice Paper Butterfly		●			●						●	●			◎
Euploea sylvester 52 Double-branded Crow							?					●			●
Euploea mulciber 53 Striped Blue Crow	●	●	●				●				●	●			○
Argyreus hyperbius 54 Indian Fritillary	○	○	○	○			○	○	○	○	○	○		○	○
Cirrochroa tyche 55 Common Yeoman												●			
Neptis hylas 56 Hylas Common Sailer											◎				○
Polygonia c-aureum 57 Asian Comma	◎	●		●							●	●			●
Vanessa cardui 58 Painted Lady	○	○		○	○		○	○	○	○	○	○			○
Vanessa indica 59 Indian Red Admiral	○	○	○	○	○		○	○	○	○	○	○			○
Kaniska canace 60 Blue Admiral	○	○	○	○			○	○	○	○	○	○		○	○
Junonia orithya 61 Blue Pansy	●	●		●			●				●	●			●
Junonia almana 62 Peacock Pansy	○	○	○		○×		○×	◎	○×	○×	●	○×			○
Hypolimnas misippus 63 Danaid Eggfly	●	●	●				●		●	●	●	●			●
Hypolimnas bolina 64 Common Eggfly	●	●	●	●			●		●	●	●	●			●
Hypolimnas anomala 65 Crow Eggfly	●	●	●				●		●	●	●	●			●
Cyrestis thyodamas 66 Common Map	○	○	○	◎	○		○	○	○	○	○	○			○
Hestina assimilis 67 Red-ring Circe							●				●				○
Melanitis leda 68 Common Evening Brown	◎	○	◎	○			○			○	○	○			○
Melanitis phedima 69 Dark Evening Brown	○	○	○				◎	●	?			●			○

1862) (Restricted Demon)

Although this species has been recorded only from Kuchino-shima and Nakano-shima, larval food plants are available throughout Tokara. Presence of *Alpina formosana* K. Schum. is reported from Akuseki-jima and Takara-jima (SHIUCHI and HOTTA 2015), *Alpina intermedia* Gagnep. from all islands other than Kogajya-jima, *Alpinia japonica* (Thunb.) Miq. from Kuchino-shima, Nakano-shima, and Suwanose-jima, whereas *Alpinia zerumbet* (Pers.) B. L. Burtt et R. M. Sm. (Shell Ginger) is known to be distributed on Nakano-shima, Taira-jima, and Takara-jima (Toshimamura Village 1995; SHIUCHI and HOTTA, 2015). On Kuchino-shima, we confirmed the presence of cultivated *A. zerumbet* to note here (KANAI and MORIYAMA, unpublished data). Therefore, also on islands where this species has not been recorded, it is necessary to search for it carefully.

Papilionidae

12) *Papilio protenor* Cramer, [1775] (Spangle)

In surveys in recent years, there have been only 2 confirmed records of this species. Among the eggs and larvae brought back from Nakanoshims in October 2010, 1 was of this species (KANAI and MORIYAMA 2010). The other record was of a female captured on Kuchino-shima in October 2011 (KANAI and MORIYAMA 2013). This is one of the species to be watched carefully to check residency in Tokara

Fig. 1. Straight Swift (*Parnara guttata*).

Pieridae

17) *Colias erate* (Esper, [1805]) (Eastern Pale Clouded Yellow)

Among the populated islands, Nakano-shima and Taira-jima have no record of this species. However, as this species shows a high mobility, probably it will be recorded in future. Many fabaceous plants (Fabaceae) are usable as larval food plants: species escaped from cultivation, e.g. *Trifolium repens* L. (White Clover), *Melilotus officinalis* (L.) Pall., *Medicago lupulina* L. *Medicago lupulina* L., and native *Kummerowa striata* (Thunb.) Schindl.

20) *Eurema mandarina* (de l'Orza, 1869) (Mandarin Grass Yellow)

This is a rare species in Tokara. It is regarded as resident ○ only on Nakano-shima, whereas on Suwanose-jima, Akuseki-jima, Kodakara-jima, and Takara-jima, its residency status (resident or temporary visitor) cannot be judged ◎.

21) *Eurema hecabe* (Linnaeus, 1758) (Common Grass Yellow)

There are a limited number of reliable capture records for this species. The Tokara Islands need further accumulation of information on *Eurema* spp. regarding their distributions and life history. Although they are relatively small in number, accumulation of specimens for further study is necessary.

25) *Pieris rapae* (Linnaeus, 1758) (Cabbage White)

This species has been confirmed on all the populated islands. However, is there any island in Tokara, where brassicaceous plants are available for larvae to grow for successive generations all the year round? As this species has high mobility, check on each island in all seasons is required regarding the growth of larvae and availability of their food plants.

Lycaenidae

29) *Arhopala japonica* (Murray, 1875) (Japaneses Oakblue)

The distribution of the larval food plant oaks (*Quercus* spp.) in Tokara is as follows.

Toshimamura Village (1995) states that *Quercus glauca* Thunb. (Japanese Blue Oak) occurs in Gajya-jima, Nakano-shima, Suwanose-jima, and Akuseki-jima. SHIUCHI and HOTTA (2015) added Kuchino-shima to the above, and regarded that all found in the Tokara Islands were of planted origin. *Quercus phillyraeoides* A. Gray f. *wrightii* (Nakai) Makino *Quercus phillyreoides* A. Gray f. *wrightii* (Nakai) Makino occurr on Nakano-shima and Takara-jima (Toshimamura Village 1995; SHIUCHI and HOTTA 2015). *Quercus acutissima* Carruth., though recorded from Nakano-shima, is regarded as of planted origin (SHIUCHI and HOTTA 2015). As chinquapins, Toshimamura Village (1995) listed *Castanopsis sieboldii* (Makino) Hatus. ex T. Yamaz. et Mashiba, SHIUCHI and HOTTA (2015) listed *Castanopsis sieboldii* (Makino) Hatus. ex T. Yamaz. et Mashiba subsp. *lutchuensis* (Koidz.) H. Ohba to occur on Kuchino-shima, Nakano-shima, Gajya-jima, Taira-jima, Suwanose-jima, Akuseki-jima, and Takara-jima.

Nakano-shima has many records of this species likely to suggest its residency there. The occurrence of such larval food plants above suggests discovery of this butterfly species on some other islands as well. Therefore, further attention is desirable in search of this species hereafter.

30) *Arhopala bazalus* (Hewitson, 1862) (Powdered Oakblue)
Lithocarpus edulis (Makino) Nakai, recorded as a larval food plant of this species, has been stated by Toshimamura Village (1995) to occur on Kuchino-shima, Nakano-shima, and Suwanose-jima. SHIUCHI and HOTTA (2015), besides these 3 islands, stated that planted ones were found also on Taira-jima.

On the islands where no *Lithocarpus edulis* (Makino) Nakai grows, this butterfly is most likely an accidental temporary visitor. On Nakano-shima, many larvae feeding on *Lithocarpus edulis* (Makino) Nakai in the wild were collected and led us to conclude the resident status ○ for this species.

37) *Celastrina argiolus* (Linnaeus, 1758) (Holly Blue)
Specimens of this species, though small in number,

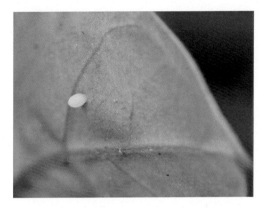

Fig. 2. An egg of Ceylon Blue Glassy Tiger (*Ideopsis similis*).

have been captured. However, its residency must be carefully judged in future after continued observation. *Lespedeza* spp. or similar road-side growing fabaceous species, therefore, need to be checked in various seasons for their possible use as larval food plants of this species to support its residency all the year round.

38) *Megisba malaya* (Horsfield, [1828]) (Malayan)
Mallotus japonicus (L.f.) Müll. Arg., a larval food plant for this species, has been recorded from almost all the islands in Tokara. However, the key to its residency all the year round is suspected to be the presence of *Mallotus phillippensis* (Lam.) Müll. Arg., which bloom in winter too (FUKUDA 2012a). Without fixed overwintering stage, this species cannot pass winter in the larval stage, if it depends only on *M. japonicus,* which bloom only from April to October.

Toshimamura Village (1995) states that Takara-jima is the northern limit of occurrence for *Mallotus phillippensis* (Lam.) Müll. Arg. SHIUCHI and HOTTA (2015), besides Takara-jima, added Akuseki-jima to the distribution range of *M. phillippensis*. Akuseki-jima, however, has been surveyed only insufficiently. Therefore, this species must be paid attention in future survey.

42) *Curetis acuta* Moore, 1877 (Angled Sunbeam)
Is there any spring inflorescence of fabaceous plant on which overwintered adult females of this species can oviposit in the Tokara Islands?

Therefore, as we cannot judge its residency status (resident or temporary visitor), we mark it with ◎. We would like to await accumulation of records in future for the judgement of residency status of this species to revise.

Nymphalidae

45) *Ideopsis similis* (Linnaeus, 1758) (Ceylon Blue Glassy Tiger) (Fig 2)

Although this species is often found from April to autumn, confirmed observations in winter of adults and larvae, in particular in March, have been scanty. On Akuseki-jima, a male was captured and 2 larvae were found on 18 March 1992 (KIRINO 1993), and in March 2019, eggs were found on the same island (KANAI, unpublished data).

68) *Melanitis leda* (Linnaeus, 1758) (Common Evening Brown)

This species, though not great in number, is regarded resident in the Tokara Islands.It is a noteworthy species for continued investigation.

2.2. Species with unstable distribution
Papilionidae

11) *Papilio polytes* Linnaeus, 1758 (Common Mormon)

Formerly, this species was regarded resident ○ from Nakano-shima southward. However, since the prefectural museum started renewed surveys of the area around 2007, only a single male has been captured on 24 August 2013 on Nakano-shima (MORIYAMA and KANAI 2014), and it has hardly ever been seen in recent years. Therefore, as the Tokara Islands as a whole, we cannot judge its residency (resident or temporary visitor) there and mark it with ◎. On Amami-Oshima, however, this species seems to be in increase. Therefore, its re-entry in the Tokara Islands in future is probable.

Pieridae

28) *Hebomoia glaucippe* (Linnaeus, 1758) (Great Orange Tip)

This species has been recorded on the populated islands where its larval food plant, *Crateva formosensis* (Jacobs) B. S. Sun, is distributed. Kodakara-jima did not originally have growth

of the plant. However, when planted there, this butterfly flew and now occurs there (Iwashita, personal communication). On Kuchino-shima and Suwanose-jima, it has not been seen in recent years in recent years. As both islands are small with only small numbers of the food plants, for some reason, probably it once became extinct. Therefore, we judged the status of this species indeterminate between resident and temporary visitor ◎.

Lycaenidae

34) *Euchrysops cnejus* (Fabricius, 1798) (Gram Blue)

On Kodakara-jima and Takara-jima, we judged its residency status indeterminate between resident and temporary visitor ◎. In future, we need higher frequencies of surveys, to check the observability of this species all the year round.

36) *Zizina otis* (Fabricius, 1787) (Lesser Grass Blue) (Fig. 3)

At present, among Kuchino-shima, Taira-jima, Kodakara-jima, and Takara-jima, where we have records, the northern limit with its stable residency is Taira-jima. Adults fly in late March to lay eggs (eggshels found) to indicate stable emergence there (Kanai and Moriyama, 2014; Moriyama and Kanai, 2015).

On Kuchino-shima, the population site observed in October 2010 disappeared altogether with the larval food plant patches (Kanai and Moriyama, 2012; Kanai and Moriyama, 2013). Thereafter, although patches of *Kummerowa striata* (Thunb.) Schindl. on the island have been repeatedly searched, it has not been rediscovered up until 2016. This species temporarily flies to show emergence for a while, but in a state with no stable residency.

Among the other islands, Nakano-shima and Kodakara-jima have no candidate fabaceous plant patch which could allow emergence of this species. On Kodakara-jima, *Medicago lupulina* L. has been recorded (SHIUCHI and HOTTA 2015), and there is an unpublished record of a male in August 2010 (HOSOYA, personal communication). Although Suwanose-jima and Akuseki-jima have candidate fabaceous plant patches, this species has been found on neither island. This species, which flew from the south, is thought to be in a state of range expansion to areas allowing successive stable emergence. Kuchino-shima and some other islands should be watched for monitoring with a few years interval to check whether this species gets footholds for settlement.

40) *Everes lacturnus* (Godart, [1824]) (Indian Cupid)

The larval food plant of this species, *Desmodium heterocarpon* (L.) DC., is stated in Toshimamura Village (1995) to occur on all islands in Tokara including the presently unpopulated Gajya-jima and Yokoate-jima. However, SHIUCHI and HOTTA (2015) did not include either Kodakara-jima or Yokoate-jima in the listing as recorded sites of this species. At any rate, despite the widespread distribution of the larval foodplant, stable occurrence of this species is known only from Nakano-shima. On Taira-jima, a fresh female was obtained on 29 September 2007, and, thereafter, surveys have been made many times. However, this species has not been found there again.

The monophagous E. lacturnus feeds on flower buds and fruits of *Desmodium heterocarpon*. Although this species is univoltine, our surveys indicated the flowering season of the larval food plant fluctuates from year to year. If brine water gets sprayed on the plant by wind, typhoon in particular, it withers or dies (MORIYAMA 2017).

In the past when asphalt pavement of roads and concrete covering of cuts for constructions was not common, Desmodium heterocarpon grew in various environments from dry to humid places, in shades and sunny areas. Such diversity must have provided larvae of *Everes lacturnus* with food plants in various conditions, some very favorbable for growth.

However, in uniformly homogenized environment, the emergence of this butterfly species and the condition of the larval food plant lose matching, leading to the extinction of the butterfly species from any island. The absence of this species on Taira-jima, Suwanose-jima, and Akuseki-jima despite the good presence of *Desmodium heterocarpon* there may indicate such distinction cases.

Fig. 3. Lesser Grass Blue (*Zizina otis*).

In future, in the emergence season, some adults may fly to such islands from Nakano-shima or Tanega-shima. If *Desmodium heterocarpon* patches are retained in good conditions, possibility of re-entry of the species leading to stable habitation remains. Therefore, it is necessary to monitor the area for this species every several years.

Nymphalidae

62) *Junonia almana* (Linnaeus, 1758) (Peacock Pansy)

Formerly, this species was given the residency status of temporary visitor ● on Kodakara-jima, whereas on the other populated islands resident ○. However, in surveys in recent years, none has been found. Therefore, the islands other than Taira-jima have been re-evaluated as in areas where it has disappeared ○×. As the cause of the decline of this species, we suspect that abandoned rice paddy fields, where the major larval food plant, *Lindernia antipoda* (L.) Alston grows, have increased. *Phyla nodiflora* (L.) Greene (Frog Fruit), another larval food plant, is distributed on Nakano-shima, Taira-jima, Suwanose-jima, Kodakara-jima, and Takara-jima (Toshimamura Village 1995, SHIUCHI and HOTTA 2015). Although this species was thought to have disappeared on Taira-jima too, 2 male specimens were obtained in 2016 after 9 years without any record (MORIYAMA and KANAI 2017), and here we treat Taira-jima is in the area with indeterminate residency ◎ (either resident or temporary visitor).

69) *Melanitis phedima* (Cramer, [1780]) (Dark Evening Brown)

Differing from those which expanded ranges northward in the climatic warming trend, this species has been regarded as a species expanded its range southward to Amami-Oshima (FUKUDA 1992). As many have been captured on Nakano-shima too, we regard this species thereof as indeterminate ◎ (either resident or temporary visitor). It is a species noteworthy for attention in future.

2.3. Species with possible taxonomical change in future

Lycaenidae

35) *Zizeeria maha* (Kollar, [1844]) (Pale Grass Blue)

For this species, the population north of Nakano-shima is regarded of the mainland Japan subspecies *Z. m. argia* (Ménétriès, 1857), whereas those on Takara-jima and further south is regarded of the subspecies of the Nansei Islands, *Z. m. okinawana* (MATSUMURA 1929). However, we, though still in an attempt to elucidate, have not reached any conclusion regarding how to treat those on Taira-jima, Suwanose-jima, and Akuseki-jima.

Nymphalidae

43) *Libythea lepita* Moore, [1858] (Nettle-tree Butterfly)

Celtis boninensis Koidz., which occur on Nakano-shima, Akuseki-jima, Kodakara-jima, and Takara-

Fig. 4. The Tokara subspecies of the Chinese Peacock (*Papilio dehaanii tokaraensis*).

jima (Toshimamura Village 1995, SHIUCHI and HOTTA 2015), shows agreement with the islands where this species have been recorded. In recent years, however, on Takara-jima, which has large trees of *Celtis boninensis*, this species is not seen at present ○×.

Those occurring north of Yaku-shima and Tanega-shima are included in the subspecies occurring in mainland Japan, *L. l. celtoides* Fruhstorfer [1909], whereas those from Amami-Oshima Is. to Okinawa Islands, and the Yaeyama Islands are put in the subspecies of the Nansei Islands, *L. l. amamiana* Shirôzu, 1956 (SHIRÔZU 2006). However, the subspecific distinction of those from the Tokara Islands is still suspended (INOMATA *et al.*, 2010-2013).

3. Concluding Remarks

In the Tokara Islands, notable beetles (Coleoptera) among others are *Dicerca nishidai* Toyama, 1986, of Nakano-shima, and *Baryrhynchus tokarensis* Ohbayashi & Satô, 1966, of Akuseki-jima, both of which are unique indigenous species. However, among butterflies, no unique indigenous species is present, but, as a unique subspecies, only the Tokara subspecies of the Chinese Peacock (*Papilio dehaanii tokaraensis* Fujioka, 1975) is known (Fig. 4). This is probably because the butterflies have relatively high potential of dispersal, with much mobility. Also regarding a number of species, subspecies are distinguished between mainland Kyushu and the Nansei Islands, the Tokara Islands are proposed to be the distributional border. Therefore, it is necessary to confirm the validity of the boundary.

Nevertheless, investigation has been far from being sufficient for each of the Tokara Islands. On many islands, evidence is too scanty to judge any species as resident or non-resident. Biological species in the Tokara Islands have attained the present state, since the formation of the islands, through repeated destruction and recovery of vegetation by eruption, invasion and extinction of animals. This is not yet in any stable state. Even hereafter, changes would continue. Regional monitoring of this area, if continued, would provide invaluable information for elucidating how the regional biological species have evolved to form the unique flora and fauna, since the Ryukyus Archipelago was formed.

Acknowledgements

For each survey, Toshimamura Village kindly issued us permission for capturing insects. Mr. Hideyuki IWASHITA, resident on Kodakara-jima Is., and Mr. Kazuki YAMAMURO, resident on Amami-Oshima Is., provided us helpful information. Mr. Haruo FUKUDA always gave us invaluable and timely advices to facilitate this study. Prof. Hiroyuki TAKASAKI at Okayama University of Science helped us draft the English translation of the text. To these people and institutions, we make grateful acknowledgement.

References

(for full citation list, see KANAI and MORIYAMA (2018), of which abridged translation is this article; only the titles referred to for updating the information herein are listed below.)

INOMATA, T., UÉMURA, Y., YAGO, M., JIMBO, U. and UEDA, U. 2010–2013. *Nihonsan Chôrui Wamei Gakumei Binran* (The Current Checklist of Japanese Butterflies. (in Japanese) Retrieved on June 30, 2019, from http://binran.lepimages.jp/

KANAI, K. and MORIYAMA, T. 2018. *Tokara-retto no chôrui* (Butterflies in the Tokara Islands). Bulletin of the Kagoshima Prefectural Museum, 37: 19–30. (in Japanese)

NAGASHIMA, S. (ed) 2019. *Nippon-nesia-ron* (Japanesia theory). 477 pp., Fujiwara-shoten, Tokyo. (in Japanese)

YONEKURA, K. and KAJITA, T. 2003–. *BG Plants Wamei-gakumei indekkusu* (YList) (BG Plants Japanese name-scientific name index). (in Japanese) Retrieved on June 30, 2019, from http://ylist.info

OTSUKA, Y., TERADA, R. and NISHIMURA, S. (eds.), *The Tokara Islands*
Kagoshima University International Center for Island Studies; Hokuto Shobo Publishing, Tokyo. 10 March 2020.

Chapter 14
Control of Black Fly in Nakano-shima Island

Yasushi OTSUKA

1. Introduction

Black flies belong to the family Simuliidae of the order Diptera. 2,328 and 76 species of black flies were recorded in the world and Japan, respectively (ADLER 2019). Female adults suck blood of birds and mammals including human for producing their eggs. They are found in any location in which running freshwater streams or rivers suitable for the habitat of their aquatic stages (egg, larva and pupa) are available. The blood-sucking habits of female black flies are responsible for considerable deleterious effects on humans and their economic welfare (CROSSKEY 1990). The medical and socioeconomic impacts associated with black flies include reduced levels of tourism, the death of domesticated birds and mammals, and the transmission of viral, protozoan and filarial diseases (ADLER *et al.* 2004). In particular, black flies are well known as vectors of *Onchocerca volvulus*, the causative filarial species of human onchocerciasis or 'river blindness' endemic in Africa and Central and South America (CROSSKEY 1990). Although such notorious black fly-borne diseases are absent in Japan, in 1989 a case of zoonotic onchocerciasis was first reported in Oita, Kyushu, Japan. Zoonotic onchocercosis is an emerging human infection caused by animal parasitic *Onchocerca* species, which are transmitted by black flies or biting midges. Recently, the numbers of infected individuals have increased worldwide. A total of 36 cases in humans have now been reported, with 13 in North America (11 in the USA and two in Canada), 11 in Japan, six in Europe, three in Turkey, and one each in Kuwait, Tunisia, and Iran. Five *Onchocerca* species (*O. gutturosa, O. cervicalis, O. dewittei japonica, O. jakutensis*, and *O. lupi*) have been identified as the causative agents. In all the Japanese cases, the causative agent was *O. dewittei japonica*. This filarial worm is naturally parasitic in the Japanese wild boar (*Sus scrofa leucomystax*). In Oita, Kyushu, its transmission vector was found to be the anthropophilic, zoophilic black fly, *Simulium bidentatum* (TAKAOKA *et al.* 2012, FUKUDA *et al.* 2019). By contrast with human onchocerciasis, in which microfilariae produced from gravid female worms cause severe dermal and ocular lesions, zoonotic onchocerciasis is in general caused by a single immature adult female or male worm and thus no microfilariae are produced. However, despite the absence of the conspicuous clinical symptoms caused by microfilariae, conjunctivitis and other ocular lesions caused by an invading adult worm in the ocular or periocular tissue regions (ocular zoonotic onchocerciasis), or a subcutaneous nodule formed around the worm in various parts of the body, can be of clinical importance. The disease is diagnosed by detecting an *Onchocerca* worm or its parts in ocular tissue or a resected subcutaneous nodule.

Table 1. Distribution of black fly in the Tokara islands.

	Kuchino-shima Is.	Nakano-shima Is.	Taira-jima Is.	Takara-jima Is.
S. aureohirtum	+	+	+	+
S. japonicum	+	+		
S. morisonoi	+	+		
S. tokarense		+		

No record in the other islands of the Tokara Islands.

Fortunately, zoonotic onchocerciasis has been not found in the Tokara Islands, but it has long suffered from black fly sucking. This chapter reports the distribution of black fly in the Tokara Islands and the history and current status of black fly control in Nakano-shima Is.

2. Distribution of black fly in the Tokara Islands

In the Tokara Islands, four species of black fly are distributed, and belong to genus *Simulium* Latreille s. l. (Table 1). *Simulium aureohirtum* Brunetti, 1911 and *S. morisonoi* Takaoka, 1973 belong to subgenus *Nevermannia* Enderlein. *Simulium japonicum* Matsumura, 1931 and *S. tokarense* Takaoka, 1973 belong to subgenus subgenus *Simulium* Latreille s. str. and *Gomphostilbia* Enderlein, respectively. Four islands (Kuchino-shima Is., Nakano-shima Is., Taira-jima Is. and Takara-jima Is., Table 1) are known for habitats of black fly (TAKAOKA 1973, TAKAOKA 2002, NODA 2008). *Simlulim morisonoi* and *S. tokarense* were known only in the Tokara Islands.

Of four species in the Tokara Islands, only *S. japonicum* bites human (Fig. 1). *Simulium japonicum* is distributed in Japan, China, Korea and Siberia. In Japan, *S. japonicum* is widely distributed from Okinawa island to Hokkaido. *Simulium japonicum* was described by Shonen Matsumura in 1931 based on specimens from Hokkaido. SIRAKI (1935) described *S. oshimanum* using specmens from Amami-Oshima Is, although OGATA (1956) and TAKAOKA (1977) considered that *S. oshimanum* a synonym of *S. japonicum*. *Simulium japonicum* of Nakano-shima Is. is very similar to that of Hokkaido. However, it can be clearly distinguished from the form of the respiratory thread. The larvae from Nakano-shima Is. are generally pale in color and have a clear head marking. The shape of cleft also varies greatly in Nakano-shima Is., and some of them have reached hypostomium. The number of annual generations of *S. japonicum* is two in Hokkaido, having six months for larva growth in winter generation, and three months for summer generation. On the other hand, larvae and adult are collected all year round in Nakano-shima Is., which seems to have

Fig. 1. Adule female of *Simulium japonicum.*

occurred year after year. The larvae period was assumed to be about four weeks in Nakano-shima Is., presumed from the results that adult was not found within three weeks after the application of the insecticide and that adults appeared four weeks later (SUZUKI 1983). The damage to human beings caused by *S. japonicum* is also known in some islands of the Nansei archipelago, Amami-Oshima Is., Tokuno-shima Is, and Okinawa Is. However, no biting damage has been reported in the mainland of Japan. As *S. japonicum* has large morphological and ecological variations as described above, it is necessary to conduct a nationwide survey and re-examine the taxonomic status of *S. japonicum*.

3. Biting damages in Nakano-shima Is.

Among the Tokara Islands, Kuchino-shima Is. and Nakano-shima Is., where *S. japonicum* inhabits, suffer from blood-sucking of blck fly. Especially, Nakano-shima Is. has long been known for its severe blood-sucking damage. In Nakano-shima Is., there are also legends about black fly. Nakano-shima Is. has a big stone, *Yosuke Iwa* (Fig. 2). In the middle of the 16th century, the Pirate Hyuga, Yosuke, had been robbing in the Tokara Islands for a long time. Taking beautiful girls as decoys, the governor of the Tokara islands held a drinking party to invite Yosuke. Yosuke was drunk with much alcohol, then killed by Tokara's people. After that, the soul and body of Yosuke turned into a big stone and ashes, respectively. The ashes finally turned into blood-sucking insects, black flies, which suffer the people of Nakano-shima Is. In addition, although it is not currently performed, there was a splendid dance in the Nakano-shima *Bon Odori* called "Yosuke Dance".

According to questionnaire surveys conducted on Nakano-shima Is. in the 1970s, most people have knowledge about black fly, and have been sucked by black fly (Table 2). In addition, it is surprised that more than 90% of the population have been bitten by black fly within a week. In subsequent collection surveys, more than 1,500 black flies came for blood feeding within three hours (Fig. 3). Black fly sucks blood during the day and has peaks in the morning and evening. But, in Nakano-shima Is., the peck of adult black fly was around 3 pm. The black blood sucking damage of black fly is generally outdoors, but the fact that it comes to blood sucking indoors in Nakano-shima Is. suggests that the impact on their lives was very severe.

The blood sucking damage of *S. japonicum* is also seen in Amami-Oshima Is. and Tokuno-shima Is. However, the blood-sucking damages in those islands are limited in the mountain area, and there is almost no blood-sucking damage by *S. japonicum* in residential areas. In general, the larva pupae of *S. japonicum* live in a relatively high-altitude and fast-flowing river, and are often far from residential areas. However, Nakano-shima Is., Kuchino-shima Is, and Kuro-shima Is., where blood sucking damages by *S. japonicum* are known in Mishima Village, are adjacent the habitats of *S. japonicum* and humans. The blood-feeding damage of black fly has existed for a long time in Nakano-shima Is., but it is thought that one of the reasons for the increase of blood-feeding damage in recent years is that the breeding of cattle on the island has increased and the number of blood-sucking sources has increased.

4. Black fly control in Nakano-shima Is.

In the 1980s, the control of black fly started in Nakano-shima Is. by Hiroshi Suzuki (Suzuki 1983). In Japan, control of larvae of black fly has been taken in areas where bools sucking damages by black fly were severe (Ogata and Sasa 1955). The control has been taken to distribute DDT (Di chlorodiphenyltrichloroethane, an organochlorine which was originally developed as an insecticide), to rivers inhabiting black fly larvae since the 1950s, but Abate (Temefos, an organophosphate larvicide) has been used since the 1970s due to environmental concerns of DDT. Abate was known to have significantly less effect on humans and fish than DDT. However, no control has been taken to target only *S. japonicum* in the mainland of Japan. Because, the blood-sucking damage to humans by *S. japonicum* is not severe in the mainland.

In April 1982, the introduction of the insecticide Abate into five rivers in Nakano-shima

Fig. 2. *Yosuke iwa* in Nakano-shima Is.

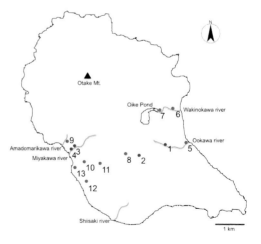

Fig. 3. A map of Nakano-shima Is. Numbers indicate the collection sites. Circles show the sites where black fly larvae were collected (red) and not collected (blue).

Table 2. Questionnaire about black fly in Nakano-shima Is.

		1972 (%)*	1977 (%)**
Do you know black fly? (yes)		100	100
Have you ever been bitten by black fly? (yes)		100	100
Have you ever been bitten by black fly within a week? (yes)		96.4	92.5
Where do you get bitten by black fly?	A: outdoor	66.4	81.5
	B: indoor	33.6	18.5
When do you get bitten by black fly?	A: morning	22.4	21.9
	B: daytime	4.3	32.8
	C: evening	69.8	45.2
	D: night	3.4	0

*Conducted in November 1972 by H. TAKAOKA; **conducted in April 1977 by H. SUZUKI (modified from SUZUKI 1983)

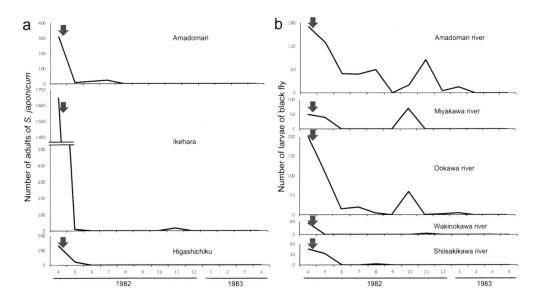

Fig. 4. Adults (a) and larvae (b) of black fly collected in Nakano-shima Is. from April 1982 to April 1983. Adult of *S. japonicum* was collected using single human bait from 13:00 to 16:00 at three sites. Laval collection was made at the five rivers for 10 minutes. Red arrows indicate the start of using the insecticide. (modified from SUZUKI 1983).

Is. (Amadomarikawa river, Miyakawa river, Shiisaki river, Ookawa river and Wakinokawa river) was started (Figs. 3, 4). The dose was 1 ppm based on the amount of water per 10 minutes of the rivers. Introductions of the insecticide were made every three weeks from April to September and once a month from October to March. Larvae were collected for 10 minutes immediately before and one day after the injection of the insecticide. In addition, adults of black fly were collected before and after the introduction of the insecticide. Fig. 4 shows the results of the collection of

black fly. Adults have been dramatically reduced with introduction of the insecticide. Larvae also generally decreased, although they fluctuated by month. The introduction of the insecticide successfully reduced the blood-sucking of black fly.

The tremendous decrease in blood-sucking damage by the introduction of the insecticide has greatly surprised the people of Nakano-shima Is. Some people said "Until then, only long sleeves were worn in order to avoid blood-sucking of black fly, but now it is possible to wear short sleeves" and "Our grandchildren never came to Nakano-shima Is. due to black fly before, but they came to this island for the first time". The people of Nakano-shima Is. gave great appreciations to H. SUZUKI (SUZUKI 1999). When I surveyed in Nakano-shima Is. about the damage of black fly in 2015, I encountered many people who were still grateful to H. Suzuki deeply. It seemed to be a huge event for the people of Nakano-shima Is. to have experienced the decrease in black fly due to the insecticide.

5. Current status of black fly control

Even after the success in reducing black fly by using the insecticide, Nakano-shima Is. and Kuchino-shima Is. continued to exterminate black fly with assistance from Kagoshima Prefecture. The insecticide was changed to Midi (Diflubenzuron, an insecticide of the benzoylurea class) from 2000, because Abate became difficult to obtain in Japan. From 2014, BT has begun to be used in Nakanoshoma Is. BT is delta endotoxins, pore-forming toxins produced by *Bacillus thuringiensis* species of bacteria. Abate was also exterminating other river-dwelling insects of the order Ephemeridae (Suzuki 1983). The range of effect of BT is limited to the order Diptera, especially mosquito and black fly, having less effect on other insects than Abate. Noda (2011) surveyed to evaluate the efficacy of insecticide (Abate) were

carried out during the period from 2007 to 2010, concluding that the number of black flies has been kept relatively low level, but it is necessary to continue regular use of insecticides. But, after insecticide changed to BT, there is no survey of the efficacy of BT in Nakano-shima Is. Therefore, in order to confirm the effect of BT, larvae and pupae of black fly were collected in running freshwater streams and rivers where the insecticide was used in October 2018. Surveys were made at 13 sites, then larvae and pupae were collected at four sites (Fig. 3). It could not be collected at the other nine locations. The collected larvae were 55 of *S. tokarense*, seven of *S. japonicum* and two of *S. morisonoi* (Fig. 5, Table 3). The collected pupae were six of *S. tokarense* and one of *S. japonicum*. Three of the four sites where black fly larvae and pupae were collected were the upstream of where the insecticide was introduced, indicating that the insecticide is working effectively at most sites.

Before using the insecticide in the 1980s, more than 1,500 of black fly came to suck blood in 3 hours, but recently not so many black flies have come to blood feeding. Recently, in Nakano-shima Is., the insecticide is poured into the rivers twice a month (Fig. 6). However, it is impossible to completely extinct *S. japonicum* by using the insecticide. Sometimes the amount of black flies increases. Larvae of black fly may live in the upstream where the insecticide is poured or

Fig. 5. Ookawa river in Nakano-shima Is. To pour the insecticide, workers need to climb a steep river and go upstream of the river.

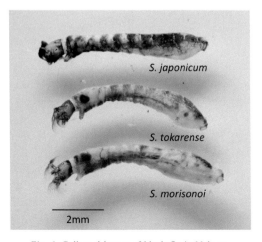

Fig. 6. Collected larvae of black fly in Nakano-shima Is.

Table 3. Collection of larvae of black fly larva in Nakano-shima Is.

Collection site*	S. aureohirtum	S. japonicum	S. morisonoi	S. tokarense
1 Ookawa river		4		7 (4)†
2 Hinode water source		3 (1)†	1	35 (2)†
3 West district water source		2	1	
4 Downstream of West district water source				11

*The numbers of collection sites correspond to numbers of Fig. 3. † The numbers in parentheses are the number of collected pupae.

in rivers where the insecticide is not sufficiently distributed. In addition, in some rivers of the southern part of Nakano-shima Is., the insecticide has not been poured in recent years. So, there is a possibility that black fly will always occur in those rivers, and black fly of the rivers may be a source for other rivers. The number of larvae of *S. japonicum* was less than that of other species (Table 3), because the peak of *S. japonicum* is from May to June. The currently using insecticide is BT, which is thought to have less effect on insects other than black fly than other insecticides. However, in order to avoid excessive insecticide application in consideration of environmental effects, insecticide application should be carried out after monitoring the number of black flies and evaluating effects on the other insects.

Acknowledgements

This study was supported in part by JSPS KAKENHI Grant Number JP 19K06421 and "Establishment of Research and Education Network on Biodiversity and Its Conservation in the Satsunan Islands" project of Kagoshima University adopted by the Ministry of Education, Culture, Sports, Science and Technology, Japan.

References

ADLER, P. H. 2019. World Blackflies (Diptera: Simuliidae): A Comprehensive Revision of the Taxonomic and Geographical Inventory [2019]. 139 pp., https://biomia.sites.clemson.edu/pdfs/blackflyinventory.pdf (Accessed on 25 October 2019).

ADLER, P. H., CURRIE, D.C. and WOOD, D. M. 2004. The Black Flies (Simuliidae) of North America. xv + 941 pp., Cornell University Press, Ithaca, New York.

CROSSKEY, R. W. 1990 The Natural History of Blackflies. John Wiley & Sons Inc., Chichester.

FUKUDA, M., UNI, S., IGARI, T., UTSUMI, Y., OTSUKA, Y., NAKATANI, J., UGAC, S., HARAI, T., HASEGAWA, H. and TAKAOKA, H. 2019. Human Case of *Onchocerca dewittei japonica* Infection in Fukushima, Northeastern Honshu, Japan. Parasitology international, 72: 101943.

NODA, S. 2008. Blackflies on Nakanoshima Is. and Kuchinoshima Is. of Tokara Islands. Medical Entomology and Zoology, 59(Suppl.): 35. (in Japanese)

NODA, S. 2011. Control of Black Fly in Nakanoshima Island, Tokara Archipelago. Occasional Papers, Research Center for the Pacific Islands, Kagoshima University, 52: 57–64. (in Japanese with English abstract)

OGATA, K. 1956. Notes on Simuliidae of the Ryukyu Islands (Diptera). Japanese Journal of Medical Science and Biology, 9(1-2): 59–69.

OGATA, K. and SASA, M. 1955. Keys to the Adult Females and Pupae of Japanese Simuliidae and Notes on the Control of Black Fly Larvae Insecticides. Japanese Journal of Sanitary Zoology, 6(1): 10–18. (in Japanese)

SHIRAKI, T. 1935. Simuliidae of the Japanese Empire. Memoirs of the Faculty of Science and Agriculture; Taihoku Imperial University, 16: 1–90.

SUZUKI, H. 1983. *Tokara rettou no idoubutugakuteki kenkyu* (Studies of Medical Zoology in the Tokara Islands). Reports of Grants-in-Aid for Scientific Research from Ministry of Education. (in Japanese)

SUZUKI, H. 1992. *Nettai no hitobito*. 302 pp., Shinjuku Shobo, Tokyo. (in Japanese)

TAKAOKA, H. 1973. Descriptions of 2 New Species of Blackflies, *Simulium* (*Gomphostilbia*) *tokarense* and *S.* (*Eusimulium*) *morisonoi* (Diptera: Simuliidae), from the Tokara Islands, Japan. Japanese Journal of Sanitary Zoology, 23(3): 201–207.

TAKAOKA, H. 1977. Studies on Black Flies of the Nansei Islands, Japan (Simuliidae; Diptera): III. On Six Species of the Subgenus *Simulium* Latreille. Japanese Journal of Sanitary Zoology, 28(2): 193–217.

TAKAOKA, H. 2002. Review on the Classification, Distribution and Ecology of the Black Flies (Diptera: Simuliidae) of the Nansei Islands in Japan, with Techniques for Collection, Slide-preparation, Microscopic Observation, and Identification of Adult, Pupal and Larval Black flies. Medical Entomology and Zoology, 53 (Suppl. 2): 55–80. (in Japanese with English abstract)

TAKAOKA, H., FUKUDA, M., OTSUKA, Y., AOKI, C., UNI, S. and BAIN, O. 2012. Blackfly Vectors of Zoonotic Onchocerciasis in Japan. Medical and veterinary entomology, 26(4): 372–378.

OTSUKA, Y., TERADA, R. and NISHIMURA, S. (eds.), *The Tokara Islands*
Kagoshima University International Center for Island Studies; Hokuto Shobo Publishing, Tokyo. 10 March 2020.

Chapter 15

Surveillance of Tsutsugamushi Disease and Acari-borne Diseases in the Tokara Islands

Masako ANDOH, Mutsuyo GOKUDEN, Toshiro HONDA, Hiromi FUJITA, Seigo YAMAMOTO, Teruki KADOSAKA, Ai TAKANO, Yasuhiro YANO, Nobuhiro TAKADA, Hiroki KAWABATA and Shuji ANDO

1. Introduction

Tsutsugamushi disease (TD), known as Scrub typhus, and Japanese spotted fever (JSF) are the two major acari-borne rickettsial infections, and are notifiable infectious diseases in Japan. TD is an infection caused by *Orientia tsutsugamushi* (Ot) and transmitted by the larva of trombiculid mites (*Leptotrombidium* spp.); rodents maintain the rickettsiae in nature (KELLY *et al.* 2009). JSF is a *Rickettsia japonica* (Rj) infection that is transmitted by different species of hard ticks, especially the *Haemaphysalis* species of Japan that are also a reservoir (PAROLA *et al.* 2013). Clinical symptoms of the two diseases have commonalities: high fever, systemic skin rash, and characteristic eschar in the site of the vector bite. The diseases are treatable with specific antibiotics (tetracyclines are used worldwide); however, severe cases such as those that develop disseminated intravascular

coagulation adopt a fatal course, as reported every year (National Institute of Infectious Diseases 2017). Delay of suitable treatment is a major factor predisposing the patients to an adverse outcome; therefore, epidemiological information is important to warn the community regarding a possible endemic for prevention, prompt diagnoses, and treatment.

The Kagoshima Prefecture, which is one of the top five highest prefectures, reports a high number of cases of both diseases every year. Environmental surveillance of the agents (Ot and Rj) and their vectors (ticks and chigger mites) responsible for the diseases has been conducted in the main land of the Kagoshima Prefecture by the effort of the Kagoshima Prefectural Institute for Environmental Research and Public Health, National Institute of Infectious Diseases, and other researchers. In the main land of Kagoshima

Table 1. Patients reports of Tsutsugamushi disease and Japanese spotted fever in the Kagoshima prefecture.

Geography	Island	Tsutsugamushi disease	Japanese spotted fever
Mainland		+	+
Osumi islands	Tanega-shima Island	+	−
	Yaku-shima Island	+	−
Tokara islands	Kuchino-shima Island	+	−
	Nakano-shima Island	+	−
	Suwanose-jima Island	+	−
	Taira-jima Island	−	−
	Akuseki-jima Island	+	−
	Kodakara-jima Island	−	−
	Takara-jima Island	−	−
Amami islands	Amami-Oshima Island	−	+
	Tokuno-shima Island	−	+

Prefecture, the distribution of TD was reported from the entire region during 2011 and 2012, but JSF was mainly distributed in the Osumi peninsula (Table 1, Fig. 1). In addition, JSF has been reported in patients in the Amami-Oshima and Tokuno-shima Islands as the presence of Rj in the hard tick *Haemaphysalis hystricis* from the Amami-Oshima Island was confirmed by specific gene detection and Rj isolation (Table 1, Fig. 1). In addition, another spotted fever group (SFG) of rickettsiae, also categorized under the same group of Rj, has been isolated or genetically detected from the hard tick *Ixodes asanumai* in Amami-Oshima Island. However, information of the prevalence of TD and JSF in other remote islands of the Kagoshima Prefecture has been very limited.

The Tokara islands are located within Yaku-shima and Amami islands (Fig. 1). Seven of the 12 islands are not inhabited by a permanent medical doctor. Before the 1990s, TD and JSF have not been reported south of the mainland of Kagoshima. Thereafter in 1993, JSF has been reported in patients in the Amami islands (Amami-Oshima Island and Tokuno-shima Island) that are located southward of the Tokara islands (Fig. 1). TD was reported in patients southward of mainland Kagoshima in Yaku-shima Island in 2001. There has been no report of JSF until now in the Tokara islands; however, severe cases of TD have been reported during 2001 and 2004 in Kuchino-shima Island, Suwanose-jima Island, Nakano-shima Island, and Akuseki-jima Island. Now, TD is an emerging disease in islands southward of the Kagoshima Prefecture including the Tokara islands. Therefore, epidemiological surveillance for pathogenic *Rickettsiae* and the presence of their vectors has started. According to the emergence of Rickettsial infection in Tokara islands, other pathogenic agents that could be carried in the same vector animals such as *Leptospira*, *Borrelia*, *Anaplasma*, *Ehrlichia*, and *Coxiella* species were also investigated.

This is a summary of the epidemiology for TD and JSF with regard to their arthropod vector and mammalian reservoir in the Tokara islands conducted between 2004 and 2016 (GOKUDEN *et al.* 2012, 2013, 2014, HONDA *et al.* 2008).

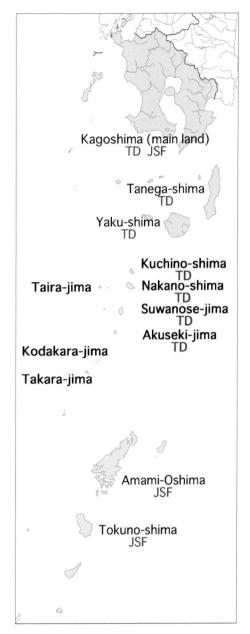

Fig. 1. Geographic distribution of Tsutsugamushi-disease (TD) and Japanese spotted fever (SFG) in the Kagoshima Prefecture.

2. Surveillance

Environmental surveillance for each island was conducted on several different occasions. Ticks and chigger mite surveys were conducted by mouse trapping to collect animals infested with ticks and mites, flagging to collect ticks in the vegetation

(Fig. 2), the black cloth sampling method (Fig. 3), or soil collection followed by the Tullgren funnel to collect chigger mites in the soil.

2.1. *Orientia tsutsugamushi* surveillance in the Tsutsugamushi disease-reported islands: Kuchino-shima Island, Nakano-shima Island, Suwanose-jima Island, and Akuseki-jima Island

Surveillance was conducted three times in Kuchino-shima Island, seven times in Nakano-shima Island, two times in Suwanose-jima Island, and five times in Akuseki-jima Island where TD was reported. The major vector of TD in the main land of the Kagoshima Prefecture is *Leptotrombidium scutellare*, and the same species was found in Kuchino-shima Island, Nakano-shima Island, and Akuseki-jima Island. Presence of *L. scutellare* in Akuseki-jima Island was confirmed in 2013 by collecting approximately 1,000 chigger mites in the island. Akuseki-jima Island is now considered the southern limit for *L. scutellare* distribution. In later analyses, *Leptotrombidium* spp. and *L. deliense* collected

in Nakano-shima Island was identified as a new species and was named *L. suzukii* (TAKAHASHI *et al.* 2014). Later, *Leptotrombidium deliense* collected in Kuchino-shima Island and Akuseki- jima Island was identified as *L. suzukii*.

From the rodent *Apodemus speciosus* in Nakano-shima Island, an Ot-specific gene was detected from the spleen. An Ot-specific antibody was detected from rodents captured in Akuseki-jima Island, which supports the presence of pathogenic Ot in the island. However, there was no evidence of Ot in Suwanose-jima Island. Distribution and population of the pathogen may vary in these islands. No Ot was isolated from the materials collected during the study.

Along with Ot, the presence of Rj was also searched for. Tick species collected from captured animals and vegetation are listed in Table 1. Rj was not isolated. However, *Rickettsia* sp In 56 was isolated from *I. asanumai* (16/21 ticks). In addition, *R. tamurae* was isolated from *A. testidinium* (2/3 ticks). Three *R. rattus* in Akuseki-jima Island had specific antibody against to Rj and other SFG *Rickettsia*, which supports the theory of the presence of pathogenic *Rickettsiae* in the Tokara islands.

2.2. Surveillance of *Rickettsiae* in Tsutsugamushi disease in unreported islands: Taira-jima Island, Kodakara-jima Island, and Takara-jima Island

Surveillance was also conducted in Taira-jima

Fig. 2. Flagging method to collect ticks from the vegetation. December 2011 in Takara-jima.

Fig. 3. Black cloth sampling method to collect chiggar mites from the soil surface. January 2013 in Akuseki-jima.

Island, Kodakara-jima Island, and Takara-jima Island where TD has not been reported (Table 2). *Rattus rattus* captured for the first time in Takara-jima Island had a specific antibody against Ot (serotype Karp and Kato), but no gene detection nor isolation of the pathogen was performed. Other evidence for *Rickettsiae* causing human diseases was neither found in Taira-jima Island, Kodakara-jima Island, nor in Takara-jima Island. SFG *Rickettsia* gene was found in *I. asanumai* in Takara-jima Island. *I. asanumai* was confirmed for the first time in Kodakara-jima Island.

2.3. Other pathogenic microorganisms in the Tokara islands

In the series of studies, the presence of other pathogenic or possibly pathogenic microorganisms was also investigated. *Francisella*, *Borrelia*, *Anaplasma*, *Babesia*, and *Trypanosoma* are the agents of tick-borne diseases that could be found in ticks and rodents. *Leptospira* that cause leptospirosis in humans and animals (especially in dogs as of veterinary importance) was isolated from *R. rattus* in Kuchino-shima Island (1/7 animals), Suwanose-jima Island (7/7 animals), and Akuseki-jima Island (9/18 animals). *Borrelia* was isolated from *A. speciosus* (1/7 animals) in Kuchino-shima Island and *R. rattus* (1/16 animals) in Nakano-shima Island. *Trypanosoma* was observed under light microscopy in the blood smear of *A. speciosus* in Nakano-shima Island. *Candidatus* Neoehrlichia mikurensis, a member of the family Anaplasmacetae, was detected from *Crocidura dsinezumi* in Kuchino-shima Island (NAKAMURA *et al.* 2018). *Francisella* and *Babesia* were not found.

3. Summary

Evidence for the presence of the pathogenic agent of TD and its vector has been found in patients presenting with TD in the islands of Kuchino-shima Island, Nakano-shima Island, Suwanose-jima Island, and Akuseki-jima Island. Confirmation of *L. scutellare*, vector and host of Ot in the main land of the Kagoshima Prefecture, is important information to speculate the Ot serotype that may correlate with disease severity.

However, this evidence was not found in other parts of the Tokara islands so far. Distribution of TD may be limited in certain islands. Outreach for TD and acari-borne diseases becomes increasingly important for early diagnosis and to prevent contact with vectors. Surveillance and research in these islands has unique limitations, specifically very limited transportation methods with long traveling time, which makes it difficult to study the differences between islands in different seasons. Seasonal investigations are important for TD and SFG because of the seasonality of their vector activities. Continual surveillance for the pathogen and vectors in remote islands will provide important information on emerging acari-borne disease epidemiology.

Acknowledgments

We are deeply grateful to all the researchers who participated in the study, who shared a memorable time together in the islands and in the Ferry Toshima. This study was partially supported by grants from the Japanese Ministry of Health, Labour and Welfare (H-18-Shinkou-Ippan-014 and H24-Shinkou-Ippan-008).

References

GOKUDEN, M., HAMADA, M., ISHITANI, K., KAMIMURA, A., MINODA, S. and FUJISAKI, R. 2012. Rickettsiosis of Kyushu and Okinawa Area. Annual Reports of Kagoshima Prefectural Institute for Environmental Research and Public Health, 13. (in Japanese)

GOKUDEN, M., IWAMOTO, Y., HAMADA, Y., HAMADA, M., ISHITANI, K. and IWAKIRI, T. 2014. Surveillance of Tsutsugamushi Disease and Japanese Spotted Fever. Annual Reports of Kagoshima Prefectural Institute for Environmental Research and Public Health, 15. (in Japanese)

GOKUDEN, M., HAMADA, M., HAMADA, Y., KAMIMURA, A., ISHITANI, K. and IWAKIRI., T. 2013. Research study of Tsutsugamushi Disease and Japanese Spotted Fever Patients and their Pathogenic Agents in Kagoshima Prefecture. Annual Reports of Kagoshima Prefectural Institute for Environmental Research and Public Health, 14. (in Japanese)

HONDA, T., GOKUDEN, M., FUJITA, H., KADOSAKA, T., KAWABATA, H., TAKANO, A., YAMAMOTO, S., OIKAWA, Y., YANO, Y. and TAKADA, N. 2008. Survey for Pathogen from Wild Rodents and Ticks in Kagoshima Prefecture. 2008. Annual Reports of Kagoshima Prefectural Institute for Environmental Research and Public Health, 9. (in Japanese)

KELLY, D. J., FUERST, P. A, CHING, W. M., RICHARDS, A. L.

Table 2. *Rickettsia* and potential host and vector for rickettsial diseases found in the Tokara islands.

Island	Year, month	Host and vector			Pathogen		
		Mouse trapping	Ticks	Chigger mites	Orientia tsutsugamushi	Rickettsia japonica	Other Rickettsia
Kuchino-shima	2008, January 2015, May 2016, June	*Apodemus speciosus* *Crocidura dsinezumi* *Rattus norvegicus* *Rattus rattus*	*Amblyomma testudinarium* *Ixodes asanumai* *Ixodes granulatus* *Ixodes turdus* *Haemaphysalis cornigera* *Haemaphysalis flava* *Haemaphysalis formosensis* *Haemaphysalis longicornis* *Haemaphysalis mageshimanensis* *Rhipicephalus microplus*	*Leptotrombidium scutellare* *Leptotrombidium suzukii*	Not confirmed	Not confirmed	SFG *Rickettsia* gene detection from *I. asanumai*. SFG *Rickettsia* isolation from *I. asanumai* and *I. granulatus*. *Candidatus* Neoehrlichia mikurensis detection from *C. dsinezumi*.
Nakano-shima	2004, October 2007, July 2012, July 2013, December 2014, January 2014, July 2015, January	*Apodemus speciosus* *Crocidura dsinezumi* *Rattus rattus*	*Amblyomma testudinarium* *Haemaphysalis flava* *Haemaphysalis hystricis* *Haemaphysalis longicornis* *Haemaphysalis mageshimaensis*	*Helenicula miyagawai* *Leptotrombidium scutellare* *Leptotrombidium suzukii* (*Leptotrombidium deliense*)	Gene (Kuroki serotype) detection from spleen of *A. speciosus*	Not confirmed	*R. tamurae* isolation from *A. testudinarium*. SFG *Rickettsia* isolation from *I. asanumai*.
Taira-jima	2008, January	*Rattus norvegicus* *Rattus rattus*	*Ixodes turdus* *Haemaphysalis cornigera* *Haemaphysalis flava* *Haemaphysalis formosensis* *Haemaphysalis mageshimanensis* *Haemaphysalis longicornis* *Rhipicephalus microplus*	Not confirmed	Not confirmed	Not confirmed	
Suwanose-jima	2007, December 2013, December	*Rattus rattus*	*Haemaphysalis flava* *Haemaphysalis longicornis*	Not confirmed	Not confirmed	Not confirmed	
Akuseki-jima	2007, July 2007, December 2012, December 2013, January 2013, December	*Rattus norvegicus* *Rattus rattus*	*Ixodes asanumai* *Haemaphysalis flava* *Haemaphysalis formosensis* *Haemaphysalis hystricis* *Haemaphysalis longicornis* *Haemaphysalis mageshimanensis*	*Helenicula miyagawai* *Leptotrombidium scutellare* *Leptotrombidium suzukii* (*Leptotrombidium deliense*)	Not confirmed	Rj antibody detection from *R. rattus*.	SFG *Rickettsia* isolation from *I. asanumai*
Kodakara-jima	2013, January		*Ixodes asanumai* *Haemaphysalis flava* *Haemaphysalis longicornis* *Haemaphysalis mageshimanensis* *Rhipicephalus microplus*	*Helenicula* sp. *Leptotrombidium burnsi*	Not confirmed	Not confirmed	
Takara-jima	2007, July 2011, July 2011, December	*Rattus rattus*	*Ixodes asanumai* *Haemaphysalis formosensis*	*Leptotrombidium deliense*	Ot antibody in *R. rattus*	Not confirmed	SFG *Rickettsia* gene isolation from *I. asanumai*

2019. Scrub Typhus: the Geographic Distribution of Phenotypic ad Genotypic Variants of *Orientia tsutsugamushi*. Clinical Infectious Diseases 48(3): 203-230.

NAKAMURA, T., TODA, M., GOKUDEN, M., YAMAMOTO, S., FUJITA, H., FUJITA, N., HONDA, T., ISHIHARA, K. and ANDOH, M. 2018. Survey of Pathogenic Bacteria in wild Animals and Ticks in Kuchinoshima Island, Tokara Islands. Medical Entomology and Zoology, 69(2): 123. (in Japanese)

National Institute of Infectious Diseases 2017. Tsutsugamushi disease and Japanese spotted fever, 2007 ~ 2016. Infectious Agents Surveillance Report, 38(6): 109–112.

PAROLA, P., PADDOCK, C. D., SOCOLOVSCHI, C., LABRUNA, M. B., MEDIANNIKOV, O., KERNIF, T., ABDAD, M. Y., STENOS, J., BITAM, I., FOURNIER, P. E. and RAOULT, D. 2013. Update on Tick-borne Rickettsioses around the World: A Geographic Approach. Clinical Microbiogy Review, 26(4): 657–702.

TAKAHASHI, M., MISUMI, H. and NODA, S. 2014. *Leptotrombidium suzukii* (Acari, Trombiculidae): A New Species of Chigger Mite Found on *Apodemus speciosus* (Rodentia, Muridae) on Nakanoshima Island in the Tokara Islands, Kagoshima Prefecture, Japan. Bulletin of the National Museum of Nature and Science Series A (Zoology), 40(4): 191–199.

OTSUKA, Y., TERADA, R. and NISHIMURA, S. (eds.), *The Tokara Islands*
Kagoshima University International Center for Island Studies; Hokuto Shobo Publishing, Tokyo. 10 March 2020.

Chapter 16
The Kuroshio around the Tokara Strait

Hirohiko NAKAMURA

1. Introduction

The Tokara Strait between Yaku-shima Island and Amami-oshima Island, with a sill depth of ~690 m and a width of ~150 km, is a major strait connecting the East China Sea (ECS) and the North Pacific Ocean (Fig. 1). Because the Kuroshio (literally, the "Black Current") passes through the Tokara Strait as it flows out of the ECS into the North Pacific Ocean, this strait has been historically regarded as the most suitable location where we can monitor the Kuroshio variation over a long time (e.g., YAMASHIRO and KAWABE 1996, ZHU *et al.* 2017), and we can understand its tendencies well (e.g., YAMASHIRO and KAWABE 2002, NAKAMURA *et al.* 2006, LIU *et al.* 2019). As the Tokara Strait is also characterized by the presence of many small islands and seamounts, the Kuroshio is strongly affected by such complex topographies as it flows through the strait. When the Kuroshio impinges on these islands or rides over the seamounts, it generates vortices, internal waves, and intensive turbulent mixing on the lee side of these islands and seamounts (TSUTSUMI *et al.* 2017, NAGAI *et al.* 2017). These effects play an important role in dissipating the kinetic energy of the Kuroshio. Surprisingly, our recent estimates (as yet unpublished) indicate that such intensive turbulent mixing can consume the kinetic energy of the Kuroshio within the Tokara Strait in only about 10 days and make it disappear completely, unless more kinetic energy is supplied from upstream.

Strong turbulent mixing due to small islands and seamounts around the Tokara Strait also plays an important role in maintaining the oceanic ecosystem within the Kuroshio. This is because vertical mixing entrains nutrient-rich thermocline water, carries it into the shallower euphotic zone where photosynthesis can occur, and activates primary euphotic production. This effect is often called the island mass effect (HASEGAWA 2019). For this reason, Japanese physical and biological oceanographers, especially those from Kagoshima University, recently have concluded that the Tokara Strait is a hotspot of nutrient-rich water, which provides growing grounds within the Kuroshio for several fish species via the tropic linkage (KOBARI *et al.* 2019).

In the present chapter, I introduce the studies on the Kuroshio in the Tokara Strait that have been performed mainly by myself and my colleagues for most of the past 10 years. Namely, I explain how we have observed the variation of the Kuroshio in the Tokara Strait in section 2, and what we have concluded about it in section 3. More concretely, I examine the state of the Kuroshio around the Tokara Strait with respect to intensity, path, and stability, particularly for seasonal variations (section 3.1) and the Kuroshio's interaction with the Tokara Strait bottom topography (section 3.2). I finally provide information on recent topics in section 4. One is an ongoing project that aims to utilize the Kuroshio's kinetic energy in the Tokara Strait for electric power, and the other is a disaster in which the Tokara Islands were polluted by oil spilled from the *Sanchi* oil tanker during January to March in 2018. The oil was spread by the combined effects of the Kuroshio flow and winter monsoon wind from the upstream continental slope area in the ECS, where the *Sanchi* sank. Relating to these topics, I show how often and how well we used the T/V *Kagoshima-maru*, owned by Kagoshima University, for oceanographic observations, emphasizing that this ship brings a large benefit to the marine sciences.

To understand this chapter, the reader needs

basic knowledge about the Kuroshio. As its detailed explanation is beyond the scope of this chapter, I here provide a brief summary of the physical aspects of the Kuroshio. The Kuroshio is a northward component of the North Pacific subtropical gyre, which is mainly driven by the prevailing winds over the North Pacific Ocean, such as the westerlies and the trade winds. A distinctive characteristic of the subtropical gyre is the westward intensification of the current. The Kuroshio is, therefore, the strongest current in the North Pacific Ocean. The subtropical gyre is an approximately steady flow, which is characterized by a form of motion called a "geostrophic current," in which the pressure gradient force is balanced by the Coriolis force due to the earth's rotation. Because of this principle, the surface water rotates clockwise in the subtropical gyre along a contour with the same sea surface height (i.e., isobar), and the sea surface height area increases on the contour's right side in the Northern Hemisphere. The sea surface height across the Kuroshio, therefore, is higher on the offshore side than on the inshore side. We can see analogous phenomena in the atmosphere in the form of typhoons and cyclones.

To the readers who need additional general explanation, I recommend reading my previous article (NAKAMURA 2013), "The Kuroshio: its physical aspect and roles in Kagoshima's nature and culture," which was included in the book *The Islands of Kagoshima* published in 2013 by Kagoshima University Research Center of the Pacific Islands. Indeed, I wrote the previous paper to provide general and useful information about the Kuroshio to persons without any previous knowledge of this current, such as visitors from foreign countries. The readers can, therefore, find general explanations of the Kuroshio from a physical oceanographic point of view, and regional features of the current in the seas of Kagoshima, such as the spatial patterns, temporal variations, water properties, and water colors. The present chapter is regarded as a sequel to the 2013 article, and it focuses on my recent studies on the Kuroshio around the Tokara Strait. Furthermore, to the readers who desire specialized knowledge about

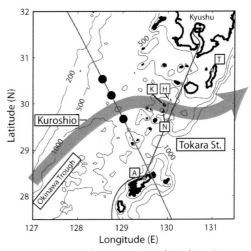

T: Tanegashima Is.   K: Kuchinoshima Is.
N: Nakanoshima Is.   A: Amami-oshima Is.
H: Hira-se Seamount

Fig. 1. Typical flow pattern of the Kuroshio superimposed on the bottom topography around the Tokara Strait, along with information on tide gage stations (closed green circles), satellite altimetry track (solid red line), and current meter moorings (closed black circles) related to the author's project during the period June 2009 to June 2010. The ferryboat *Naminoue* route is also shown (solid blue line).

the Kuroshio, I recommend the review article about the Kuroshio that I recently wrote, which will be published in the near future by Springer Books as NAKAMURA (2019): *Changing Kuroshio and Its Affected Shelf Sea: A Physical View, in Changing Asia-Pacific Marginal Seas*, edited by C.-T. A. CHEN and X. GUO.

2. Measurement of the Kuroshio around the Tokara Strait

Temporal and spatial variations of the Kuroshio have been observed for a long time in the Tokara Strait. This is because the Tokara Strait is geographically the most suitable location for the measurement of the Kuroshio in Japanese coastal regions adjacent to the Kuroshio. In this section, we consider how this strait is suitable for the measurement of the Kuroshio variation and what methods are used to measure it.

A fundamental method for measuring the velocity of a persistent current, such as the Kuroshio, is to use its tendency to coincide with the geostrophic current, in which the pressure gradient force is balanced by the Coriolis force. A simplest way to observe the geostrophic current at the sea surface is to measure the sea surface height (SSH) that causes the pressure gradient force. There exist two methods to measure it: One is the historical method in which the SSH is measured at a coastal tide gage station. As of December 2019, there are 188 coastal tide gage stations along Japanese coasts from Hokkaido to the Nanseishoto Island chain; these stations are owned by Japanese government agencies, such as Japan Meteorological Agency (https://www.jma.go.jp/jp/choi/list1. html). Some stations have continuous measurement records going back over 100 years. The other method was introduced recently by new technology, in which the SSH is measured from orbit. The satellites, named TOPEX/Poseidon, measuring the SSH over the global oceans were first launched in 1992. Because nearly 25 years have passed since satellite measurements began, a sufficiently large amount of data has been accumulated for analysis.

In addition to the methods based on SSH measurement, the in situ current velocity can be measured by current meters directly. Current meters are moored in the sea and mounted to vessels. In the following paragraphs, I explain how these methods are used in the Tokara Strait and provide specific examples based on my experiences.

2.1. Tide gage stations

The Tokara Strait is the best location to observe the Kuroshio on the whole Japanese coast, because the tide gage stations have been in place for a long time at some islands, including Tanega-shima (since 1965), Nakano-shima (since 1984), and Amami-oshima Islands (since 1965) (see Fig. 1), that are located across the Kuroshio from its inshore to offshore side. Using this geographical merit, KAWABE (1995) developed methods to monitor the daily current speed and current position of the Kuroshio using the sea level (SL) records from these three islands. With the assumption that the Kuroshio is a geostrophic current, the

current speed of the Kuroshio at the sea surface is estimated from the SL difference between Naze in Amami-oshima Island and Nishinoomote in Tanega-shima Island (Naze minus Nishinoomote). A positive value for the SL difference indicates an eastward current speed averaged over the entire width of the Kuroshio in the Tokara Strait, and a negative SL difference indicates a corresponding westward current. In addition, the current position of the Kuroshio can be identified by the ratio between two SL differences, that is, the northern SL difference (Nakano-shima minus Nishinoomote) / the southern SL difference (Naze minus Nakano-shima). This ratio is often called the Kuroshio Position Index (KPI). YAMASHIRO and KAWABE (1996) established an equation to transfer the KPI to the actual position of the Kuroshio axis, which corresponds to a location with the maximum eastward current speed at a depth of 200 m.

In addition, it is worth noting some complexities. The SL variation is caused not only by geostrophic current but also by tides, atmospheric pressure change, and thermal expansion of the sea water. It is, therefore, necessary to remove the latter effects to estimate the geostrophic current accurately. The harmonic analysis, which is a method to decompose a time series into many individual oscillations, each with a specified period, is generally used to remove tidal constituents from the SL time series. The oscillation periods of tidal constituents are well known from astronomical studies. The SL variations due to tidal motions can be estimated in the Tokara Strait accurately, because the SL has been recorded in the Tokara Strait at least since 1984, which is long enough to apply harmonic analysis.

2.2. Satellite altimetry

The ongoing global ocean observing altimetry satellite mission started in October 1992. Since 1992, a spatially gridded dataset of global SSH distribution has been available from the Archiving Validation and Interpretation of Satellite Oceanography (AVISO) Data Center. The temporal interval of the data is ~10 days and its spatial resolution is ~25 km. This dataset is very useful for understanding the behaviors of mesoscale

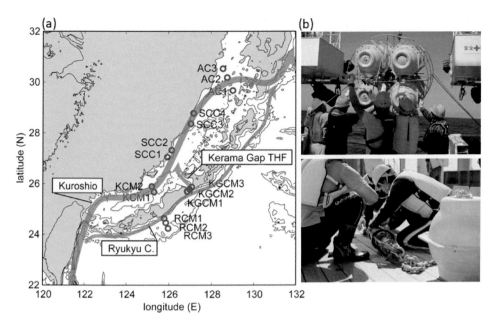

Fig. 2. (a) Locations of long-term current meter moorings, which were deployed during 2004 to 2019 during the author's studies using the T/V *Kagoshima-maru*. Based on these moored meter observations, the current features of the Kuroshio, the Ryukyu Current, and the Kerama Gap Throughflow have been investigated. (b) Photos of ADCP deployment onboard the T/V *Kagoshima-maru* in June 2015 at KCM1 (see Fig. 2a), which was carried out as an international research collaboration, the Joint Kuroshio-Ryukyu Current System Study, between Japan, China, and South Korea.

eddies and currents at scales of several hundred kilometers and several tens of days. This dataset is, therefore, used not only in academic fields but also in commercial fields. For example, fishermen fishing in the pelagic seas often use this dataset to obtain information on their fishing grounds, which tend to form near the convergence zone along the perimeter of the mesoscale eddy or the current.

From the SSH map provided by AVISO, we have reliable information on large-scale motions of the Kuroshio, such as the behavior of the large meander south of Honshu, the largest island of Japan. The meandering motion of the Kuroshio in the ECS is, however, one order of magnitude smaller in spatial scale than that south of Honshu. The use of this dataset, therefore, is unsuitable for the study of the temporal and spatial variations of the Kuroshio position within the ECS. Instead of this dataset, I therefore used the SSH data measured along a satellite altimetry track west of the Tokara Strait (see Fig. 1) to capture seasonal variations of the Kuroshio's position and stability

(NAKAMURA *et al*. 2012). The along-track SSH data has a high spatial resolution of 6.2 km even though its temporal resolution is the same 10 days as that of the AVISO gridded dataset.

Here, I explain two issues that needed to be overcome when I used the along-track SSH data. One issue is that the satellite altimetry data provide only the SSH variation relative to a long-term average SSH distribution because the earth's geoid, that is, the shape of the ocean surface without the influence of winds and tides, cannot be accurately determined by current technology. To solve the problem that the satellite altimetry provides only the relative SSH variation, I measured velocity distributions along the satellite track several times from the T/V *Kagoshima-maru*, which ran along the satellite track with a ship-mounted current meter (NAKAMURA *et al*. 2012). The time series of the relative geostrophic current distribution derived from the relative SSH distribution along the satellite track were best-fitted to the absolute velocity distributions measured by the ship-mounted current meter.

The other issue is aliasing, which is a phenomenon that manifests itself as an artificial oscillation appearing in a time series without a time interval sufficient to resolve a real oscillation. The Kuroshio meander motion west of the Tokara Strait typically has a period from 10 to 90 days, so that the temporal resolution (10 days) of the satellite altimetry SSH time series is not sufficient to examine the actual meander variation. Therefore, I had to prove that my data analysis did not suffer from aliasing. For this purpose, I compared the satellite altimetry SSH time series with the current-meter records having short time intervals, which were observed by current meters moored at three locations on the satellite track (NAKAMURA *et al.* 2012).

2.3. Current meter moorings placed by the T/V *Kagoshima-maru*

Moored current meters provide a direct method for measuring in situ current over short time intervals, and thus this method is the most reliable for current measurement. However, mooring observation is not appropriate for understanding the entire horizontal structure of the current or the eddy. This is because it is hard to deploy a sufficient number of moorings over the entire study area. The deployment of a mooring system, especially in the deep ocean, is difficult work that can be done only with a ship equipped with heavy machinery, such as cranes and winches.

Fortunately, I have the advantage of being able to deploy current meter moorings with high observational ability because I can use the T/V *Kagoshima-maru* in my research. Since the middle 2000s, I have conducted a cruise of about 2 weeks duration twice yearly, together with my colleagues at Kagoshima University. These cruises combine onboard training of students and specialized oceanographic research. Figure 2 shows the locations of long-term moorings (over 1 year) that I, together with many Japanese and international collaborators, have deployed around the Okinawa Trough using the T/V *Kagoshima-maru* since 2004. The number of locations is 15, and 6 foreign research institutes have used the T/V *Kagoshima-maru*: Graduate

School of Oceanography/University of Rhode Island (USA), Second Institute of Oceanography/Ministry of Natural Resources (China), Korea Institute of Ocean Science & Technology (Korea), Inha University (Korea), Seoul National University (Korea), and Applied Physics Laboratory/University of Washington (USA).

To obtain seasonal and interannual variations in the ocean with moored current meters, we usually maintain the mooring for more than 2 years. Therefore, a mooring system deployed in the sea is recovered about 1 year later and redeployed immediately after a rapid maintenance of the onboard instruments and hardware. When we go to the sea to recover such a mooring once a year, we are extremely worried whether the mooring is present and can be safely recovered. Mooring systems are sometimes missing because the mooring line is accidentally cut by fishing gear. In addition, there are rare cases in which the acoustic releaser, which is the instrument that makes the mooring system separate from its anchor, does not work. If we fail to recover the mooring system, we lose not only a year's worth of data but also expensive oceanographic instruments, which we may not be able to purchase again.

2.4. The ferryboat Naminoue

Kagoshima City is a hub port for the ferryboats that transport goods and people from Kyushu to the Nanseishoto Islands. The ferryboat Naminoue made round trips between Kagoshima and Naha in Okinawa Island via Amami-oshima, Tokuno-shima, Okinoerabu-jima, and Yoron-jima Islands (see Fig. 1). The round-trip time of the Naminoue was 4 days. My laboratory mounted an acoustic Doppler current profiler (ADCP) on this ship and conducted a long-term current survey during 2003 to 2012. The ADCP is an instrument that measures the vertical profile of current velocity based on the following fundamental principle: the velocity of particles, such as plankton, carried by the current in the sea water can be calculated with the Doppler-shifted frequency between the sound wave emitted from the ADCP into the sea water and that returned to the ADCP after being reflected by the particles. If the ADCP is mounted at the bottom of the ship, the vertical velocity profiles are sampled as the ship runs along its course. With voluntary collaboration kindly provided by the company that owned the Naminoue, my group collected a total of 1,234 velocity cross-sections across the Kuroshio in the Tokara Strait and analyzed the Kuroshio flow variation (ZHU *et al.* 2017, LIU *et al.* 2017, LIU *et al.* 2019).

3. What Is Known about the Kuroshio around the Tokara Strait?

3.1. Seasonal variations in intensity, path, and stability of the Kuroshio

Since the middle 2000s, I have actively studied several types of seasonal Kuroshio variations, such as intensity, path, and stability in the ECS. My first interest among these factors was stability, because I was aware that the Kuroshio in the northeastern ECS tends to be stable in the summer-

fall period but unstable in the winter-spring period (Fig. 3). Thus, I analyzed comprehensive datasets consisting of readings from moored current meters placed along the continental slope, the KPI time series in the Tokara Strait, and satellite sea surface temperature (SST) images over the northeastern ECS (NAKAMURA *et al.* 2003). Before the middle 2000s, most physical oceanographers focused on the dynamics by which the stable Kuroshio flow develops into the Kuroshio meandering motion, that is, an unstable flow. My interest, however, aimed at understanding seasonal dependency of the instability rather than the instability itself (NAKAMURA *et al.* 2006, NAKAMUA *et al.* 2008).

This topic was very exciting for me because the mechanism causing the seasonal nature of the Kuroshio destabilization was thought to be a local process driven by the Northeast Asian Monsoon wind. This hypothesis (NAKAMURA *et al.* 2010) has

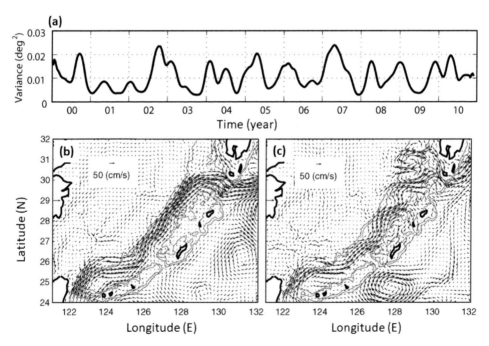

Fig. 3. (a) Index to express the Kuroshio's meandering activity west of the Tokara Strait: specifically, the 20- to 80-day variance for the satellite altimetry-derived Kuroshio axis position west of the Tokara Strait (the solid red line in Fig. 1 shows the satellite track). The time series reveals the presence of seasonal variation, in which the activity is high in the winter-spring period but low in the summer-fall period. (b, c) Typical Kuroshio surface current states: (b) unstable state for the winter-spring period and (c) stable state for the summer-fall period. Specifically, these are snapshots of surface current vectors from a realistic high-resolution ocean general circulation model simulation for (a) 2 October 2003 and (b) 11 March 1998.

a special meaning for physical oceanographers because it contradicts the traditional theory, in which seasonal variations in the Kuroshio are explained as a remote process caused by planetary waves that propagate from the North Pacific interior region to the western boundary region, which are excited by seasonal variations in the prevailing winds over the North Pacific Ocean. To confirm the monsoon wind hypothesis, as reported in NAKAMURA *et al.* (2012), I analyzed the combined data of the satellite altimetry SSH time series along the satellite track west of the Tokara Strait and the records of current meters moored along the satellite track (see Figs. 1 and 3). Based on this study, I believe that the seasonal nature of the Kuroshio destabilization in the northeastern ECS is generated by seasonal local wind variation due to the Northeast Asian Monsoon.

After the stability problem was addressed, my interest shifted to the study of the seasonal variation of the Kuroshio path around the Tokara Strait. More specifically, I examined the small meander off the southeastern coast of Kyushu that was known to appear in the winter-spring period. This problem has attracted many Japanese physical oceanographers, because this small meander propagates downstream and sometimes develops into large meanders off the southern coast of Honshu. The presence of such a seasonality was, however, questioned and debated in the middle 2000s. Therefore, I first examined whether the small meander really tends to appear in the winter-spring period, and concluded that small meanders experience phase-locking with the seasonal cycle, as occurs in the winter-spring period, even though the intensity of such phase-locking is modulated on decadal timescales (NAKAMURA *et al.* 2015). By analyzing monthly mean surface geostrophic current data from AVISO (see section 2.2) and wind stress fields, I next showed that the southwestward monsoon wind blowing against the Kuroshio in the autumn and early winter is responsible for the small meander formation (NAKAMURA *et al.* 2015). Furthermore, I succeeded in proposing the possible dynamics to explain this phenomenon, which is based on the effect of local wind over a jet with strong velocity shear, such

as the Kuroshio. Using a numerical model with idealized topography, I showed that the response of the modeled Kuroshio to the local wind stress is consistent with observational and theoretical results.

Since about 2016 up to now, my interest has aimed at the study of the seasonal variation in the Kuroshio intensity. With respect to seasonal surface velocity variation, my supervised student, Zhen-long Zhang, and I pointed out that it is stronger in summer and weaker in winter over the entire Kuroshio path, based on observational data analysis. Furthermore, through numerical experiments based on a realistic general circulation model, we also showed that its essential driving force is the local wind stress over the Kuroshio. More specifically, we showed that seasonal Kuroshio velocity variations near the surface layer are caused primarily by local responses to wind stress upon the current itself, while the deep layer seasonal Kuroshio velocity variations can be explained by the conventional remote process, named the Sverdrup balance, in which barotropic responses to the wind stress curling over the area west of the Izu-Ogasawara Ridge are responsible. We pointed out that if seasonal Kuroshio transport variations are estimated for the water column from the sea surface to depths over 1,000 m, a semiannual cycle with maxima in winter and summer will be detected as a combined feature of both responses, as shown for the Tokara Strait by ZHU *et al.* (2017) and LIU *et al.* (2019). The latest results are now being prepared for publication.

My study of the seasonal variation of the Kuroshio in terms of stability, path, and intensity has convinced me that there is a common mechanism governing the three types of variations, namely the local response of the Kuroshio to the Northeast Asian Monsoon wind. Confirming this mechanism will establish a new paradigm that explains the Kuroshio variation, because the conventional theory is based on the remote response of the Kuroshio to the prevailing winds over the North Pacific interior region. This new paradigm will play a crucial role in understanding not only in the seasonal variations but also the interannual variations of the Kuroshio.

3.2. Turbulent mixing due to Kuroshio–topography interaction

Until about 10 years ago, I had considered the turbulent mixing in the ocean as "noise" when investigating large-scale oceanic phenomena, such as temporal and spatial variations of the Kuroshio. However, this viewpoint changed significantly when my colleagues and I discovered the Kerama Gap overflow, which is a near-bottom current over the sill of the Kerama Gap, a narrow (~50 km wide) but deep channel (sill depth of 1,100 m) connecting the Okinawa Trough to the Philippine Sea (NAKAMURA *et al.* 2013). Specifically, upwelling caused by strong turbulent mixing within the Okinawa Trough draws the Kerama Gap overflow from the Philippine Sea into the Okinawa Trough. This phenomenon has an important meaning not only in the circulation system but also in the ecosystem in the Okinawa Trough, because nutrient-rich Philippine Sea intermediate water is sucked up into the lower thermocline below the Kuroshio in the Okinawa Trough.

After this experience, I clearly recognized the importance of turbulent mixing in understanding physical and biological problems in the Okinawa Trough. At that time, during 2015 to 2019, I had been involved in a large research project, named "Ocean Mixing Processes: Impact on Biogeochemistry, Climate and Ecosystem (OMIX)," which was supported with a Grant-in-Aid for Scientific Research in Innovative Areas by the Ministry of Education, Culture, Sport, Science and Technology. In this large project, which consists of 9 individual research groups, I belonged to a group that aimed to study turbulent mixing processes in the Kuroshio and their influence on its ecosystem. My main task in this group was to conduct in situ observations with the T/V *Kagoshima-maru* to clarify the physical and biological processes in the Tokara Strait. Six cruises almost 10 days long were carried out by the T/V *Kagoshima-maru* during 2015 to 2019 in the Tokara Strait, and physical, chemical, and biological oceanographers from several universities and institutes throughout Japan were invited.

The central purpose of this observational study consisted of three parts: 1) to clarify turbulent mixing processes due to interactions of the Kuroshio and tidal currents with the bottom topography in the Tokara Strait, 2) to estimate the energy dissipation rate due to turbulent mixing integrated over the Tokara Strait, and 3) to clarify the role of the Tokara Strait in the low-trophic-level ecosystem in the Kuroshio.

For the first purpose, Dr. Tsutsumi from Kyushu University (currently of Univ. of Tokyo), analyzed data from the 2015 cruise and revealed the first direct evidence that strong turbulence with eddy diffusivity of the order 10^{-1} m^2 s^{-1} is generated on the lee (downstream) side of the Hira-se Seamount in the Tokara Strait when the Kuroshio impinges it (TSUTSUMI *et al.* 2017). This magnitude of eddy diffusivity is ~1,000 times larger than the canonical value of the world ocean average (MUNK and WUNSCH 1998). After this discovery, we focused on the phenomena near the Hira-se Seamount (see Fig. 1) during the OMIX project. Using data from the 2016 cruise, Dr. Nagai (Tokyo University of Marine Science and Technology) next observed coherent band-like structures with lateral scales more than the order 10 km between strong turbulent layers and near-inertial internal wave shears in the Tokara Strait (NAGAI *et al.* 2017). This evidence suggested that the breaking of near-inertial internal waves is an essential cause of strong turbulent mixing occurring in the Tokara Strait. Furthermore, using data from the 2018 cruise, Dr. Nagai found evidence that the near-inertial internal waves were generated around the Hira-se Seamount through inertial–symmetric instability, which is due to interaction of the Kuroshio with the seamount bottom topography. For the second purpose, a rough estimate by Drs. Lien and Kunze from the University of Washington, using data from the 2019 cruise, indicated that intensive turbulent mixing in the Tokara Strait can consume the kinetic energy of the Kuroshio in this location in only about 10 days.

For the third purpose, Dr. KOBARI (Kagoshima Univ.) and Dr. YOSHIE (Ehime Univ.) joined the OMIX project to establish a hypothesis that may provide a key for solving the Kuroshio Paradox, that is, that "the surface water of the Kuroshio is nutrient-depleted and has relatively low primary productivity, yet abundant fish populations are supported in the region" (Saito 2019). Their hypothesis is as follows: The Tokara Strait is a hotspot of nutrient supply to the surface water of the Kuroshio because of strong turbulent mixing. This nutrient supply acts to maintain the low-trophic ecosystem in the Kuroshio downstream of the Tokara Strait, specifically, off the eastern coast of Kyushu Island and off the southern coast of Shikoku Island. Based on their previous observations performed around the Kuroshio region in the ECS, they had known that the standing stock of zooplankton is high within the Kuroshio while that of phytoplankton is low, compared with the coastal areas inshore of the Kuroshio. To explain this fact, they made a working hypothesis that zooplankton rapidly consumes phytoplankton within the Kuroshio, which is a unique characteristic of the Kuroshio's low-trophic ecosystem. They have carried out many experiments onboard the T/V *Kagoshima-maru*, where zooplankton and phytoplankton were incubated in bottles of sea water obtained from the Kuroshio. For these incubation experiments, they controlled the amount of nutrients that were

artificially supplied into the bottled sea water in the range around a standard value measured in the Tokara Strait. The results of the experiments support their current hypothesis (Abe *et al.* 2019, Kobari *et al.* 2019).

The observational study on the enhanced turbulent mixing in the Tokara Strait is continuing with a further extension after the OMIX project is finished in March 2020. A new collaborative research project with the Applied Physics Laboratory/University of Washington was started in November 2019 with a plan to carry out three T/V *Kagoshima-maru* cruises near the Hira-se Seamount until June 2021. The project name of this collaboration research is "The Kuroshio Interaction of Tokara Strait Topography," the nickname of which is KITTY.

4. Other recent topics for the Kuroshio around the Tokara Strait

4.1. The Kuroshio as a clean energy resource
As already explained in the previous sections, the Kuroshio, which has a width of ~100 km and a depth of ~1,000 m, is one of the largest ocean currents. Furthermore, its speed exceeds 1 m s^{-1}

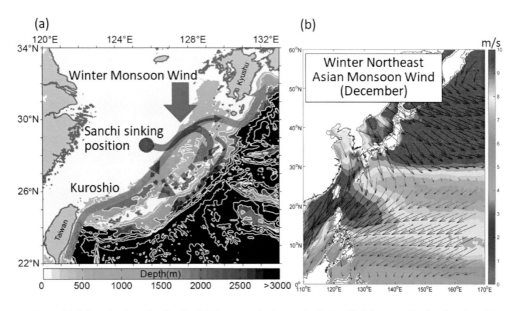

Fig. 4. (a) Schematic view showing the drifting routes (red arrows) of oil spilled from the *Sanchi* oil tanker. (b) Winter monsoon wind speed (colors) and direction (arrows), specifically, December mean sea-surface winds from the NASA Quick Scatterometer for the period September 1999 to August 2007.

near the sea surface. This means that the current motion can provide a relatively inexhaustible source of energy. The Kuroshio is, therefore, regarded as an important resource for clean energy to replace fossil fuels, such as oil.

After the Great East Japan Earthquake on 11 March 2011, Japanese marine scientists and engineers began to develop technology to convert the energy of the Kuroshio flow to electric power. The Tokara Strait was considered as one of the most suitable locations to locate electric power stations, which consist of multiple turbines, in the Kuroshio. This is because the Kuroshio flows through shallow seas near the Tokara Strait, while it flows through deep seas and significantly shifts its location by meandering motion off the southern coast of Honshu. Therefore, a first Japanese test plant, using a turbine with a capacity of 100 kW of electric power generation, was started by IHI Co., Ltd. in the coastal sea of Kuchino-shima Island ("K" in Fig. 1) in summer of 2019. However, drawbacks have been pointed out for plans to construct an electric plant in the Tokara Strait. One problem is that the Kuroshio's current speed is about 30% weaker in the Tokara Strait than off the southern coast of Honshu, because the islands in the strait disperse the Kuroshio and the strong turbulent mixing dissipates its energy. Another drawback is that the sea area near the Hira-se Seamount, where the Kuroshio's mainstream is likely to flow all year round, and hence the most suitable location for an electric plant, is too far from the mainland of Kyushu to install an underwater electric transmission cable. Therefore, it may be more realistic to develop small electric plants that supply energy to each island.

4.2. Oil spill from Sanchi oil tanker

Another topic is also related to energy, not clean energy, but oil. The Sanchi, a Panamanian oil tanker, collided with another ship, caught fire, and sank on 14 January 2018 on the continental shelf edge ~300 km west of Amami-oshima Island, which is close to the inshore flank of the Kuroshio. Although the ship was believed to carry ~110,000 tons of natural-gas condensate, it was unclear where the condensate that spilled from the ship

went. A plausible view was that most condensate evaporated when the ship burned. Moreover, some of the ship's fuel oil first drifted ashore on the coast of Kodakara-jima Island on 28 January, and then it drifted southwestward along the Nanseishoto Island chain, arriving at the western coast of Amami-oshima Island on 1 February and the western coast of Okinawa Island on 9 February (Fig. 4).

I was surprised to hear of the news that a large amount of oil drifted ashore on Kodakara-jima Island, because this meant that oil patches were able to drift across the Kuroshio from its inshore side to its offshore side. However, Dr. Kako at Kagoshima University, using a realistic ocean circulation model, succeeded in simulating the drift of oil patches from the location where the *Sanchi* sank to Nanseishoto Islands such as Kodakara-jima, Amami-oshima, and Okinawa. In addition to the Kuroshio flow, the wind played an important role in the movement of drifting oil patches. More specifically, wind can push oil, which is known as the sailing effect, and the wind-induced sea surface waves can carry oil forward in the same direction as the wind, which is called the Stokes drifting effect. The velocity of oil propelled by the sum of both effects is about 4% of the wind speed. A strong outbreak of cold winter air had covered the Kuroshio region where many oil patches were drifting, and the associated strong northerly wind, which exceeded 10 m s^{-1}, carried oil patches southward across the Kuroshio in the area west of Kyushu (see Fig. 4).

This disaster unexpectedly gave us some new information: namely, that we can make material floating on the sea surface drift across the Kuroshio in the Tokara Strait if the material is pushed by an appropriate wind. Here, there exists a folk story that ancient fishermen in the Yayoi era (~BC/300–AC/300) moved between Kyushu and Okinawa islands along the Nanseishoto Islands chain by rowing their boat without a sail (KINOSHITA 2000). Although they must have moved across the Kuroshio, with its strong current with speed of more than 1 m s^{-1} and ~100 km width in the Tokara Strait, how did they make such a voyage successfully? The wind must be the key to solving this mystery.

References

ABE, M., KOBARI, T., HONMA, T., KANAYAMA, T., KARU, F., YOSHIE, N., *et al.* 2019. Changes in Plankton Community Structure, Standing Stocks and Productivity from Upstream to Downstream of the Kuroshio Across the Tokara Strait. Bulletin on Coastal Oceanography, 57(1): 65–72. (in Japanese)

HASEGAWA, D. 2019. Island Mass Effect. In: Kuroshio Current, Physical, Biogeochemical and Ecosystem Dynamics, Geophysical Monograph 243 (eds. NAGAI, T., SAITO, H., SUZUKI, K. and TAKAHASHI, M.), pp. 163–174, John Wiley & Sons, Hoboken.

KAWABE, M. 1995. Variations of Current Path, Velocity, and Volume Transport of the Kuroshio in Relation with the Large Meander. Journal of Physical Oceanography, 25: 3103–3117.

KINOSHITA, N. 2000. An Archaeological Interpretation of an Ancient Fishermen's Folktale. Departmental Bulletin Paper, Faculty of Letters, Kumamoto University, 71–96. (in Japanese)

KOBARI, T., HONMA, T. HASEGAWA, D., YOSHIE, N., TSUTSUMI, E., MATSUNO, T., *et al.* 2019. Phytoplankton Growth and Consumption by Microzooplankton Stimulated by Turbulent Nitrate Flux Suggest Rapid Trophic Transfer in the Oligotrophic Kuroshio. Biogeosciences, in review.

LIU, Z. J., NAKAMURA, H., ZHU, X. H., NISHINA, A. and DONG, M. 2017. Tidal and Residual Currents Across the Northern Ryukyu Island Chain Observed by Ferryboat ADCP. Journal of Geophysical Research: Oceans, 122: 7198–67217.

LIU, Z. J., NAKAMURA, H., ZHU, X. H., NISHINA, A., GUO, X. and DONG, M. 2019, Tempo-spatial Variations of the Kuroshio Current in the Tokara Strait Based on Long-term Ferryboat ADCP Data. Journal of Geophysical Research: Oceans, 124: 6030–6049.

MUNK, W. and WUNSCH, C. 1998. Abyssal Recipes II: Energetics of Tidal and Wind Mixing. Deep Sea Research Part I, 45: 1977–2010.

NAGAI, T., HASEGAWA, D., TANAKA, T., NAKAMURA, H., TSUTSUMI, E., INOUE, R. and YAMASHIRO, T. 2017. First Evidence of Coherent Bands of Strong Turbulent Layers Associated with High-Wavenumber Internal-Wave Shear in the Upstream Kuroshio. Scientific Reports, 7: 14555.

NAKAMURA, H. 2013. The Kuroshio - its Physical Aspect and Roles in Kagoshima's Nature and Culture -. In: The Islands of Kagoshima: Culture, Society, Industry and Nature (eds. KAWAI, K., TERADA, R. and KUWAHARA, S.), pp. 118–127, Kagoshima University Research Center for the Pacific Islands, Kagoshima.

NAKAMURA, H., HIRANAKA, R., AMBE, D. and SAITO, T. 2015. Local Wind Effect on the Kuroshio Path State off the Southeastern Coast of Kyushu. Journal of Oceanography, 71: 575–596.

NAKAMURA, H., ICHIKAWA, H., NISHINA, A. and LIE, H. J. 2003. Kuroshio Path Meander between the Continental Slope and the Tokara Strait in the East China Sea. Journal of Geophysical Research: Oceans, 108: 3360.

NAKAMURA, H., NISHINA, A., ICHIKAWA, H., NONAKA, M. and SASAKI, H. 2008. Deep Countercurrent Beneath the Kuroshio in the Okinawa Trough. Journal of Geophysical Research: Oceans, 113: C06030.

NAKAMURA, H., NISHINA, A., LIU, Z., TANAKA, F., WIMBUSH, M. and PARK, J. H. 2013. Intermediate and Deep Water Formation in the Okinawa Trough. Journal of Geophysical Research: Oceans, 118: 6881–6893.

NAKAMURA, H., NISHINA, A., TABATA, K., HIGASHI, M., HABANO, A. and YAMASHIRO, Y. 2012. Surface Velocity Time Series Derived from Satellite Altimetry Data in a Section Across the Kuroshio Southwest of Kyushu. Journal of Oceanography, 68: 321–336.

NAKAMURA, H., NONAKA, M. and SASAKI, H. 2010. Seasonality of the Kuroshio Path Destabilization Phenomenon in the Okinawa Trough: A Numerical Study of its Mechanism. Journal of Physical Oceanography, 40: 530–550.

NAKAMURA, H., YAMASHIRO, T., NISHINA, A. and ICHIKAWA, H. 2006. Time-frequency Variability of Kuroshio Meanders in Tokara Strait. Geophysical research letters, 33: L21605.

SAITO, H. 2019. The Kuroshio: its Recognition, Scientific Activities and Emerging Issues. In: Kuroshio Current, Physical, Biogeochemical and Ecosystem Dynamics, Geophysical Monograph 243 (eds. NAGAI, T., SAITO, H., SUZUKI, K. and TAKAHASHI, M.), pp. 1–11, John Wiley & Sons, Hoboken.

TSUTSUMI, E., MATSUNO, T., LIEN, R. C., NAKAMURA, H., SENJYU, T. and GUO, X. 2017. Turbulent Mixing within the Kuroshio in the Tokara Strait. Journal of Geophysical Research: Oceans, 122: 7082–7094.

YAMASHIRO, T. and KAWABE, M. 2002. Variation of the Kuroshio Axis South of Kyushu in Relation to the Large Meander of the Kuroshio. Journal of Oceanography, 58: 487–503.

YAMASHIRO, T. and KAWABE, M. 1996. Monitoring of Position of the Kuroshio Axis in the Tokara Strait Using Sea Level Data. Journal of Oceanography, 52: 675–687.

ZHU, X. H., NAKAMURA, H., DONG, M., NISHINA, A. and YAMASHIRO, T. 2017. Tidal Currents and Kuroshio Transport Variations in the Tokara Strait Estimated from Ferryboat A DCP data. Journal of Geophysical Research: Oceans, 122: 2120–2142.

Chapter 17
Review of the Ichthyofaunal Studies in the Tokara Islands, Southern Japan

Hiroyuki MOTOMURA

1. Introduction

The Tokara Islands, located in the northern Ryukyu Islands, between the Osumi and Amami islands, southern Japan, comprises 12 islands, including five uninhabited. The 12 islands extend northeast to southwest across a range of 160 km. The largest is Nakano-shima Island with an area of ca. 34 km^2 and a population of 150 people.

In terms of marine biology, the Tokara Islands is one of the most unexplored regions in Japanese waters because of its inaccessibility (no airports or high-speed vessels) and lack of experimental and diving facilities. The only public transport to the islands is a car ferry, but this service is frequently canceled due to adverse weather conditions especially during summer (tropical cyclones, including typhoons) and winter (prevailing westerlies) seasons.

Although it is hard for ichthyologists to conduct fish surveys in the islands, the region is biogeographically interesting because the Kuroshio Current, a warm, strong-water current, flows uniquely across the island chain (MOTOMURA 2012, 2015). Few fishes have been collected and recorded from the Tokara Islands, compared with neighboring well-surveyed islands: e.g., 1,615 species recorded from Amami-oshima Island (south of Tokara Islands) (NAKAE *et al.* 2018) and 1,277 species from Yaku-shima Island (north of Tokara Islands) (MOTOMURA and HARAZAKI 2017).

In this chapter, the history of ichthyofaunal studies in the Tokara Islands is reviewed and recent specimen-based records from the islands are listed.

2. Material and methods

Standard and total lengths are abbreviated as SL and TL respectively. The systematic arrangement of families generally follows NELSON (2006). Scientific names generally follow FRICKE *et al.* (2019), with some modifications following recently published or unpublished taxonomic studies. Within families, species are arranged in alphabetical order of the scientific name. Standard Japanese names generally follow NAKABO (2013), having been transliterated using the Hepburn system. Each species record was compiled from published literature with voucher specimens. Registration number, mm in SL or TL, and locality (island name) are listed in each species record. Specimens collected far off the Tokara Islands are not listed.

Institutional codes used in this paper are as follows: BSKU (Laboratory of Marine Biology, Faculty of Science, Kochi University, Kochi, Japan), KAUM (Kagoshima University Museum, Kagoshima, Japan), NSMT (National Museum of Nature and Science, Tsukuba, Japan), URM (Faculty of Science, University of the Ryukyus, Okinawa, Japan; specimens currently transferred to Okinawa Churaumi Aquarium, Okinawa, Japan), and YCM (Yokosuka City Museum, Kanagawa, Japan).

3. History of ichthyofaunal studies in the Tokara Islands

After World War II and until February 1952, the Tokara Islands were under the rule of several United States Military Governments, including the Provisional Government of Northern Ryukyu Islands, the United States Military Government of the Ryukyu Islands, and the Ryukyu Provisional Central Government. One year after the administrative rights of Tokara Islands returned to Japan, the first comprehensive scientific survey, including zoology, botany, geology, meteorology, and cultural anthropology, in the Tokara Islands was carried out by the Osaka Municipal Natural Science Museum (currently Osaka Museum of Natural History) with the support of the Kagoshima Prefectural Government and the Asahi Shimbun in May–June 1953 (KAMOHARA 1955). During the survey, 124 fish species were collected by Dr. T. KAMOHARA from Takara-jima Island (26 May to 1 June) and Nakano-shima Island (4 to 13 June), 14 of which represented the first records from Japan (KAMOHARA 1954). KAMOHARA (1954) proposed new Japanese names for the 14 newly recorded species, with the following six names still in use as standard names: Hoshisusukibera for *Anampses twistii* Bleeker 1856; Seitembera for *Halichoeres scapularis* (Bennett 1832); Onibera for *Stethojulis trilineata* (Bloch and Schneider 1801); Aotengimpo for *Blenniella caudolineata* (Günther 1877); Nisekaeruuo for *Istiblennius edentulus* (Forster and Schneider 1801); and Mondarumagarei for *Bothus mancus* (Broussonet 1782). All of KAMOHARA's Tokara specimens were deposited at the Osaka Museum of Natural History and Kochi University, and some have been re-examined and published by recent authors (see list below).

After KAMOHARA (1954), no comprehensive ichthyofaunal surveys were made in the Tokara Islands until SAKAI *et al.* (2005, 2009) who reported a total of 304 fish species from the islands (Kuchino-shima, Nakano-shima, Taira-jima, Kodakara-jima islands) on the basis of underwater photographs. Because their photographs are not currently available to public and no specimens were collected, the accuracy of their identifications are somewhat doubtful; e.g., *Scorpaenopsis cirrosa*, which is absent from the Ryukyu Islands (MOTOMURA *et al.* 2004), was listed as occurring in Taira-jima Island, but was most likely a mis-identification of *S. papuensis*, *S. oxycephala*, *S. possi*, or *S. ramaraoi*. Incidentally, although SHINOMIYA and SHIMADA (1980) reported a list of 82 species (including unidentified species) from the Kagoshima mainland (Nezime), Osumi Islands (Iwo-jima and Kuchierabu-jima islands), Tokara Islands (Nakano-shima and Suwanose-jima islands) and Amami-oshima Island, they provided

only a list of fish names without locality of each species and voucher specimens have been lost.

Recently, the Kagoshima University Museum actively surveyed the ichthyofauna of the Tokara Islands, and since 2011 about 2,000 specimens from the islands have been collected and deposited in the museum's fish collection. Some specimens have already been examined and the information published (see list below), and the remaining data will be published as a checklist or field guide in the near future. As part of this research, three new species were described from the Tokara Islands (Fig. 1): *Syngnathus chihiroe* Matsunuma 2017 (type locality: north of Kuchino-shima Island), *Epinnula pacifica* Ho, Motomura, Hata and Jiang 2017 (Taira-jima Island), and *Plectranthias maekawa* Wada, Senou and Motomura 2018 (Gaja-jima Island). No further new species have been described on the basis of primary type specimens collected from the Tokara Islands. In addition to the new species, seven species (members of Serranidae, Pseudochromidae, Pomacentridae, Pinguipedidae, Tripterygiidae, and Acanthuridae) were reported from the Tokara Islands between 2013 and 2019 as the first records from Japan (see list below).

4. Published records of fishes from the Tokara Islands

A list of 66 fish species recorded over the last 10 years on the basis of specimens collected from the Tokara Islands is provided below.

HETERODONTIDAE
Heterodontus japonicus Miklouho-Maclay and Macleay 1884
[Jpn name: Nekozame]
NAKAMURA and MOTOMURA (2019): KAUM–I. 129109, 866.0 mm TL, Taira-jima Island.

BERYCIDAE
Beryx splendens Lowe 1843
[Jpn name: Kimmedai]
HATA *et al.* (2016b): KAUM–I. 54896, 209.0 mm SL, Kuchino-shima Island.

HOLOCENTRIDAE

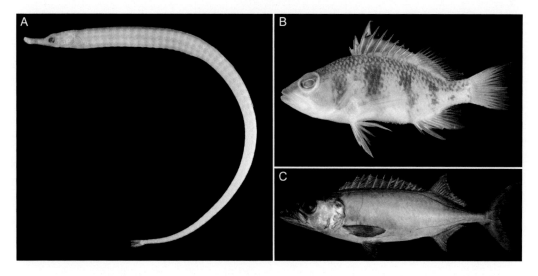

Fig. 1. Photographs of holotypes of species originally described from the Tokara Islands. A: *Syngnathus chihiroe* (NSMT-P 106296, 92.0 mm SL, north of Kuchino-shima Island; photo by M. MATSUNUMA); B: *Plectranthias maekawa* (KAUM–I. 110144, 58.2 mm SL, Gaja-jima Island); C: *Epinnula pacifica* (KAUM–I. 72269, 710.0 mm SL, Taira-jima Island).

Myripristis berndti Jordan and Evermann 1903
[Jpn name: Akamatsukasa]
EGUCHI and MOTOMURA (2016): KAUM–I. 63193, 148.0 mm SL, north of Kuchino-shima Island; KAUM–I. 63362, 163.2 mm SL, Nakano-shima Island.

Myripristis botche Cuvier 1829
[Jpn name: Urokomatsukasa]
EGUCHI and MOTOMURA (2016): KAUM–I. 66612, 149.6 mm SL, Nakano-shima Island.

Myripristis kuntee Valenciennes 1831
[Jpn name: Kuroobimatsukasa]
EGUCHI and MOTOMURA (2016): KAUM–I. 63192, 139.4 mm SL, north of Kuchino-shima Island; KAUM–I. 78191, 149.4 mm SL, Kuchino-shima Island; KAUM–I. 63594, 140.6 mm SL, Nakano-shima Island.

Myripristis murdjan (Forsskål 1775)
[Jpn name: Yogorematsukasa]
EGUCHI and MOTOMURA (2016): KAUM–I. 63357, 132.4 mm SL, KAUM–I. 63363, 108.7 mm SL, Nakano-shima Island.

Ostichthys japonicus (Cuvier 1829)
[Jpn name: Ebisudai]
EGUCHI and MOTOMURA (2016): KAUM–I. 62463, 274.7 mm SL, south of Suwanose-jima Island. MATSUNUMA *et al.* (2018): same specimen with EGUCHI and MOTOMURA (2016).

Sargocentron ittodai (Jordan and Fowler 1902)
[Jpn name: Teriebisu]
EGUCHI and MOTOMURA (2016): KAUM–I. 63351, 130.6 mm SL, KAUM–I. 63418, 115.6 mm SL, Nakano-shima Island; URM-P 32340, 155.6 mm SL, Kodakara-jima Island.

Sargocentron praslin (Lacepède 1802)
[Jpn name: Kuroobiebisu]
EGUCHI and MOTOMURA (2016): KAUM–I. 63424, 160.0 mm SL, Nakano-shima Island.

Sargocentron punctatissimum (Cuvier 1829)
[Jpn name: Hoshiebisu]
EGUCHI and MOTOMURA (2016): URM-P 32341, 93.8 mm SL, Kodakara-jima Island.

CAPROIDAE
Antigonia capros Lowe 1843

[Jpn name: Hishidai]

Hata *et al.* (2015c): KAUM–I. 66172, 150.3 mm SL, KAUM–I. 66173, 151.4 mm SL, KAUM–I. 66174, 159.6 mm SL, east of Nakano-shima Island.

SYNGNATHIDAE

Syngnathus chihiroe Matsunuma 2017

[Jpn name: Chihiroyoji]

Matsunuma (2017): NSMT-P 106296, holotype, 92.0 mm SL, north of Kuchino-shima Island (described as new species).

SCORPAENIDAE

Dendrochirus zebra (Cuvier 1829)

[Jpn name: Kirimmino]

Matsunuma and Motomura (2019): BSKU 63780, 62.8 mm SL, Suwanose-jima Island; KAUM–I. 77956, 84.0 mm SL, Kuchino-shima Island.

Hozukius emblemarius (Jordan and Starks 1904)

[Jpn name: Hozuki]

Matsunuma and Motomura (2014): KAUM–I. 54894, 157.1 mm SL, Kuchino-shima Island; KAUM–I. 58299, 457.0 mm SL, vicinity of Yokoate-jima and Akuseki-jima islands.

Pterois antennata (Bloch 1787)

[Jpn name: Nettaiminokasago]

Matsunuma and Motomura (2011): BSKU 51076, 58.5 mm SL, Kuchino-shima Island. Matsunuma *et al.* (2011): referred to Matsunuma and Motomura (2011: fig. 2B) and provided a distribution map. Matsunuma and Motomura (2018): BSKU 51076, 58.5 mm SL, KAUM–I. 77955, 74.9 mm SL, Kuchino-shima Island.

Pterois radiata Cuvier 1829

[Jpn name: Kimiokoze]

Matsunuma and Motomura (2015): BSKU 2712, 66.8 mm SL, BSKU 3239, 57.7 mm SL, BSKU 3317, 46.4 mm SL, Takara-jima Island; BSKU 63779, 61.6 mm SL, Suwanose-jima Island; KAUM–I. 63356, 76.1 mm SL, Nakano-shima Island.

Scorpaena neglecta Temminck and Schlegel 1843

[Jpn name: Izukasago]

Wibowo and Motomura (2019): BSKU 33744, 177.6 mm SL, west of Tokara Islands.

SEBASTIDAE

Sebastiscus tertius (Barsukov and Chen 1978)

[Jpn name: Ukkarikasago]

Morishita *et al.* (2018): KAUM–I. 29288, 247.3 mm SL, Tokara Islands.

APLOACTINIDAE

Cocotropus possi Imamura and Shinohara 2008

[Jpn name: Higemojaokoze]

Koeda and Motomura (2018): KAUM–I. 86964, 22.9 mm SL, Taira-jima Island.

ACROPOMATIDAE

Verilus pacificus (Mochizuki 1979)

[Jpn name: Bakemutsu]

Inaba *et al.* (2016): KAUM–I. 69733, 246.6 mm SL, north of Kuchino-shima Island; KAUM–I. 68444, 328.3 mm SL, Taira-jima Island (recorded as *Neoscombrops pacificus*).

SERRANIDAE

Cephalopholis aurantia (Valenciennes 1828)

[Jpn name: Hanahata]

Koeda and Motomura (2015a): KAUM–I. 70640, 223.4 mm SL, south of Tokara Islands.

Epinephelus fasciatus (Forsskål 1775)

[Jpn name: Akahata]

Kuriiwa *et al.* (2014): 10 specimens, Kuchino-shima Island; 20 specimens, Gaja-jima Island; 16 specimens, Kodakara-jima Island (all specimens deposited at NSMT).

Epinephelus retouti Bleeker 1868

[Jpn name: Akahatamodoki]

Hata and Motomura (2015): KAUM–I. 76694, 280.0 mm SL, KAUM–I. 77543, 296.0 mm SL, north of Kuchino-shima Island; KAUM–I. 56200, 311.0 mm SL, Nakano-shima Island.

Gracila albomarginata (Fowler and Bean 1930)

[Jpn name: Tatesujihata]

Hata *et al.* (2018a): KAUM–I. 200430, 311.7 mm SL, north of Gaja-jima Island.

Niphon spinosus Cuvier 1828
[Jpn name: Ara]
Hata and Motomura (2019): KAUM–I. 96800, 310.0 mm SL, Kuchino-shima Island.

Odontanthias unimaculatus (Tanaka 1917)
[Jpn name: Ittensakuradai]
Tashiro *et al.* (2018): KAUM–I. 78672, 136.5 mm SL, northwest of Kuchino-shima Island; KAUM–I. 82934, 116.8 mm SL, south of Gaja-jima Island; KAUM–I. 78930, 137.2 mm SL, Yakushin Bank, east of Nakano-shima Island; KAUM–I. 110612, 128.4 mm SL, KAUM–I. 110613, 120.1 mm SL, KAUM–I. 110614, 158.6 mm SL, Gon Bank, northwest of Taira-jima Island.

Plectranthias longimanus (Weber 1913)
[Jpn name: Muramomijihanadai]
Kawaji *et al.* (2019): KAUM–I. 63271, 25.1 mm SL, Nakano-shima Island.

Plectranthias maekawa Wada, Senou and Motomura 2018
[Jpn name: Ayameizuhanadai]
Wada *et al.* (2018): KAUM–I. 110114, holotype, 58.2 mm SL, Gaja-jima Island; KAUM–I. 96644, paratype, 65.1 mm SL, KAUM–I. 96645, paratype, 62.3 mm SL, Nakano-shima Island (described as new species).

Plectranthias nanus Randall 1980
[Jpn name: Chibihanadai]
Kawaji *et al.* (2019): KAUM–I. 99030, 19.3 mm SL, KAUM–I. 99097, 22.6 mm SL, Akuseki-jima Island (described as first Japanese record).

Plectranthias sheni Chen and Shao 2002
[Jpn name: Kiobiizuhanadai]
Fujiwara *et al.* (2017b): KAUM–I. 83683, 93.4 mm SL, KAUM–I. 83684, 107.1 mm SL, KAUM–I. 83685, 89.4 mm SL, KAUM–I. 83686, 87.8 mm SL, Nakano-shima Island; KAUM–I. 78928, 123.3 mm SL, KAUM–I. 78929, 118.5 mm SL, KAUM–I. 89482, 124.1 mm SL, Yakushin Bank, east of Nakano-shima Island (described as first Japanese records).

Plectranthias wheeleri Randall 1980
[Jpn name: Fujinahanadai]
Tashiro *et al.* (2017): KAUM–I. 91349, 65.1 mm SL, west of Suwanose-jima Island (described as second Japanese record). Wada *et al.* (2018): KAUM–I. 110597, 86.3 mm SL, Gon Bank, northwest of Taira-jima Island; KAUM–I. 91349, 65.1 mm SL, west of Suwanose-jima Island.

Plectropomus powelli (Smith 1964)
[Jpn name: Yamabukihata]
Hata and Motomura (2015): KAUM–I. 56119, 316.0 mm SL, KAUM–I. 72787, 330.0 mm SL, north of Kuchino-shima Island; KAUM–I. 74329, 386.0 mm SL, east of Nakano-shima Island (recorded as Saloptia powelli).

Sacura margaritacea (Hilgendorf 1879)
[Jpn name: Sakuradai]
Yoshida *et al.* (2017): KAUM–I. 96640, 141.9 mm SL, KAUM–I. 96754, 128.1 mm SL, west of Nakano-shima.

GIGANTHIIDAE
Giganthias immaculatus Katayama 1954
[Jpn name: Miharahanadai]
Delloro and Motomura (2018): KAUM–I. 77357, 231.6 mm SL, KAUM–I. 77358, 251.4 mm SL, north of Kuchino-shima Island; KAUM–I. 89491, 258.4 mm SL, Yakushin Bank, east of Nakano-shima Island; KAUM–I. 51148, 260.9 mm SL, Kodakara-jima Island; KAUM–I. 54482, 284.0 mm SL, KAUM–I. 54485, 220.9 mm SL, KAUM–I. 54486, 264 mm SL, Takara-jima Island; KAUM–I. 54133, 282.0 mm SL, KAUM–I. 54144, 283.3 mm SL, KAUM–I. 54145. 249.5 mm SL, Tokara Islands.

PSEUDOCHROMIDAE
Pseudoplesiops immaculatus Gill and Edwards 2002
[Jpn name: Hanasakitanabatamegisu]
Koeda *et al.* (2017): KAUM–I. 86962, 30.4 mm SL, Taira-jima Island (described as first Japanese record).

CARANGIDAE

Caranx lugubris Poey 1860

[Jpn name: Kappore]

HATA *et al.* (2015b): KAUM–I. 69396, 440.0 mm SL, north of Tokara Islands.

BRAMIDAE

Brama orcini Cuvier 1831

[Jpn name: Marubarashimagatsuo]

HATA and MOTOMURA (2016b): KAUM–I. 74354, 27.0 mm SL, Nakano-shima Island [collected from stomach of *Scomber australasicus* (KAUM–I. 74324, 314.2 mm SL)]. KOEDA and MOTOMURA (2017): same specimen with HATA and MOTOMURA (2016b).

EMMELICHTHYIDAE

Emmelichthys struhsakeri Heemstra and Randall 1977

[Jpn name: Rosokuchibiki]

HATA *et al.* (2016c): KAUM–I. 82932, 223.4 mm SL, south of Kogaja-jima Island; KAUM–I. 83688, 226.3 mm SL, east of Nakano-shima Island.

LUTJANIDAE

Etelis radiosus Anderson 1981

[Jpn name: Okuchihamadai]

HATA *et al.* (2015a): KAUM–I. 68890, 517.0 mm SL, north of Tokara Islands.

Paracaesio stonei Raj and Seeto 1983

[Jpn name: Yambarushimaaodai]

HATA *et al.* (2017b): KAUM–I. 82741, 407.8 mm SL, Taira-jima Island; KAUM–I. 54128, 379.7 mm SL, Kodakara-jima Island.

Pristipomoides auricilla (Jordan, Evermann and Tanaka 1927)

[Jpn name: Kimadarahimedai]

HATA *et al.* (2017a): KAUM–I. 51077, 348.5 mm SL, Gaja-jima Island.

Pristipomoides flavipinnis Shinohara 1963

[Jpn name: Kimmehimedai]

HATA and MOTOMURA (2016a): KAUM–I. 45510, 363.0 mm SL, off Tokara Islands; KAUM–I. 77538, 290.0 mm SL, KAUM–I. 77539, 326.0 mm

SL, Kodakara-jima Island.

NEMIPTERIDAE

Parascolopsis eriomma (Jordan and Richardson 1909)

[Jpn name: Akatamagashira]

FUJIWARA *et al.* (2014): KAUM–I. 55567, 266.0 mm SL, KAUM–I. 55568, 256.4 mm SL, KAUM–I. 55569, 261.0 mm SL, Suwanose-jima Island.

LETHRINIDAE

Lethrinus amboinensis Bleeker 1854

[Jpn name: Yokoshimafuefuki]

HATA and MOTOMURA (2017): KAUM–I. 71918, 343.0 mm SL, KAUM–I. 95740, 330.0 mm SL, north of Kuchino-shima Island.

Lethrinus erythracanthus Valenciennes 1830

[Jpn name: Amakuchibi]

HATA *et al.* (2018b): KAUM–I. 107801, 479.0 mm SL, west of Takara-jima Island (described as northernmost record for this species).

PEMPHERIDAE

Pempheris adusta Bleeker 1877

[Jpn name: Ryukyuhatampo]

KOEDA and MOTOMURA (2015b): KAUM–I. 63360, 122.3 mm SL, KAUM–I. 63361, 127.9 mm SL, Nakano-shima Island.

Pempheris oualensis Cuvier 1831

[Jpn name: Yumehatampo]

KOEDA *et al.* (2015): KAUM–I. 63425, 173.4 mm SL, Nakano-shima Island.

GLAUCOSOMATIDAE

Glaucosoma buergeri Richardson 1845

[Jpn name: Aobadai]

HATA *et al.* (2016d): KAUM–I. 68567, 480.0 mm SL, north of Kuchino-shima Island.

POMACENTRIDAE

Abudefduf nigrimargo Wibowo, Koeda, Muto and Motomura 2018

[Jpn name: Amimeoyabitcha]

UEJO *et al.* (2018): KAUM–I. 115057, 137.1 mm SL, Suwanose-jima Island (described as first

Japanese record).

Abudefduf vaigiensis (Quoy and Gaimard 1825)
[Jpn name: Oyabitcha]
WIBOWO *et al.* (2017): KAUM–I. 78006, 120.7 mm SL, KAUM–I. 78007, 118.2 mm SL, KAUM–I. 78012, 121.3 mm SL, KAUM–I. 78190, 116.7 mm SL, Kuchino-shima Island; KAUM–I. 63413, 75.6 mm SL, KAUM–I. 63414, 84.5 mm SL, Nakano-shima Island.

ARIOMMATIDAE
Ariomma brevimanum (Klunzinger 1884)
[Jpn name: Minamimedai]
HATA *et al.* (2016a): KAUM–I. 77464, ca. 739 mm SL (snout damaged), north of Kuchino-shima Island.

LABRIDAE
Bodianus tanyokidus Gomon and Madden 1981
[Jpn name: Zunagaakabo]
HATA *et al.* (2015d): KAUM–I. 78687, 145.3 mm SL, Kuchino-shima Island (described as northernmost record).

PINGUIPEDIDAE
Parapercis kentingensis Ho, Chang and Shao 2012
[Jpn name: Yamayuritoragisu]
MATSUO *et al.* (2018): KAUM–I. 78688, 133.6 mm SL, KAUM–I. 78689, 114.9 mm SL, KAUM–I. 78690, 116.5 mm S, northwest of Kuchino-shima Island; KAUM–I. 78932, 123.5 mm SL, Yakushin Bank, east of Nakano-shima Island (described as first Japanese records).

TRIPTERYGIIDAE
Enneapterygius fuscoventer Fricke 1997
[Jpn name: Mitsudarehebigimpo]
TASHIRO and MOTOMURA (2018a): KAUM–I. 63407, 18.7 mm SL, KAUM–I. 63408, 19.0 mm SL, Nakano-shima Island (described as first Japanese records).

Helcogramma fuscipectoris (Fowler 1946)
[Jpn name: Kuromasuku]
TASHIRO and MOTOMURA (2014): KAUM–I. 63398, 22.6 mm SL, KAUM–I. 63399, 24.2 mm SL,

KAUM–I. 63400, 15.2 mm SL, Nakano-shima Island.

Helcogramma inclinata (Fowler 1946)
[Jpn name: Ayahebigimpo]
TASHIRO and MOTOMURA (2014): YCM-P 26990, Nakano-shima Island; KAUM–I. 2037, 39.4 mm SL, Takara-jima Island.

Helcogramma rhinoceros Hansen 1986
[Jpn name: Tenguhebigimpo]
TASHIRO and MOTOMURA (2014): KAUM–I. 63252, 30.3 mm SL, KAUM–I. 63467, 29.4 mm SL, Nakano-shima Island. TASHIRO and MOTOMURA (2018b): KAUM–I. 63466, Nakano-shima Island.

Helcogramma striata Hansen 1986
[Jpn name: Tatejimahebigimpo]
TASHIRO and MOTOMURA (2014): KAUM–I. 63256, 24.4 mm SL, KAUM–I. 63265, 23.6 mm SL, KAUM–I. 63289, 21.7 mm SL, KAUM–I. 63290, 20.1 mm SL, KAUM–I. 63291, 13.8 mm SL, Nakano-shima Island.

BLENNIIDAE
Meiacanthus atrodorsalis (Günther 1877)
[Jpn name: Ogonnijigimpo]
MORISHITA and MOTOMURA (2018): KAUM–I. 115043, 64.4 mm SL, Suwanose-jima Island.

Meiacanthus grammistes (Valenciennes 1836)
[Jpn name: Higenijigimpo]
MORISHITA and MOTOMURA (2018): KAUM–I. 129110, 66.5 mm SL, Taira-jima Island.

GOBIESOCIDAE
Lepadichthys misakius (Tanaka 1908)
[Jpn name: Misakiubauo]
FUJIWARA and MOTOMURA (2019): KAUM–I. 114855, 16.0 mm SL, Suwanose-jima Island.

GOBIIDAE
Eviota flavipinnata Suzuki, Greenfield and Motomura 2015
[Jpn name: Kibureisohaze]
FUJIWARA *et al.* (2018): KAUM–I. 77947, 19.3 mm SL, Kuchino-shima; KAUM–I. 86933, 16.7 mm

SL, KAUM–I. 86959, 17.6 mm SL, Taira-jima Island.

Vanderhorstia puncticeps (Deng and Xiong 1980)
[Jpn name: Hoobeniotohimehaze]
FUJIWARA *et al.* (2017a): KAUM–I. 88828, 33.7 mm SL, west of Tokara Islands.

ACANTHURIDAE
Naso tergus Ho, Shen and Chang 2011
[Jpn name: Shinobitenguhagi]
MATSUNUMA and MOTOMURA (2013): KAUM–I. 52262, 363.0 mm SL, Nakano-shima Island (described as first Japanese record).

GEMPYLIDAE
Epinnula pacifica Ho, Motomura, Hata and Jiang 2017
[Jpn name: Aosumiyaki]
HATA and MOTOMURA (2016c): KAUM–I. 72269, 710.0 mm SL, Taira-jima Island (recorded as *Epinnula magistralis*). Ho *et al.* (2017): KAUM–I. 72269, holotype, 710.0 mm SL, Taira-jima Island (described as new species).

TETRAODONTIDAE
Arothron firmamentum (Temminck and Schlegel 1850)
[Jpn name: Hoshifugu]
FUKUI and MOTOMURA (2017): KAUM–I. 96703, 141.6 mm SL, KAUM–I. 96704, 140.8 mm SL, KAUM–I. 96705, 155.6 mm SL, KAUM–I. 96706, 155.5 mm SL, KAUM–I. 96707, 144.2 mm SL, Gaja-jima Island.

Acknowledgments

I am grateful to Y. HARAGUCHI, other volunteers, and students of KAUM for their curatorial assistance, M. MATSUNUMA (Kindai Univ., Nara) for providing a specimen photograph of *Syngnathus chihiroe*, and G. YEARSLEY (Australia) for comments on the manuscript. This study was supported in part by JSPS KAKENHI Grant Numbers JP19770067, JP26241027, JP24370041, JP23580259, and JP26450265; the JSPS Core-to-Core Program: B Asia-Africa Science Platforms; the "Biological Properties of Biodiversity Hotspots in Japan" project of the National Museum of Nature and Science, Tsukuba, Japan; "Establishment of Research and Education Network on Biodiversity and Its Conservation in the Satsunan Islands" project of Kagoshima University adopted by the Ministry of Education, Culture, Sports, Science and Technology, Japan; and the "Island Research" project of Kagoshima University.

References

DELLORO, E. S. Jr. and MOTOMURA, H. 2018. First Records of *Giganthias immaculatus* (Perciformes: Giganthiidae) from the Osumi and Tokara Islands, Kagoshima Prefecture, Japan, with Notes on Sexual Dimorphism. Nature of Kagoshima, 45: 21–25. (free PDF available at http://www.kagoshima-nature.org/)

EGUCHI, K. and MOTOMURA, H. 2016. Holocentrid Fishes of the Ryukyu Islands, Japan. Nature of Kagoshima, 42: 57–112. (in Japanese; free PDF available at http://www.kagoshima-nature.org/)

FRICKE, R., ESCHMEYER, W. N. and VAN DER LAAN, R. (eds.). 2019. Eschmeyer's Catalog of Fishes: Genera, Species, References. Retrieved on October 7, 2019, from http://researcharchive.calacademy.org/research/ichthyology/catalog/fishcatmain.asp

FUJIWARA, K., HATA, H. and MOTOMURA, H. 2014. Nemipterid Fishes of Kagoshima Prefecture, Southern Japan. Nature of Kagoshima, 40: 59–67. (in Japanese; free PDF available at http://www.kagoshima-nature.org/)

FUJIWARA, K. and MOTOMURA, H. 2019. Validity of *Lepadichthys misakius* (Tanaka 1908) and Redescription of *Lepadichthys frenatus* Waite 1904 (Gobiesocidae: Diademichthyinae). Zootaxa, 4551(3): 275–298.

FUJIWARA, K., OKAMOTO, M. and MOTOMURA, H. 2017a. First Record of *Vanderhorstia puncticeps* (Gobiidae: Gobiinae) from off the Ryukyu Islands, Japan. Nature of Kagoshima, 43: 231–234. (in Japanese; free PDF available at http://www.kagoshima-nature.org/)

FUJIWARA, K., SUZUKI, T. and MOTOMURA, H. 2018. Review of Japanese Records of *Eviota afelei* and *Eviota flavipinnata* (Teleostei: Gobiidae). Nature of Kagoshima, 45: 89–97. (in Japanese; free PDF available at http://www.kagoshima-nature.org/)

FUJIWARA, K., TASHIRO, S., TAKAYAMA, M., SENOU, H. and MOTOMURA, H. 2017b. Records of the Anthiine Fish *Plectranthias sheni* from Japan and Proposal of a New Standard Japanese Name. Japanese Journal of Ichthyology, 64: 121–129. (in Japanese)

FUKUI, Y. and MOTOMURA, H. 2017. Reproductive Behavior of *Arothron firmamentum* (Tetraodontiformes: Tetraodontidae) from Gaja-jima Island, Tokara Islands, Southern Japan. Nature of Kagoshima, 43: 243–247. (in Japanese; free PDF available at http://www.kagoshima-nature.org/)

HATA, H., HARAGUCHI, Y. and MOTOMURA, H. 2015a. First Record of *Etelis radiosus* (Perciformes: Lutjanidae) from the Tokara Islands in the Ryukyu Islands,

Southern Japan. Nature of Kagoshima, 41: 95–99. (in Japanese; free PDF available at http://www.kagoshima-nature.org/)

HATA, H., HARAGUCHI, Y. and MOTOMURA, H. 2015b. First Record of *Caranx lugubris* (Perciformes: Carangidae) from the Tokara Islands, Kagoshima Prefecture, Southern Japan. Nature of Kagoshima, 41: 69–72. (in Japanese; free PDF available at http://www.kagoshima-nature.org/)

HATA, H., ITOU, M. and MOTOMURA, H. 2016a. *Ariomma brevimanum* (Perciformes: Ariommatidae) from Kagoshima Prefecture, Southern Japan. Nanki-seibutsu, 58: 44–47. (in Japanese)

HATA, H., IWATSUBO, H., HARAGUCHI, Y., MORI, K. and MOTOMURA, H. 2016b. A Synopsis of Alfonsinos (Beryciformes: Berycidae) in Kagoshima Prefecture, Japan. Nature of Kagoshima, 42: 49–56. (in Japanese; free PDF available at http://www.kagoshima-nature.org/)

HATA, H., IWATSUBO, H. and MOTOMURA, H. 2017a. First Specimen-based Records of *Pristipomoides auricilla* (Perciformes: Lutjanidae) from the Satsunan Islands, Japan. Biological Magazine Okinawa, 55: 19–26.

HATA, H., IWATSUBO, H. and MOTOMURA, H. 2017b. First Records of the Cocoa Snapper *Paracaesio stonei* (Perciformes: Lutjanidae) from the Satsunan Islands, Japan. Fauna Ryukyuana, 36: 55–62. (free PDF available at http://w3.u-ryukyu.ac.jp/naruse/lab/Fauna_Ryukyuana.html)

HATA, H., IWATSUBO, H. and MOTOMURA, H. 2018a. First Record of *Gracila albomarginata* (Perciformes: Serranidae) from the Tokara Islands, Japan. Biological Magazine Okinawa, 56: 33–38.

HATA, H. and MOTOMURA, H. 2015. Records of Two Groupers, *Epinephelus retouti* and *Saloptia powelli* (Perciformes: Serranidae), from the Satsunan Islands, Kagoshima Prefecture, Southern Japan. Memoirs of the Faculty of Fisheries, Kagoshima University, 64: 1–9. (in Japanese; free PDF available at https://ir.kagoshima-u.ac.jp/?action=repository_opensearch&index_id=262)

HATA, H. and MOTOMURA, H. 2016a. First Specimen-based Records of *Pristipomoides flavipinnis* (Perciformes: Lutjanidae) from the Tokara and Amami Islands, Japan. South Pacific Studies, 36: 103–110. (free PDF available at http://cpi.kagoshima-u.ac.jp/publications/southpacificstudies/archivespst.html)

HATA, H. and MOTOMURA, H. 2016b. Record of *Brama orcini* (Perciformes: Bramidae) Found in the Stomach of *Scomber australasicus* (Scombridae) from the Tokara Islands, Kagoshima Prefecture, Southern Japan. Nature of Kagoshima, 42: 203–206. (in Japanese; free PDF available at http://www.kagoshima-nature.org/)

HATA, H. and MOTOMURA, H. 2016c. First Record of the Snake Mackerel *Epinnula magistralis* (Perciformes: Gempylidae) from the Tokara Islands, Japan. Fauna Ryukyuana, 30: 11–15. (free PDF available at http://w3.u-ryukyu.ac.jp/naruse/lab/Fauna_Ryukyuana.html)

HATA, H. and MOTOMURA, H. 2017. First Records of *Lethrinus amnoineneis* (Perciformes: Lethrinidae) from the Tokara Islands, Kagoshima Prefecture, Southern Japan. Nature of Kagoshima, 43: 169–174. (in Japanese; free PDF available at http://www.kagoshima-nature.org/)

HATA, H. and MOTOMURA, H. 2019. First Records of the Perciform Fish *Niphon spinosus* from the Satsunan Islands, Northern Ryukyu Islands, Japan. Biological Magazine Okinawa, 57: 201–209.

HATA, H., OHTOMI, J. and MOTOMURA, H. 2018b. First and Northernmost Records of *Lethrinus erythracanthus* (Perciformes: Lethrinidae) from Kagoshima Prefecture, Southern Japan. Nature of Kagoshima, 44: 95–99. (in Japanese; free PDF available at http://www.kagoshima-nature.org/)

HATA, H., TAKAYAMA, M. and MOTOMURA, H. 2015c. Records of *Antigonia capros* (Perciformes: Carproidae) from the Satsunan Islands, Southern Japan. Nature of Kagoshima, 41: 171–175. (in Japanese; free PDF available at http://www.kagoshima-nature.org/)

HATA, H., TAKAYAMA, M. and MOTOMURA, H. 2015d. The Northernmost Record of a Wrasse, *Bodianus tanyokidus* (Perciformes: Labridae), from the Tokara Islands, Kagoshima Prefecture, Southern Japan. Bulletin of the Biogeographical Society of Japan, 70: 193–196. (in Japanese)

HATA, H., TAKAYAMA, M. and MOTOMURA, H. 2016c. First Records of *Emmelichthys struhsakeri* (Perciformes: Emmelichthyidae) from the Tokara Islands, Kagoshima Prefecture, Southern Japan. Nature of Kagoshima, 42: 207–211. (in Japanese; free PDF available at http://www.kagoshima-nature.org/)

HATA, H., TAKAYAMA, M. and MOTOMURA, H. 2016d. First Records of *Glaucosoma buergeri* (Perciformes: Glaucosomatidae) from the Osumi and Tokara Islands, Kagoshima Prefecture, Southern Japan. Nature of Kagoshima, 42: 269–273. (in Japanese; free PDF available at http://www.kagoshima-nature.org/)

HO, H.-C., MOTOMURA, H., HATA, H. and JIANG, W.-C. 2017. Review of the Fish Genus *Epinnula* Poey (Perciformes: Gempylidae), with Description of a New Species from the Pacific Ocean. Zootaxa, 4363(3): 393–408.

INABA, T, HATA, H. and MOTOMURA, H. 2016. First Records of *Neoscombrops pacificus* (Perciformes: Acropomatidae) from Kagoshima Prefecture, Southern Japan. Nature of Kagoshima, 42: 129–133. (in Japanese; free PDF available at http://www.kagoshima-nature.org/)

KAMOHARA, T. 1954. A List of Fishes from the Tokara Islands, Kagoshima Prefecture, Japan. Publications of the Seto Marine Biological Laboratory, 3(3): 265–299.

KAMOHARA, T. 1955. *Tokara no sakana* (Fishes of the Tokara Islands). Research Reports of the Kôchi University, 4(8): 1–11. (in Japanese)

KAWAJI, Y., SENOU, H., MUTO, N. and MOTOMURA, H. 2019. Records of Three Anthiadine Species, *Plectranthias longimanus*, *P. nanus*, and *P. winniensis*, from Japanese Waters, with Morphological and Genetic Comparisons (Perciformes: Serranidae). Japanese Journal of Ichthyology, doi: 10.11369/jji.19-004. (in Japanese)

KOEDA, K., KABURAGI, K. and MOTOMURA, H. 2015. Records of *Pempheris oualensis* (Perciformes: Pempheridae) from the Satsunan Islands, Ryukyu Archipelago, Japan. Bulletin of the Biogeographical Society of Japan, 70: 275–282. (in Japanese)

KOEDA, K. and MOTOMURA, H. 2015a. First Record of

Cephalopholis aurantia (Perciformes: Serranidae) from Tanega-shima Island and the Tokara Islands, Kagoshima, Japan. Nature of Kagoshima, 41: 47–52. (in Japanese; free PDF available at http://www.kagoshima-nature.org/)

KOEDA, K. and MOTOMURA, H. 2015b. First Records of *Pempheris adusta* (Perciformes: Pempheridae) from Kuchierabu-jima, Nakano-shima, and Tokuno-shima Islands in the Satsunan Islands and the Kagoshima mainland, Southern Japan with some Biological Comments. Nature of Kagoshima, 41: 139–144. (in Japanese; free PDF available at http://www.kagoshima-nature.org/)

KOEDA, K. and MOTOMURA, H. 2017. Annotated List of Fish Specimens Taken from Fish Stomach Deposited at the Kagoshima University Museum, Japan. Nature of Kagoshima, 43: 257–269. (in Japanese; free PDF available at http://www.kagoshima-nature.org/)

KOEDA, K. and MOTOMURA, H. 2018. Third Specimen and Northernmost Records of the Rare Velvetfish *Cocotropus possi* from Taira-jima Island, Tokara Islands, Japan, with a fresh color description. Japanese Journal of Ichthyology, doi: 10.11369/jji.18-004. (in Japanese)

KOEDA, K., YOSHIDA, T. and MOTOMURA, H. 2017. First Japanese and Northernmost Distributional Record of *Pseudoplesiops immaculatus* (Perciformes: Pseudochromidae: Pseudoplesiopinae) from the Tokara Islands. Biogeography, 19: 55–60.

KURIIWA, K., CHIBA, S. N., MOTOMURA, H. and MATSUURA, K. 2014. Phylogeography of Blacktip Grouper, *Epinephelus fasciatus* (Perciformes: Serranidae), and Influence of the Kuroshio Current on Cryptic Lineages and Genetic Population Structure. Ichthyological Research, doi: 10.1007/s10228-014-0408-9.

MATSUNUMA, M. 2017. *Syngnathus chihiroe*, a New Species of Pipefish (Syngnathidae) from Southern Japan. Zootaxa, 4232(3): 385–396.

MATSUNUMA, M., AIZAWA, M., SAKURAI, Y. and MOTOMURA, H. 2011. Record of a Lionfish, *Pterois mombasae*, from Yaku-shima Island, Southern Japan, and Notes on Distributional Implications of the Species and *P. antennata* in Japan (Scorpaenidae). Nature of Kagoshima, 37: 3–8. (in Japanese; free PDF available at http://www.kagoshima-nature.org/)

MATSUNUMA, M., FUKUI, Y. and MOTOMURA, H. 2018. Review of the *Ostichthys japonicus* Complex (Perciformes: Holocentridae: Myripristinae) in the Northwestern Pacific Ocean, with Description of a New Species. Ichthyological Research, doi: 10.1007/s10228-018-0625-8.

MATSUNUMA, M. and MOTOMURA, H. 2011. First Records of a Lionfish, *Pterois mombasae* (Scorpaenidae: Pteroinae), from Japan, and Morphological Comparisons with *P. antennata*. Japanese Journal of Ichthyology, 58: 27–40. (in Japanese)

MATSUNUMA, M. and MOTOMURA, H. 2013. First Japanese Record of *Naso tergus* (Perciformes: Acanthuridae) from the Tokara Islands, Southern Japan. Japanese Journal of Ichthyology, 60: 103–110. (in Japanese)

MATSUNUMA, M. and MOTOMURA, H. 2014. First Records of

Hozukius emblemarius (Sebastidae) from the Amami and Tokara Islands, Kagoshima Prefecture, Southern Japan. Nature of Kagoshima, 40: 29–33. (in Japanese; free PDF available at http://www.kagoshima-nature.org/)

MATSUNUMA, M. and MOTOMURA, H. 2015. Redescriptions of *Pterois radiata* and *Pterois cincta* (Scorpaenidae: Pteroinae) with Notes on Geographic Morphological Variations in *P. radiata*. Ichthyological Research, doi: 10.1007/s10228-015-0483-6.

MATSUNUMA, M. and MOTOMURA, H. 2018. Redescription and Geographic Variations of *Pterois antennata* and First Record of *Pterois Paucispinula* from French Polynesia (Scorpaenidae: Pteroinae). Species Diversity, 23: 95–114. (free PDF available at https://www.jstage.jst.go.jp/browse/specdiv)

MATSUNUMA, M. and MOTOMURA, H. 2019. Redescription of *Dendrochirus zebra* (Scorpaenidae: Pteroinae) with a New Species of *Dendrochirus* from the Ogasawara Islands, Japan. Ichthyological Research, doi: 10.1007/s10228-019-00681-1.

MATSUO, R., MATSUNUMA, M., MOTOMURA, H. and KIMURA, S. 2018. Records of *Parapercis kentingensis* (Perciformes: Pinguipedidae) from Japan. Japanese Journal of Ichthyology, doi: 10.11369/jji.17-036. (in Japanese)

MORISHITA, S., KAWAI, T. and MOTOMURA, H. 2018. *Sebastiscus vibrantus*, a New Species of Rockfish (Sebastidae) from Indonesia and Taiwan. Ichthyological Research, doi: 10.1007/s10228-018-0632-9.

MORISHITA, S. and MOTOMURA, H. 2018. First Record of *Meiacanthus atrodorsalis* (Perchiforms: Blenniidae) from the Tokara Islands, Kagoshima Prefecture, Southern Japan. Nature of Kagoshima, 45: 63–67. (in Japanese; free PDF available at http://www.kagoshima-nature.org/)

MORISHITA, S. and MOTOMURA, H. 2019. First Specimen-based Record of *Meiacanthus grammistes* (Perciformes: Blenniidae) from the Tokara Islands, Kagoshima Prefecture, Southern Japan. Nature of Kagoshima, 45: 381–384. (in Japanese; free PDF available at http://www.kagoshima-nature.org/)

MOTOMURA, H. 2012. *Kuroshio ga hagukumu Kagoshima-ken no gyorui tayousei* (Fish Diversity in Kagoshima Influenced by the Kuroshio Current). In: Kuroshio no sakana-tachi (Fishes in the Kuroshio Current) (ed. MATSUURA, K.), pp. 19–45, Tokai University Press, Tokyo. (in Japanese)

MOTOMURA, H. 2015. *Ryukyu-rettou no gyorui tayousei* (Fish Species Diversity in the Ryukyu Islands). In: *Nansei-shotou no seibutsu tayousei, sono seiritsu to hozen* (Biodiversity, Formation History, and Conservation in the Nansei Islands) Ecology Lectures 8 (ed. Ecological Society of Japan), pp. 56–63, Nanpou Shinsha, Kagoshima. (in Japanese)

MOTOMURA, H. and HARAZAKI, S. 2017. Annotated Checklist of Marine and Freshwater Fishes of Yaku-shima Island in the Osumi Islands, Kagoshima, Southern Japan, with 129 New Records. Bulletin of the Kagoshima University Museum, 9: 1–183. (free PDF available at https://www.museum.kagoshima-u.ac.jp/staff/motomura/dl_en.html)

MOTOMURA, H., YOSHINO, T. and TAKAMURA, N. 2004.

Review of the scorpionfish genus *Scorpaenopsis* (Scorpaeniformes: Scorpaenidae) in Japanese Waters with Three New Records and an Assessment of Standard Japanese Names. Japanese Journal of Ichthyology, 51: 89–115. (in Japanese)

NAKABO, T. (ed.). 2013. Fishes of Japan with pictorial keys to the species. Third edition. 1 + 2428 pp., Tokai University Press, Hadano. (in Japanese)

NAKAE, M., MOTOMURA, H., HAGIWARA, K., SENOU, H., KOEDA, K., YOSHIDA, T., TASHIRO, S., JEONG, B., HATA, H., FUKUI, Y., FUJIWARA, K., YAMAKAWA, T., AIZAWA, M., SHINOHARA, G. and MATSUURA, K. 2018. An annotated checklist of fishes of Amami-oshima Island, the Ryukyu Islands, Japan. Memoirs of the National Museum of Nature and Science, Tokyo, 52: 205–361.

NAKAMURA, J. and MOTOMURA, H. 2019. Record of *Heterodontus japonicus* (Heterodontiformes: Heterodontidae) from Taira-jima Island, Tokara Islands, Kagoshima, Southern Japan. Nature of Kagoshima, 45: 373–375. (in Japanese; free PDF available at http://www.kagoshima-nature.org/)

NELSON, J. S. 2006. Fishes of the World. Fourth edition. xv + 601 pp., John Wiley & Sons, Inc., New Jersey.

SAKAI, Y., KADOTA, T., KIDERA, T., SAGARA, K., SHIBATA, J., SHIMIZU, N., TAKEYAMA, T., FUJITA, O., HASHIMOTO, H. and GUSHIMA, K. 2005. Fish Fauna at Reefs of the Northern Tokara Islands, Southern Japan. Journal of the Graduate School of Biosphere Science, Hiroshima University, 44: 1–14. (in Japanese)

SAKAI, Y., KADOTA, T., SHIMIZU, N., TSUBOI, M., YAMAGUCHI, S., NAKAGUCHI, K., GO, A., MASUI, Y., HASHIMOTO, H. and GUSHIMA, K. 2005. Fish Fauna at Reefs of Tokara Islands, Southern Japan, Surveyed by Underwater Census during 2002–2007. Journal of the Graduate School of Biosphere Science, Hiroshima University, 48: 19–35. (in Japanese)

SHINOMIYA, A. and SHIMADA, K. 1980. *Tokara retto shuhen kaiiki no sangosho gyoruisou* (Fish fauna in coral reefs in the Tokara Islands and adjacent waters). Prompt Report, Faculty of Engineering, Kagoshima University, 29–34. (in Japanese)

TASHIRO, S. and MOTOMURA, H. 2014. The validity of *Helcogramma ishigakiensis* (Aoyagi, 1954) and a synopsis of species of *Helcogramma* from the Ryukyu Islands, Southern Japan (Perciformes: Tripterygiidae). Species Diversity, 19: 97–110. (free PDF available at https://www.jstage.jst.go.jp/browse/specdiv)

TASHIRO, S. and MOTOMURA, H. 2018a. Redescriptions of Two Western Pacific Triplefins (Perciformes: Tripterygiidae), *Enneapterygius fuscoventer* and *E. howensis*. Ichthyological Research, doi: 10.1007/s10228-017-0612-5.

TASHIRO, S. and MOTOMURA, H. 2018b. *Helcogramma melanolancea*, a New Triplefin (Perciformes: Tripterygiidae) from Bali, Indonesia. Ichthyological Research, doi: 10.1007/s10228-018-0660-5.

TASHIRO, S., TAKAYAMA, M. and MOTOMURA, H. 2017. Second Japanese Record of *Plectranthias wheeleri* (Perciformes: Serranidae) from Suwanose-jima Island, Tokara Islands, Kagoshima Prefecture, Southern Japan. Japanese Journal of Ichthyology, 64: 195–199. (in Japanese)

TASHIRO, S., TAKAYAMA, M. and MOTOMURA, H. 2018. First Records of *Odontanthias unimaculatus* (Perciformes: Serranidae) from Kagoshima Prefecture, Southern Japan. Nature of Kagoshima, 44: 347–351. (in Japanese; free PDF available at http://www.kagoshima-nature.org/)

UEJO, T., WIBOWO, K. and MOTOMURA, H. 2018. First Japanese Record of the Black Margined-scale Sergeant *Abudefduf nigrimargo* (Perciformes: Pomacentridae) from the Tokara Islands. Species Diversity, 23: 249–251. (free PDF available at https://www.jstage.jst.go.jp/browse/specdiv)

WADA, H., SENOU, H. and MOTOMURA, H. 2018. *Plectranthias maekawa*, a New Species of Perchlet from the Tokara Islands, Kagoshima, Japan with a Review of Japanese Records of *P. wheeleri* (Serranidae: Anthiadinae). Ichthyological Research, doi: 10.1007/s10228-018-0674-z.

WIBOWO, K. and MOTOMURA, H. 2019. Redescription of the Indo-West Pacific scorpionfish *Scorpaena neglecta* Temminck & Schlegel 1843, a Senior Synonym of Four Nominal Species (Teleostei: Scorpaenidae). Zootaxa, 4619(2): 311–329.

WIBOWO, K., TODA, M. and MOTOMURA, H. 2017. Validity of *Abudefduf caudobimaculatus* Okada and Ikeda 1939 and Synonymies of *Abudefduf vaigiensis* (Quoy and Gaimard 1824) (Perciformes: Pomacentridae). Ichthyological Research, doi: 10.1007/s10228-017-0594-3.

YOSHIDA, T., TAKAYAMA, M. and MOTOMURA, H. 2017. First Ryukyu Records of *Sacura margaritacea* (Perciformes: Serranidae) from Nakano-shima Island, Tokara Islands, Kagoshima Prefecture, Southern Japan. Nature of Kagoshima, 43: 111–116. (in Japanese; free PDF available at http://www.kagoshima-nature.org/)

The Tokara Islands

Culture, Society, Industry and Nature

2020年3月　初版1刷発行

編集者　　大塚　　靖
　　　　　寺田　竜太
　　　　　西村　　悟

鹿児島大学国際島嶼教育研究センター
〒890-8580　　鹿児島市郡元1-21-24
TEL 099-285-7394　FAX 099-285-6197

発行所　　㈲北斗書房
〒132-0024 東京都江戸川区一之江8-3-2
TEL 03-3674-5241　FAX 03-3674-5244

印刷所　三報社印刷㈱　定価2,000円＋税